Rethinking Commonsense Psychology

Rethinking Commonsense Psychology

A Critique of Folk Psychology, Theory of Mind and Simulation

Matthew Ratcliffe

First published 2007 by
PALGRAVE MACMILLAN
Houndmills, Basingstoke, Hampshire RG21 6XS and
175 Fifth Avenue, New York, N.Y. 10010
Companies and representatives throughout the world

PALGRAVE MACMILLAN is the global academic imprint of the Palgrave
Macmillan division of St. Martin's Press, LLC and of Palgrave Macmillan Ltd.
Macmillan® is a registered trademark in the United States, United Kingdom
and other countries. Palgrave is a registered trademark in the European
Union and other countries.

ISBN-13: 978-0-230-00710-9   hardback
ISBN-10: 0-230-00710-4   hardback

This book is printed on paper suitable for recycling and made from fully
managed and sustained forest sources.

A catalogue record for this book is available from the British Library.

Library of Congress Cataloging-in-Publication Data

Ratcliffe, Matthew, 1973–
    Rethinking commonsense psychology: a critique of folk psychology, theory of
mind, and simulation/Matthew Ratcliffe.
        p. cm.
    Includes bibliographical references and index.
    ISBN-13: 978-0-230-00710-9
    ISBN-10: 0-230-00710-4
        1. Psychology–Philosophy. 2. Ethnopsychology. 3. Philosophy of mind. 4. Cognitive
science. I. Title.

BF38.R338 2007
150.1–dc22

                                                                2006049328

10   9   8   7   6   5   4   3   2   1
16   15   14   13   12   11   10   09   08   07
Transferred to Digital Printing 2008

This book is dedicated to Huxley and Lilu, who don't believe very much at all and desire only food and sleep. They provided me with much needed support whilst I was writing the book, by sitting on my lap and purring.

Contents

Preface		ix
1	Commonsense Psychology, Theory of Mind and Simulation	1
	Belief-desire psychology	3
	Theory or simulation?	8
	Development and evolution	16
	A place to start	20
2	Where is the Commonsense in Commonsense Psychology?	27
	Natural born dualists?	29
	Commonsense as taken-for-granted reality	36
	The origins of 'folk psychology'	42
	What do the folk have to say?	46
	Science and folk psychology	52
3	The World We Live in	58
	The commonsense world	59
	Heidegger's world	62
	Heidegger on other people	70
	Gurwitsch on situations and roles	74
	Encountering others	78
4	Letting the World Do the Work	85
	Norms, roles and functions	86
	Situations are reasons	96
	The development of social ability	98
	Social interaction as embodied, embedded cognition	107
	Social situations and belief-desire psychology	118
5	Perceiving Actions	121
	Experiencing others	123
	Evidence from neuroscience	129

The mirror system: applications and limitations 139

Emotion in expression and meaning in gesture 143

Explaining action without FP 149

6   The Second Person 152

Wherefore art Thou? 154

Sartre on intersubjectivity 158

Interaction 164

Conversational interaction 173

Simulation or simulated interaction? 180

Denying people 184

7   Beliefs and Desires 186

Everyday 'belief' and 'desire' 187

'Belief' and 'desire' in FP 190

Experience and belief 197

Beliefs, desires and commitments 199

Beliefs as indeterminate dispositions 205

Narratives 211

Understanding reasoning 216

8   The Personal Stance 222

Evolution and development 224

The impersonal personal stance 230

Phenomenology, science and naturalism 234

Notes 245

References 255

Index 265

Preface

The assumption that people understand each other by employing a 'commonsense' or 'folk' psychology is currently pervasive in philosophy of mind, cognitive science and various other disciplines. Folk psychology is almost always taken to consist primarily of an ability to attribute internal propositional attitude states, principally beliefs and desires, in order to predict and explain behaviour. The emphasis of recent debates has not been on *whether* we do this but on which mechanisms enable us to do it, how they arise during development and how they might have evolved.

In this book, I propose a series of interconnected arguments against the view that we have such a folk psychology. I start off by observing that proponents of the view are not clear about what is meant by the terms 'folk' and 'commonsense'. I go on to argue that an understanding of shared social situations often does most or all of the interpretive work that belief-desire psychology is claimed to do. Then I challenge the view that mental states are understood by people to be 'internal', 'unobservable' causes of behaviour. Many mental states are, I suggest, perceivable. And some are partly constituted by behaviour, rather than being hidden causes of behaviour. I go on to emphasise the extent to which social life involves interaction and relatedness between people. 'Folk psychology', I claim, misconstrues an understanding that is inextricable from contexts of interaction as a matter of socially removed individual observers deploying their internal cognitive mechanisms in order to predict and explain the behaviour of others. Finally, I argue that the terms 'belief' and 'desire' do not pick out unitary kinds of mental state that people attribute to each other. Instead, they are abstract placeholders for a range of different states that are subtly distinguished by everyday narratives but not by the kinds of examples routinely offered on behalf of 'folk psychology'. I bring these criticisms together to conclude that 'folk psychology', as generally described, is a somewhat misleading abstraction from social life, which is wrongly asserted to be 'commonsense' or 'what the folk think'.

Through my critique, I develop the beginnings of an alternative account. According to this account, a distinctive kind of bodily relatedness between people is constitutive of the ability to appreciate someone as a *person*. In addition, relations and interactions between people are

ix

structured and regulated by shared, normatively organised social environments. These environments are ordinarily taken for granted as enabling backgrounds for interpersonal interpretation, interaction and coordination. 'Folk psychology', I argue, fails to accommodate the manner in which people are understood as *people*, rather than as complex mechanisms. It also confuses an understanding of social environments with an understanding of the internal mental states of individual organisms.

My thinking on this topic has benefited from interactions with several people. I am especially grateful to Daniel Hutto, with whom I have spent many hours discussing the shortcomings of folk psychology, and to Shaun Gallagher, whose insightful criticisms of folk psychology inspired me to investigate this topic in the first place.

I would like to thank many great colleagues, past and present, for illuminating discussions of this topic. These include David Cooper, Matthew Eddy, Andy Hamilton, Simon James, Benedict Smith and several others. I am especially grateful to Robin Hendry and Jonathan Lowe, with whom I have had many thought-provoking conversations about folk psychology and related themes. I have also had really helpful conversations with some very talented postgraduate students, including Richard Clarkson (who read the entire manuscript and offered many helpful comments), Matthew Conduct, Beth Hannon, Donnchadh O'Conaill, Francis O'Sullivan and others. In addition, I am grateful to two anonymous referees for offering constructive criticisms and helpful suggestions.

Material from this book was presented at conferences in Orlando, Vienna, Bristol and Leuven, in talks given at the Universities of Cambridge, Hull and Lancaster and in a Royal Institute of Philosophy Lecture I gave in London. I am grateful to all these audiences for helpful criticisms and suggestions. Some passages in Chapters 5 and 8 are adapted from my article 'Phenomenology, Neuroscience and Intersubjectivity'. I am grateful to Blackwell publishers for granting permission to reproduce this work. Chapter 6 is very loosely based on my articles 'Folk Psychology and the Biological Basis of Intersubjectivity' and 'Folk Psychology is not Folk Psychology'. Some of the arguments of Chapters 2 and 7 are also addressed in my 'From Folk Psychology to Commonsense'.

Completion of this book was facilitated by an award from the Arts and Humanities Research Council Research Leave Scheme. This allowed me to spend three months, from 1st April until 30th June 2006 working exclusively on the book, when I would otherwise have been up to my neck in marking. I am very grateful indeed for the opportunity they gave me to complete this project.

My greatest debt I leave until last; I thank my wife Beth for her love, support and tolerance. During the time I spent writing this book, she not only put up with my non-stop nattering about folk psychology but also read the entire manuscript and offered helpful suggestions. Sorry, Beth, for dedicating this book to our cats; you get the next one.

1
Commonsense Psychology, Theory of Mind and Simulation

What is distinctive about understanding and interacting with other people? Our social relations are diverse in nature; people are encountered as strangers, the holders of certain social roles and statuses, neighbours, competitors, lovers, friends or family. And we interact with each other in all sorts of ways. Negotiating one's way along a busy shopping street alongside several hundred others, with the occasional exchange of nods, smiles or frowns, is very different from a free-flowing conversation with a good friend about assorted trivia. Playing a well-matched and familiar opponent at chess is far removed from answering a request for directions from a stranger. And, despite the diversity of social life, it seems that all our relations with people are somehow different in character from our interactions with inanimate objects. We do not ordinarily experience, understand and interact with each other in the same way that we do rocks, artefacts or (most) non-human animals.[1]

This book is an exploration of the structure of interpersonal understanding. Are there any practical skills, concepts, patterns of reasoning, experiences, feelings and so forth that are specific to our ability to understand and interact with people? If so, which are most central and how do the various elements of interpersonal understanding interconnect? A comprehensive answer to such questions is likely to cast considerable light on our conception of what it is to *be* a person.[2] Given the assumption that interpersonal relations are not just a matter of non-conceptual practical skills but also of applying certain concepts, it seems likely that the concepts we employ to interpret and interact with people will be closely related to, if not the same as, the concepts that constitute our sense of what people are.

So where do we start? Despite the apparent heterogeneity of social life, there is a remarkable degree of consensus concerning what interpersonal

1

understanding most centrally involves. The same account is explicitly stated or implicitly assumed throughout much recent work in philosophy of mind, cognitive science, developmental psychology and several other disciplines. According to this account, interpersonal understanding is accomplished by means of a 'folk' or 'commonsense' psychology. The terms 'folk' and 'commonsense' are used interchangeably to indicate that it involves an intuitive, *everyday* ability that we acquire independently of what scientific theorising might tell us about mind and behaviour. The term 'psychology' indicates that it is an understanding of *mental states*, involving the deployment of psychological concepts. As Churchland (1998a, p. 3) puts it, folk psychology is 'the prescientific, commonsense conceptual framework that all normally socialized human beings deploy in order to comprehend, predict, explain, and manipulate the behaviour of humans and the higher animals'.

Almost all those who claim or assume that we understand people by employing a folk psychology also agree on (a) what the fundamental constituents of folk psychology are and (b) what its primary role is. In this chapter, I will begin by outlining the orthodox conception of folk psychology and will then offer an overview of issues that arise concerning the cognitive abilities that facilitate it, how they develop during childhood and how they might have evolved. In so doing, my primary aim is to show that, despite heated debates concerning the mechanisms that enable folk psychology, their development and their evolution, almost all participants in these debates share the same view of what folk or commonsense psychology consists of. Although this view is often stated by its proponents in such a way as to make it seem so obvious as to require no justification, it is a view that I have increasingly come to doubt, and this book is the culmination of those doubts. My approach throughout the book is to explore the structure of interpersonal understanding through a critique of commonplace descriptions of folk psychology. The positive account of interpersonal understanding that I develop through this critique is not an elaboration, revision or supplementation of the orthodox account of folk psychology. Instead, it departs from that account in just about every respect, the implication being that what is labelled an 'everyday', 'commonsense' or 'folk' psychology and routinely accepted as the core of human social life is actually nothing of the sort and bears little relation to how people understand each other. A more detailed summary of my various arguments and conclusions is provided in the final section of this chapter.

Belief-desire psychology

How do we understand each other in everyday life? Folk psychology is generally taken to consist primarily of an ability to attribute internal mental states to people on the basis of behavioural observations. The emphasis is on intentional states, including beliefs, desires, perceptions, memories and emotions, and it is generally agreed that the concepts of 'belief' and 'desire' are central. For example, Fodor (1987, x) refers to a 'commonsense belief/desire psychology', indicating that commonsense psychology is most fundamentally a matter of possessing and competently applying the concepts of 'belief' and 'desire'. Belief, desire and other kinds of mental state posited by folk psychology are usually referred to as 'propositional attitudes', meaning that they take the form 'A believes that p', 'B desires that q', 'C remembers that r' and so forth, where p, q and r are propositions with any intelligible content you like, such as 'the car won't start', 'the Empire State Building is in New York', 'it is raining', 'cats don't like dogs' and 'human beings are rational'. As Davies and Stone (1995b, p. 2) put it:

> The conceptual repertoire constituting folk psychology includes, predominantly, the concepts of belief and desire and their kin – intention, hope, fear, and the rest – the so-called propositional attitudes.

However, not all mental states are propositional attitudes. For example, pains and itches are not communicable in the form 'B pains or itches that p'. Although such states might have perceived locations and characteristic feels, they do not seem to stand in a relation of 'aboutness' to anything. Thus it is arguable that they are not intentional states (although there is some controversy over this). Some accounts acknowledge that our conceptions of non-intentional mental states also enter into folk psychology. For instance, Goldman (1995, p. 75) enquires as to how we 'arrive at attributions of propositional attitudes (and other mental states)'. Nevertheless, all discussions make clear the centrality of propositional attitudes to interpersonal understanding. Most of them refer exclusively to propositional attitudes and some restrict themselves even more specifically to beliefs and desires. The term 'intentional state' has a more general application than 'propositional attitude', encompassing states such as emotions, which are not generally regarded as propositional attitudes. However, the two terms are sometimes employed interchangeably in the folk psychology literature and I will criticise this practice in Chapter 7.

Most authors writing on folk psychology state or assume that the 'folk' think of propositional attitudes as internal states of agents that stand in causal relations to each other and to behaviour, rather than as mere dispositions towards certain behaviours. People are taken to be realists about the internal states they attribute, rather than regarding belief-desire psychology as a useful tool with which to interpret people's behaviour. In addition, it is generally agreed that there is a clear 'folk' distinction between the roles of belief and desire. Beliefs provide information and guide action, whereas desires incorporate goals and thus motivate action.[3]

What role is folk psychology, construed in this way, said to have? The consensus is that our primary aim, when attributing propositional attitudes to someone, is to predict her behaviour. Successful social co-ordination and co-operation require each party to be able to predict what the other will do. And achieving a desirable outcome in non-co-operative and competitive exchanges, which might involve deceit or attempts to conceal intentional states on the part of one or both parties, similarly requires an ability to predict what another person is likely to do. In both kinds of case, it is claimed that the way we do so is to think about the internal causes of a person's past, current and future behaviour; her beliefs and desires.

Folk psychology is also claimed to play a key role in *explaining* behaviour, although its role in prediction is presumably much more widespread, given that we only seek to explain a small proportion of people's activities. An explanation might be offered in conjunction with a prediction or we might want to explain a behaviour that has already occurred, whether that behaviour is one's friend kicking a traffic cone five minutes ago or Napoleon invading Russia in 1812. Such explanations, it is claimed, often look something like 'B acted in such and such a way because B believed that p and desired that q' but can involve much more elaborate combinations of beliefs, desires and other intentional states, interconnected in systematic ways.

Let us assume for now that 'commonsense' belief-desire psychology is an adequate characterisation of something that we do. In which circumstances do we employ it? Consider the following scenarios:

An intimate conversation between lovers
A professional meeting with several colleagues
Buying a loaf of bread from someone in a shop
Anticipating the actions of someone approaching you on a quiet, poorly lit street

Lecturing to a group of students
A telephone conversation with an old friend
A job interview
An email exchange with an unfamiliar person
Negotiating one's way past others on a busy shopping street
Playing a game of chess
Taking an order in a restaurant
Asking for directions from a stranger
Being on holiday in a foreign country and trying to communicate with an irate stranger in the absence of a shared language
Exchanging nods with a colleague as you pass in the corridor.

Social life is not homogeneous and, at first glance, it would seem that there are many different kinds of social situation, which make quite different demands on us and are likely to draw on a wide range of abilities. One way to address the issue of where belief-desire psychology comes into play would be to rigorously classify social situations and tasks, dividing them into types and looking at the various demands that each type places upon us. However, proponents of belief-desire psychology have not done so. One reason for this omission is that many of them assume the centrality of belief-desire psychology to *all* social life, thus dispensing with the need for a more specific account of where it does and does not apply. For example, Wellman (1990, p. 1) states that 'an understanding of the mind is also fundamental to an understanding of the social world. Children come to understand that the overt actions of self and others are the products of internal mental states such as beliefs and desires'. Frith and Happé (1999, p. 2) similarly claim that belief-desire psychology 'appears to be a prerequisite for normal social interaction: in everyday life we make sense of each other's behaviour by appeal to a belief-desire psychology'. These claims and many others like them suggest that the ability to attribute internal propositional attitude states is taken to lie at the core of all the social scenarios that I listed above. Hence recent debates over folk psychology are not concerned with *whether* belief-desire psychology adequately characterises something that we do; most participants assume that its employment is very widespread or even ubiquitous. Instead, the emphasis has been on two broad issues:

(a) Whether commonsense belief-desire psychology will cohere with what empirical science tells us about the mind.
(b) Which mechanisms underlie our folk psychological abilities, how these mechanisms develop during childhood and how they evolved.

Turning first of all to (a), under the assumption that we are, in everyday life, committed to the existence of internal propositional attitude states, there is the question of whether commonsense has got it right. Fodor (1987) assumes that people are realists about propositional attitudes and also argues that folk realism is defensible, which is fortunate because he thinks that folk psychology is utterly indispensable. Although we only tend to explicitly contemplate people's beliefs and desires when things do not proceed as expected, Fodor claims that belief-psychology is also quietly at work on all those other occasions when nothing untoward happens. He remarks that, while misattributions of intentional states are the stuff of 'excellent theatre', 'the successes of commonsense psychology, by contrast, are ubiquitous and – for that very reason – practically invisible' (1987, p. 2). Hence explicit utterances of belief-desire psychology are just the tip of the iceberg. Fodor construes our largely implicit understanding of mental states as a systematic and highly complicated 'theory', which has considerable predictive power and incorporates law-like generalisations concerning the relationships between concepts such as 'belief', 'desire', 'intention' and 'action' (p. 7). This theory, he thinks, is so engrained in our psychology that we could not manage without it. To quote a well-known passage, 'if commonsense intentional psychology really were to collapse, that would be, beyond comparison, the greatest intellectual catastrophe in the history of our species' (1987, xii). He goes on to suggest that, if the concepts of representation and computation are combined, the result is compatible with what the core of commonsense psychology tells us about mental states. So our most deeply cherished theory is left largely intact.

A very different view is offered by Churchland (1981, 1998a,b), who disagrees concerning both the utility of folk psychology and the reality of psychological entities, such as propositional attitudes. Like Fodor, Churchland construes folk psychology as an everyday, pre-scientific *theory* of mindedness. He claims that this theory has considerable shortcomings. Despite the more general conceptual integration occurring between the empirical sciences, folk psychology remains isolated, cut off from an increasingly cohesive scientific picture of the world. While the sciences have progressed, folk psychology has failed to change, to expand, to accommodate new discoveries or to interact productively with the mature sciences. Furthermore, there just does not seem to be a place in current neuroscience for entities like propositional attitude states, suggesting that there are no such things to be found residing in our heads. Churchland adds that the predictive power of folk psychology is much over-rated. In fact, it has nothing informative to say about much of our mental lives, including dreams, perceptual illusions and most kinds of psychopathology.

Thus it has all the hallmarks of a degenerating research program, the scope of which is progressively narrowing. He therefore advocates 'eliminativism' concerning folk psychology, anticipating its replacement, rather than revision, once neuroscience has reached a sufficiently advanced stage.

However, there is an important sense in which Churchland does not reject the orthodox account of folk psychology. Like Fodor, he assumes that propositional attitude psychology *does* play a central role in everyday social life. In fact, he says that it 'embodies our baseline understanding of the cognitive, affective, and purposive nature of people' (1998a, p. 3). What he questions is (a) whether folk realism concerning propositional attitudes is defensible and (b) whether propositional attitude psychology is as successful as it is made out to be.[4]

A position lying somewhere in between Fodor's realism and Churchland's eliminativism is offered by Dennett (1987, 1991a), who refers to folk psychology as the adoption of an 'intentional stance'. According to Dennett, the intentional stance is a highly effective predictive device when deployed upon certain entities, especially other human beings. However, its predictive power is not due to its accuracy at detecting internal states but to its picking up on certain patterns in behaviour. These patterns do not, strictly speaking, reside *in* the behaviour or cause it, given that the same behaviour and all its causes could be comprehensively described from a purely 'physical stance' that made no reference to intentional states. However, any physical description of human behaviour able to support accurate prediction would be very complicated indeed and far too cumbersome to use in everyday social situations, where time and cognitive resources are limited. What the intentional stance manages to do is utilise much coarser, less detailed patterns that have far greater practical utility when it comes to interpreting, predicting and explaining behaviour. By analogy a simple road map is a far more effective tool for the driver than a detailed description of the environment, including every bend, tree and hill. The map incorporates less detailed but more useful patterns. The patterns revealed through an intentional stance take the form of interconnected intentional states, bound together in systematic ways by a presumption of rationality that is constitutive of belief-desire psychology.[5] Dennett describes the stance as follows:

. . . first you decide to treat the object whose behaviour is to be predicted as a rational agent; then you figure out what beliefs that agent ought to have, given its place in the world and its purpose. Then you figure out what desires it ought to have, on the same considerations, and finally you predict that this rational agent will act to further its

goals in the light of its beliefs. A little practical reasoning from the
chosen set of beliefs and desires will in many – but not all – instances
yield a decision about what the agent ought to do; that is what you
predict the agent *will* do.

(1987, p. 17)

As is clear from this passage, although Dennett is not committed to the
view that beliefs and desires are internal states of an organism, with distinct causal roles, he does accept that they are central to interpersonal
interpretation, the goal of which is to predict what an organism will do.
Furthermore, although Dennett himself is not a realist about propositional attitudes, construed as states in heads, it is unclear whether or not
he takes the 'folk' who adopt the intentional stance to be realists. One
could maintain both that people are realists about internal intentional
states when they adopt an intentional stance and that the realism integral to the intentional stance turns out to be misguided, despite it being
part of a very useful predictive device.[6]

In summary then, folk psychology is construed as an everyday, pre-
scientific ability to attribute propositional attitudes, principally beliefs
and desires. It is generally assumed that the 'folk' take these to be internal causes of behaviour, which stand in systematic relations to each
other, although whether folk realism is defensible turns out to be a
tricky philosophical issue. The ability to apply folk psychology is often
taken to be central to all social life. Even when we are not explicitly
thinking about people's mental states, we are, it is claimed, implicitly
assigning them in order to predict behaviour.

Theory or Simulation?

Recent debates concerning folk psychology do not address the question
of what we do but, rather, that of how we do it. Churchland (1981),
Fodor (1987) and many others argue that folk psychology is a matter of
possessing and applying a *theory* of mental states. In everyday life, we
are oblivious to the full complexity of the theory, as it is largely tacit.
However, everyday utterances are claimed to give us some clues as to its
structure, other aspects of which can be revealed through more rigorous
philosophical and scientific scrutiny. Simple examples along the following lines are often offered:

B desires that q.
B believes that action p will achieve q.
All other things being equal, B will do p.

This sort of example is generally taken to be an everyday 'platitude', the kind of claim that any sufficiently educated person will accept without hesitation. A vast number of such platitudes can be listed, all of which seem to incorporate structured relations between kinds of mental state and action. It is arguable that our appreciation of such platitudes is symptomatic of a unified, conceptual appreciation of the connections between mental states and actions. This appreciation, it is claimed, involves an elaborate set of law-like generalisations relating mental states to each other and to behaviour, a largely tacit theory that we ordinarily apply effortlessly when understanding other people. But what is meant by the claim that folk psychology involves possession and application of a *theory*? As already noted, Fodor emphasises concepts, law-like generalisations and predictive power. However, more recent discussions have offered further criteria for theory-hood. Botterill (1996) emphasises the need for a theory to contain *'principles that provide a systematic integration of knowledge'* (p. 107). That is, a theory must comprise a cohesive whole that unites various phenomena under a common framework and be simpler in structure than an inventory of the phenomena that it encompasses. As Botterill puts it, a theory must be more like Newtonian mechanics than the disparate snippets of advice that make up 'gardening lore' (p. 109). He lists several other criteria, including reference to unobservables, incorporation of explicitly or implicitly defined concepts, employment to predict and explain phenomena and an ability to handle counterfactuals (p. 106). Given these criteria, folk psychology seems to fit the bill. All manner of behaviours are brought together under a common framework, which is employed to predict and explain what people do. This framework is clearly conceptual, at least in part, given the explicit inclusion of concepts such as 'belief', 'desire' and 'intention'. Mental states are generally taken to be unobservable causes of behaviour. Furthermore, beliefs and desires often feature in counterfactual claims. For example, if I had not desired to study philosophy, I would have studied medicine instead.[7]

An alternative to the 'theory of mind' account of folk psychology emerged in 1986, in the guise of 'simulation theory'.[8] While 'theory of mind' or, as it is sometimes known, the 'theory theory', emphasises possession and deployment of a body of conceptual knowledge concerning mental states and their interrelations, variants of simulation theory emphasise the role of practical skills, of knowing how to do something, rather than knowing that something is the case. The basic idea is fairly simple; under the assumption that my own cognitive processes are sufficiently similar to those of other people, I can, given the right inputs, use the outputs of those processes to predict what they will do. I can do so without resorting to a theoretical knowledge of how the relevant cognitive processes work, as the assumption that I am like them in certain relevant respects takes the place of a theory of mind. As Heal puts it:

> I can harness all my complex theoretical knowledge about the world and my ability to imagine to yield an insight into other people *without any further elaborate theorizing about them*. Only one simple assumption is needed: that they are like me in being thinkers, that they possess the same fundamental cognitive capacities and propensities that I do.
>
> (1995a, p. 47)

She suggests that this procedure is particularly useful when it comes to predicting what others will do. The primary role of simulation is to get you from another person's current mental states to their predicted mental states and/or behaviour.[9] One takes the person's current mental states and feeds them into one's own practical reasoning mechanism. Instead of acting on the basis of the output, one ascribes it to the other person.

However, the question arises as to how one acquires the right input states. How does one pick up on those features of the environment that are psychologically relevant and recognise which mental states a person is likely to have in a given situation? It is arguable that simulation presupposes a background of theory, given that further procedures, which may well involve concepts, inferences, law-like generalisations and so forth, might well be needed to arrive at an appropriate starting point for the simulation. It is also arguable that theory plays a role in deciding when simulation is likely to be effective. In certain cases, it may well be that the two systems are not sufficiently similar to warrant the assumption of a common output, even given the same input states.

Others have made stronger claims on behalf of the role of simulation. For example, Goldman (1995, p. 83) maintains that it not only gets us from current to future states but is the 'fundamental method' by which we ascribe mental states to others, including non-propositional states, such as pains and emotions. To acquire knowledge of another person's current mental states, one considers what one would perceive and think in her situation and ascribes, via inference or analogy, the same or similar states to her. To predict her future mental states and actions, one just maintains the analogy and asks what one would think and do, given such a psychological starting point. An objection to this view is that it faces the charge of phenomenological implausibility. Given that we are frequently unaware of using ourselves as models in order to predict what others will think and do, what grounds are there for maintaining that such practices are widespread? Heal suggests that simulation is a 'personal level' activity; it is something that we knowingly do via an exercise of the imagination and thus something that we should be aware of doing. But phenomenological implausibility is perhaps not a problem for her, given that she takes its role to be more limited. Goldman deals with the problem by suggesting, unlike Heal, that the process often proceeds tacitly and is not always phenomenologically accessible. Furthermore, although he claims that simulation is fundamental to our understanding of others, he adds that it need not be something we always rely upon. We first come to understand another person via simulation but, with increasing familiarity, we might later rely on scripts and routines instead.

Gordon (1995a,b,c, 1996) argues that simulation plays an even more fundamental role. It not only comprises our most basic access to others' intentional states but is also the source of the concept 'belief'. He offers an account of simulation that does not include any reliance at all on inference, analogy or theory. According to this account, simulation involves two imaginative shifts. First of all, I imagine what I would do in another person's situation. The next shift is to imagine what she will do in her situation, which requires somehow adopting her perspective on the world, rather than my perspective in her situation (1995a, p. 63). Having undergone this perspectival shift, there is no additional need to simulate specific mental states or cognitive processes. Once I have adopted the other person's perspective, everything else takes care of itself; mental states arise in exactly the same way that they would if I had retained my own egocentric perspective. The shift is from self to other, rather than from having my beliefs to adopting her beliefs; an 'egocentric shift' or change of 'point of view' is what does the work (1995b, p. 56). Hence I do not entertain the thought 'B believes that p' when simulating but take it to be the case that p, from within B's perspective. The concept of belief, Gordon argues, originates in the ability to tie a statement of fact to a context of simulation. I adopt B's perspective and, in so doing, take p to be the case; 'B believes that p' means the occurrence of 'p' within a B simulation (1995a, p. 68).

One potential problem with this view is that, although theory seems to be absent, the ability to adopt another person's point of view remains unexplained. Gordon attributes it to 'our capacity for recentering our egocentric maps' (1995b, p. 63). However, there is the question of what this capacity involves. Magical transference into another's psychological predicament is presumably not an acceptable solution; what is required is an appropriate series of adjustments to my own psychology (Gordon, 1995b, p. 57). But a problem with this is that my adjusted psychology is still 'mine' and so a grasp of what it is to be 'another psychology', rather than 'a modification of my own egocentric point of view', remains unaccounted for. Even assuming that adjustments to one's own psychology can yield reliable predictions of others' behaviour, there is still the question of which adjustments to make and this opens the door for some kind of theory, given that a systematic body of knowledge could underlie the ability to achieve the right kinds of egocentric shift.

As with Goldman's account, there is also the concern of phenomenological implausibility. When I interpret and interact with other people, I seldom undergo an explicit shift in perspective. Gordon, like Goldman, suggests that simulation need not be an achievement that we are always able to verbally report. It can operate at a 'sub-verbal level', enabling us to anticipate the behaviour of others and perhaps, sometimes, our own behaviour. He states that we employ our own cognitive mechanisms 'off-line', indicating that simulation is something achieved by the mechanisms that underlie folk psychology, rather than something that we knowingly perform (1995a, p. 70).[10] However, it remains unclear how one is supposed to undergo a change in one's 'point of view' without any associated phenomenology.

Hence there are quite different conceptions of what simulation is and what it achieves, each with different limitations and shortcomings. But what appeal do any of these have over the theory theory? Heal (1995b, p. 36) stresses the relative economy of simulation. In most everyday situations, an enormous amount of information could potentially enter into our deliberations. In getting from input states to output states, any number of factors could come into play. But we somehow manage to focus on only a few of them, rather than going off in all manner of directions and getting nowhere. Our ability to interpret each other must somehow accommodate this grasp of relevance. A 'theory of relevance' would be cumbersome to say the least, and theory theorists have given little indication of whether and how such a theory might operate. A far more economical solution, Heal suggests, would be to let our own grasp of relevance do the job without relying on an additional theory of how it does that job (1996, p. 84).[11] This leaves the issue of how we achieve a grasp of relevance unresolved. However, the theory theory has to deal with both a grasp of relevance and a theory of relevance; one mystery is surely better than two.

Heal also suggests that our ability to interpret others leans heavily on the specific contents of mental states, rather than just a knowledge of the systematic connections that exist between kinds of mental state. She offers the example of whether John will think a jacket is garish (1995b, p. 39). If you know that (a) John thinks all bright colours are garish and (b) the jacket is scarlet, you will most likely conclude that John will believe the jacket to be garish. The inference requires the knowledge that 'scarlet is bright', and this knowledge is content-specific. Unless a theory of mind is also a theory of the interconnections that apply between all our concepts, it seems that simulation is a better strategy for handling content. In the simplest case, one just assumes that others will have the same conceptual knowledge as oneself.

Another problem with the theory theory is its emphasis on systematic relations that apply between types of mental state, relations that are often claimed to be constitutive of rationality. It is arguable that certain examples of practical reasoning offered by theory theorists, marketed as platitudes, are actually rather poor reflections of how people usually reason and of the kinds of conclusions people are likely to draw about actions, given certain beliefs. To quote Goldman:

> One of the favorite sorts of platitudes offered by philosophers is something like 'If x believes "p only if q" and x desires p, then x desires q'. But the relationship formulated by this 'platitude' simply does not systematically obtain.
>
> (1995, p. 79)

Goldman cites the possibility of contextually inactive beliefs and desires as a reason why such 'platitudes' might fail to apply. (I will discuss numerous further counter-examples to so-called folk psychological platitudes in Chapter 7.) An advantage of simulation is that it does not require an account of precisely how people reason. All it needs is the assumption that, regardless of how people reason, they at least reason in a similar fashion.

As theory and simulation theories have different limitations, a popular option is to maintain that they both have some role to play in enabling folk psychology. As Stone and Davies (1996, p. 136) remark:

> The mental simulation debate has reached a stage at which there is considerable agreement about the need to develop hybrid theories – theories that postulate both theory and simulation, and then spell out the way in which those two components interact.

Most theory theorists continue to maintain that simulation cannot be fundamental to our grasp of mindedness, as the ability to utilise any isomorphism between self and other will fall back on a prior understanding of relevant similarities and differences between them (for example, Carruthers, 1996, p. 22). In other words, simulation presupposes an understanding of which entities are appropriate objects for simulation. However, there is general acknowledgement that simulation will have at least some role to play, if only as 'an enrichment of the operation of theory' (Botterill and Carruthers, 1999, p. 89).

The question of how theory and simulation might relate to each other is complicated by there being several different conceptions of simulation. In order to determine the role played by theory, the kind of theoretical knowledge needed and its required level of sophistication, there is the need to ascertain what work and how much work simulation routines do. As discussed, Heal, Goldman and Gordon offer differing accounts of the role and scope of simulation. Perhaps more pressing is the concern that the nature of 'simulation' remains unclear. Gordon emphasises a perspectival transformation, whereas Heal and Goldman both focus on simulating practical reasoning. There is also disagreement as to whether simulation involves an exercise of the imagination or the operation of sub-personal mechanisms. And a further distinction can be made between simulating and being a simulation. Heal (1996, p. 76) states:

> By a simulation of X we shall understand something, Y, which is similar enough to X in its intrinsic nature for tendencies to diachronic development which are inherent in X to have parallels in Y.

However, X understanding Y in virtue of similarities between X and Y is not the same as X actively modelling Y. In more recent work, Heal employs the term 'co-cognition' rather than 'simulation', co-cognition being 'just a fancy name for the everyday notion of thinking about the same subject matter' (1998, p. 483). Co-cognition does not involve taking on another's perspective or actively modelling her psychology. Heal goes on to distinguish different versions of the simulationist claim and remarks that, if the term 'simulation' is employed to encompass them all, it will be of 'limited usefulness' (p. 479).[12]

One possibility is that several different kinds of modelling and co-cognition might support or be supported by one or more bodies of knowledge. Recent work has moved towards hybrid models that combine theory with variants of simulation in a number of different ways and there is a trend towards increasingly elaborate models of theory-simulation interaction. For example, Nichols and Stich offer what they describe as a 'motley array' of interacting mechanisms, portrayed diagrammatically as boxes in a flow chart (2003, p. 212).

It is debatable how the simulation-theory debate might relate to the prospects for eliminativism concerning folk psychology. One cannot eliminate a theory if there is no theory. However, simulation still incorporates the concepts of 'belief' and 'desire'. One can debate the reality of such entities, without assuming that they are embedded in a theory. A case could also be made for the elimination of a practice like simulation in certain contexts, if it turned out to be ineffective and was something that we had at least some control over.

Another issue is that of how the simulation-theory debate relates to intuitive distinctions between first- and third-person access to mental states. We might employ a theory of mind to interpret our own mental states, as well as those of others. Even if this is so, as many theory theorists have claimed, it is likely that the theory will be deployed more accurately and perhaps differently in the first-person case, given that we generally have much more information about our own activities, which might be accessed through means other than behavioural observation. Simulation theories, in contrast, might be construed as privileging first-person knowledge of mental states over knowledge of others' mental states, given that we use ourselves as models in order to ascribe mental states to others. However, simulation could also be argued to play a number of roles in understanding and predicting first-person mental states and behaviours. Taking our past mental states as inputs might serve to make our reasons for actions clearer to us. In addition, taking possible future situations as inputs could be of considerable help when it comes to planning behaviour. And recall that, on Gordon's view, the capacity to undergo a shift of perspective is constitutive of the concept of belief. Hence the ability to think about our own beliefs presupposes an appreciation of other people as believers. So there are various options regarding the relationship between first- and third-person theory and simulation.[13]

Despite the increasing complexity and technicality of debates over how folk psychology is enabled, how useful it is and whether it is ultimately to be usurped by empirical science, all these debates remain constrained by a shared account of what folk psychology is. The view that the principal accomplishment of folk psychology is the attribution of propositional attitudes, in the service of prediction and explanation, is as established among the simulationist camp as it is among the theory theorists. Goldman (1995, p. 81) states that his account is primarily concerned with 'intentional explanation and prediction'. Gordon (1995a) offers 'an account of the nature of folk psychology' (p. 60), accepting that 'explanations are often couched in terms of beliefs, desires, and other propositional attitudes' and that 'predictions, particularly predictions of the behaviour of others, are often made on the basis of attributions of such states' (p. 66). Heal (1995b. p. 34) similarly emphasises beliefs, desires and intentions.

Hence the term 'folk psychology' can be employed to refer to a view that is common to both simulation and theory camps, although it is sometimes used in a more specific sense, to refer to the theory theory. The term 'theory of mind' is also employed in both broad and narrow senses, to refer either to the view that everyday interpersonal understanding involves attributing propositional attitudes or to the more specific view that this is achieved by means of a theory (Carruthers and Smith, 1996, p. 1). Throughout this book, I will only use 'theory of mind' in its more restrictive sense, while using 'folk psychology' (which I take to be interchangeable with 'commonsense psychology') in a broader way, to encompass the claims that (a) we have a commonsense understanding of mindedness and (b) this understanding consists primarily of an ability to attribute internal mental states, principally beliefs and desires, in order to predict and explain behaviour. Hence 'folk psychology' is not just 'whatever everyday interpersonal understanding consists of'; it is everyday interpersonal understanding conceived of in a particular way. Throughout the remainder of this discussion, I will abbreviate 'folk psychology', understood as (a) and (b), rather than just (a), to FP.[14]

Development and evolution

The simulation-theory debate overlaps with a substantial body of work on the development and evolution of folk psychological ability. Regardless of whether one advocates a theory, simulation or hybrid account, there is the question of whether the abilities that facilitate propositional attitude attribution are innate or acquired. Most writers on the topic are of the view that FP is largely innate. Evidence for this is drawn from a variety of empirical findings, but there has been particular emphasis on variants of the false belief task, which was devised by Wimmer and Perner (1983) to test subjects' ability to attribute a false belief to a puppet, having observed the verbal and non-verbal performances of two interacting puppets. Wimmer and Perner found that the ability arose in most typical children between four and five years of age.

Later variants of the task indicate that it is present in even younger children but do not challenge the claim that it arises at around the same age in most cases (see, for example, Wellman, Cross and Watson, 2001).[15] That FP is a complex skill, which first appears at the same early age in most children without any explicit training, has been taken by many to indicate that it is innate (for example, Carruthers, 1996).

Of course, an ability to attribute beliefs and desires is not demonstrated from birth. However, there are numerous characteristics that are taken to be largely innate but which do not present themselves on day one, including teeth, language and an ability to walk. Furthermore, it is possible that younger children do possess the relevant concepts but have not yet developed the ability to apply them (Fodor, 1995).

In contrast to the view that FP is largely a matter of innate ability, Gopnik (1996a,b) argues for a version of the theory theory, according to which FP is acquired in much the same manner that we acquire scientific theories. In response to the objection that an acquired theory would be unlikely to develop at the same early age in all children, Gopnik suggests that young children have access to a massive body of shared information, which makes convergence upon a common theory almost inevitable. It is not so much that they are 'little scientists' but rather that scientific theorising is made possible by mechanisms that have the primary function of facilitating childhood learning (1996b, p. 485). The view that scientists are 'big children' or that children are 'little scientists' has been challenged by others who claim that children cannot have the cognitive skills required for theory acquisition unless they already have a concept of false belief. How could one test a theory without entertaining the possibility of its falsehood? So it is unclear how the child scientist could obtain FP via a process analogous to theorising and hypothesis testing unless she had already had FP (Carruthers, 1996, p. 23).

Closely related to the question of innateness is that of whether FP is 'modular' in nature. Empirical findings are often taken to show that the ability to attribute mental states can be selectively impaired, leaving more general intelligence largely intact. For example, autistic children tend to perform very poorly on false belief tasks, compared to children with Down's Syndrome who have a lower general intelligence (Baron-Cohen, 1995, Chapter 5).[16] Hence it has been proposed that FP ability depends upon a specialised cognitive mechanism, dedicated to the task of understanding other minds. Such task-specific mechanisms are often referred to as 'modules'. The term was coined by Fodor (1983), who conceived of modules as cognitive input systems, the operations of which are insulated from the influence of other cognitive systems. Fodorian modules have a range of distinctive properties, including domain specificity, characteristic breakdown patterns, high processing speed and a fixed neural architecture (Fodor, 1983, Chapter 3). Recent conceptions of modularity tend to be more liberal. Certain authors, including Baron-Cohen (1995), adopt an account of modularity along the lines of that suggested by Cosmides and Tooby (1992). According to this account, modules are functionally individuated cognitive systems. They are 'domain-specific', meaning that they incorporate representations and/or processes that are dedicated to the solution of specific environmental problems. However, the possibility of at least some communication between modular processes is not ruled out. Modularity, according to Cosmides and Tooby, is not restricted to input systems. Instead, they propose that our entire cognitive architecture is modular in nature. As Tooby and Cosmides put it in their preface to Baron-Cohen (1995),

> . . . our cognitive architecture resembles a confederation of hundreds or thousands of functionally dedicated computers (often called modules) designed to solve adaptive problems endemic to our hunter-gatherer ancestors.
>
> (xiii–xiv)[17]

Both simulation and theory theories are compatible with modularity. Gordon (1995a, p. 70) suggests the possibility of a cognitive module dedicated to the process of simulation. Botterill and Carruthers (1999, Chapter 3) emphasise the role of theory over simulation but also propose that the 'mind-reading system' is modular in nature.[18] If FP rests on modular abilities, it could be that several modules are involved. Baron-Cohen (1995, Chapter 4) proposes three systems that operate as developmental precursors to a fully fledged FP: an 'intentionality detector', an 'eye-direction detector' and a 'shared attention mechanism'. These come to operate in conjunction with a 'theory of mind mechanism' that develops later.[19] Happé and Loth (2002) speculate that we have different modules for processing communicative gestures and intentional actions. And Sperber and Wilson (2002) postulate a pragmatics sub-module that somehow enables us to make the contextual assumptions required to interpret speaker meaning.

It has also been argued that some ingredients of FP are non-modular in nature. Modular systems draw on a limited range of inputs and processes. But consider the task of figuring out whether someone is hiding a belief or explicitly attempting to deceive you. In coming to this conclusion, you might need to draw on information from a range of sources and piece it together in an intricate, innovative way. Thus the more demanding cases of belief attribution arguably require a degree of cognitive flexibility that cannot be achieved by a wholly modular process and draw instead on a wide range of cognitive resources (Currie and Sterelny, 2000).

The topic of modularity is closely related to that of how FP evolved. According to Cosmides and Tooby (1992), modules are functionally individuated and the function of a device is the role that it has been historically selected to perform.[20] However, even if modules are, by definition, products of natural selection, this need not entail that they are innate, in the sense of being wholly or largely specified by the genes or assembled by the time of birth. Although, as discussed, Gopnik rejects modularity, associating it with the 'innate theory' view and contrasting it with her own account of the child scientist (1996a, p. 169), it is possible to forge a middle path between the two views. A module could be acquired through a complicated developmental process, involving learning. That process could, at the same time, be significantly constrained by innate adaptations. Gopnik does acknowledge an 'initial innate theory' that the child starts off with, which is progressively revised and elaborated through learning, with FP as the usual outcome (1996a, p. 172). Given such a view, it could still be maintained that FP is an evolved adaptation. The development of any biological structure is reliant on certain environmental constants; it could be the case both that FP is a biological adaptation and that the innate structures that predispose us towards it make use of environmental factors to facilitate its assembly. Various accounts of FP development emphasise this kind of developmental complexity, suggesting that an FP module is the outcome of a series of interactions between innate abilities, learning environments and developmental stages. For example, Garfield, Peterson and Perry (2001, p. 502) suggest that FP depends on an 'acquired module', arising through progressive developmental stages which themselves depend on immersion in certain kinds of social environments. If FP develops in some such fashion, the distinction between a largely innate theory and a theory acquired through learning looks unclear to say the least. That said, perhaps the most popular view is still the one that runs a theory theory of FP together with modularity and innateness. As summarised by Davies and Stone (1995a, p. 5), it is the view that 'tacit knowledge of the theory is innate, that it is embodied in a special-purpose module of the mind, and that development is predominantly a matter of maturation rather than of learning'.[21]

Let us assume for now that FP, regardless of whether it depends on a theory or an ability to simulate, originated as an evolved adaptation specific to an understanding of mindedness. Why did it evolve? In other words, what was the historical advantage of being able to attribute beliefs and desires to conspecifics? One popular view has its origins in Humphrey (1976), who argues that the greatest environmental problems faced by our ancestors involved not the inanimate environment or other species of organism but members of one's own species. The most successful social organisms will be those that are able to detect deception, get away with deceiving others and anticipate others' behaviour to get the most out of strategic interaction. Thus Humphrey suggests that characteristically human intelligence arose as a result of selection pressures favouring strategic social abilities. Being able to detect a false belief is not the same as being able to figure out that an expressed belief differs from a concealed belief. Nor is it sufficient for instilling false beliefs in others. However, an ability to distinguish between belief and behaviour, coupled with the recognition that beliefs differ from person to person, is at least a significant step towards successful deceit and deceit detection.[22] Hence it has been argued that mind reading abilities progressively developed in response to selection pressures favouring what is often termed 'Machiavellian intelligence' (Byrne and Whiten, eds, 1988). There are several different understandings of this term. It need not encompass only deceitful strategies and can also accommodate a diversity of co-operative behaviours that ultimately lead to personal gain (Byrne and Whiten, 1997). However, even if selection pressures relating to social competition and strategic interaction did play a significant role in human cognitive evolution and, more specifically, social understanding, it is likely that numerous additional factors, associated with all sorts of circumstances, also played a role (Byrne, 1997). Nevertheless FP, with its emphasis on detecting hidden mental states, seems especially well-tailored to strategic interactions involving deceit and concealment.

A place to start

In what follows, I will not be immersing myself any further in complicated debates over whether FP is enabled by theory or simulation, whether it is modular, how it develops, why it evolved and whether it will be complemented by what science tells us about minds. Instead, I want to focus on the common presupposition that shapes all such discussions, FP itself. The reason I have included, in this first chapter, a lengthy preamble about accounts of the mechanisms that enable FP, their development and their evolution is that although they are not my primary focus, the critique of FP developed here will have various repercussions for them. An ability to attribute internal propositional attitudes on the basis of behavioural observations, so as to facilitate prediction and explanation of behaviour, is almost always accepted as a starting point for enquiry. Should it turn out that commonplace descriptions of FP are incomplete, misleading or plain wrong, accounts of the nature, evolution and development of mechanisms that enable FP and of the relationship between FP and scientific psychology will most likely need to be rejected or at least significantly revised. Some such repercussions will be indicated in later chapters.

But, one might ask, what could possibly be wrong with FP? After all, it is so engrained in philosophy of mind and cognitive science as to seem utterly uncontroversial. And how could it be controversial? It is just a simple description of something that we do. However, I begin in Chapter 2 by arguing that FP is not quite so commonsensical as it is made out to be. In so doing, I will not simply ask whether FP is commonsense but will instead enquire as to what is actually meant by the term 'commonsense'. It turns out that everyday 'folk', who have not been taught all about belief-desire psychology and told that it is commonsense, do not find FP at all obvious. Thus 'commonsense psychology' cannot mean a description of interpersonal understanding that is apparent to all. I consider various other conceptions of commonsense and conclude that FP is not 'commonsense' in any sense of the term. It is instead a philosophical position as debatable as any other. The only difference between it and most other philosophical positions is that no good arguments seem to have been offered to the effect that FP is what we actually do in everyday life.

Having established that FP is in fact a philosophical account of interpersonal understanding, in the remainder of the book I investigate the plausibility of that account, focusing on two central questions:

(a) Which social accomplishments involve FP?
(b) Is FP an adequate description of anything that we do?

Chapters 3 and 4 address the scope of FP. I suggest that much of our ability to understand and interact with one another depends not on FP but on a shared understanding of interlocking social roles, social norms and artefact functions. Frameworks of norms, roles and functions, I claim, are generally understood as features of the everyday world, and they are taken for granted by most explicit efforts at interpersonal interpretation and interaction. This kind of appreciation of the shared world is, I argue, presupposed by FP rather than accommodated by it. I also note that proponents of FP frequently miscast an understanding of the shared social world in terms of the attribution of propositional attitudes. Hence the role of FP is, at the very least, over-emphasised.

Chapters 5–7 turn from the scope of FP to the question of whether it is an adequate description of anything that we do. The claim that we attribute internal propositional attitude states on the basis of behavioural observations might seem innocent. However, descriptions of FP tend to incorporate a number of contestable assumptions. I focus on the following:

(a) Mental states cannot be perceived and must therefore be inferred on the basis of behaviour.
(b) Mental states are internal states that cause behaviour.
(c) Interpersonal understanding is best construed in terms of the detached observation of person B by person A, rather than in terms of interaction between A and B.
(d) Understanding others is a matter of deploying one's internal cognitive abilities, rather than a cognitive achievement that is partly enabled by interaction with them.
(e) Adopting the third-person perspective towards somebody and interpreting the behaviour of a 'she' or 'he' is typical of interpersonal understanding. Addressing someone in the second person, as 'you', does not involve anything extra.
(f) Everyday interpersonal understanding incorporates the concepts of 'belief' and 'desire' and a clear distinction between them.

Chapter 5 challenges (a) and (b), by suggesting that we are ordinarily able to perceive the goal structure of actions, in addition to the meanings of many gestures and expressions. Many feelings, emotions and thoughts are partially constituted by gesture, expression and action. Hence mental states are not always wholly internal causes of behaviour; they are often partly embodied in perceivable behaviour. I bring this conclusion together with the conclusions of Chapters 3 and 4, to show that perception of action, expression and gesture in a shared context of norms, roles and functions is, in many cases, all we need to understand what people are doing and why.

Chapter 6 takes issue with (c), (d) and (e). I suggest that an emphasis on those social encounters where we address each other as 'you' can provide more insight into what it is to relate to someone as a *person* than the traditional focus on detached observation of a 'he' or 'she'. I note that I-you relations are generally characterised by expressive, gestural and dialogical interaction between participants. This interaction, I argue, is itself constitutive of our ability to understand each other. Interpersonal understanding is not usually a matter of deploying internal abilities in observational contexts. Instead, the abilities partly reside in the interaction. Generalising from the I-you case, I suggest that all instances of *personal* understanding incorporate a distinctive kind of bodily responsiveness. Indeed, taking someone to be a *person* involves adopting a *personal stance*, comprised of a kind of affective, bodily relatedness. Understanding people is never detached, in the sense that observation of a rock might be. I also offer a re-interpretation of 'simulation', according to which it is not ordinarily a matter of A simulating B but of simulated interaction between A and B.

Chapter 7 addresses the assumption that the 'folk' are committed to two principal categories of mental state, belief and desire. I suggest that these terms are used to communicate a wide range of predicaments and that an intuitive appreciation of the differences between them is evident in everyday discourse. However, illustrations of how FP works, of the kind that are routinely offered by its proponents, tend to confuse these various states and lump them all together under the categories of 'belief' and 'desire'. I also show that the clear-cut distinction between belief-like and desire-like states, insisted on by FP, is not respected by everyday thought. Furthermore, many so-called 'beliefs' and 'desires' are not propositional attitudes and I offer examples of 'believing p', where p is not a proposition or series of propositions but is reliably understood by people all the same. Borrowing a term from Needham (1972), I conclude that 'belief' and 'desire' are 'peg words', very general terms used to refer to a wide range of different phenomena. The claim that they are understood by people to be distinctive kinds of internal states involves a misguided reification of abstractions.

Chapter 8 draws the argument of the preceding chapters together to suggest that FP is not, strictly speaking, *false*. It is, rather, an abstraction from social life that is misleading in various respects and has no psychological reality. At best, it is a convenient way of talking in certain areas of philosophy, which has become an entrenched and misguided philosophical institution. This final chapter concludes with a tentative diagnosis of the problem, suggesting that it stems largely from the prevalence of mechanistic naturalism. The mistake is not to postulate mechanisms but to assume that interpersonal understanding is itself somehow like mechanistic understanding and thus to miscast it in mechanistic terms, as a matter of figuring out how internal states interact in reliable ways so as to cause behaviour. This amounts to a refusal to recognise the affective, self-engaging stance through which people are encountered *as people* in the context of a shared social world and, ultimately, to a somewhat pathological denial of the personal. I also suggest that, if we admit that the personal stance involves an 'openness to others' that is quite different in character from mechanistic thinking, there are insufficient grounds for insisting that a mechanistic stance will ultimately be able to explain what is accessible through a personal stance. There may be certain truths that are just not available to one who thinks only in terms of mechanism, including truths about people.

What I do not dispute here is the view that social life relies on an ability to predict behaviour and sometimes to explain it. There is a sense in which it is trivially true that interpersonal understanding involves prediction. Our various interactions with each other certainly do involve anticipating what people are going to do next. Otherwise, navigating a busy shopping street would be impossible. However, this sense of 'prediction' need not imply that I direct any cognitive resources at all towards a specific individual in order to predict what that individual will do on a given occasion. For example, if a sign says 'turn left', I will predict that B will turn left, given my prediction that everyone in a very large crowd of which B is a part will turn left. In such cases, I may well successfully co-ordinate my own behaviour with that of B while being utterly oblivious to B. Even if I do focus specifically upon B and make the explicit prediction that she will turn left, I do not need to consider any internal characteristics of B in order to predict what she will do. My prediction rests on there being a 'turn left' sign, coupled with the general assumption that people in everyday situations tend to follow signs. So predicting B, in the liberal sense of 'prediction', need not involve any cognitive effort directed at B and can instead rely on a range of indirect methods. I do not want to challenge such a permissive sense of 'prediction'. However, we might also understand 'predicting B' in a narrower sense, as involving cognitive effort focused specifically upon B's characteristics and behaviour, with the aim of anticipating what B will do. The questions of how frequently we do this in social life and of whether, where and how our doing so relies on FP ability will need to be addressed. To further complicate matters, there are many other cases of prediction that involve not just observing a situation but intervening in it in such a way as to make it more likely that a certain person or group of people will act in a particular way. So the ability to predict might in some cases be inextricable from the ability to successfully manipulate behaviour. It is questionable whether prediction in cases of intervention and manipulation relies on the same skills as detached prediction.

Proponents of FP do not generally distinguish between different kinds of prediction. Thus it is difficult to assess how encompassing they claim the role of FP to be or what kinds of prediction it is supposed to enable. I do not directly challenge the claim that FP is involved in prediction, given that the claim is itself unclear. Rather, throughout the discussion I consider the various skills that we employ when understanding and interacting with people in different contexts to see whether and when FP might be employed, remaining sensitive to the different ways in which 'prediction', in the general sense of the term, might be accomplished.

The claim that FP plays a central role in explanation is clearer and easier to assess, as its proponents offer numerous and varied illustrations of how we explain people's activities by invoking FP. However, I take understanding, rather than explanation, as my primary focus, given that we only attempt to explain behaviour in certain cases. Understanding has a wider scope than explanation and it is important to look at all those instances where we understand and relate to people without attempting to explain what they do. Nevertheless, I do examine various examples of social explanation, in order to determine whether and how FP is involved, and the theme of explanation is particularly prominent in Chapter 7. That we sometimes explain people's behaviour is, of course, something I take for granted throughout. However, what I challenge is the assumption that explanations of why people do what they do can in most cases be fitted into the mould of FP.

In emphasising 'understanding', I use the term in a fairly permissive sense, to include the application of concepts, non-conceptual practical skills, patterns of reasoning and the ability to detect and respond to emotions and feelings. My aim is to explore what everyday interpersonal understanding involves. To assume an overly restrictive conception of understanding from the outset would be to prejudge the issue. I will discuss several different kinds of social understanding and will also consider how they relate to each other. In referring to understanding *and* experience, I do not wish to imply that experience involves no understanding. Experience, I will suggest, can incorporate practical responsiveness, affectivity and the application of concepts. However, not all social understanding is integral to experience. In addition to experiencing people and social situations, we also think about what we experience. We think about situations as we actively participate in them. We also reflect upon aspects of social life and our various social experiences from a non-participant perspective. A further distinction needs to be drawn between everyday and scientific reflection upon interpersonal relations, as the latter may turn out to be quite different from the kind of reflection that people ordinarily engage in. Hence, in discussing both experience and understanding, I do not want to suggest that they are wholly distinct; some forms of understanding are integral to social experience and others are not.

Throughout the book, I draw heavily on phenomenological descriptions, offered by the likes of Husserl, Heidegger, Scheler, Gurwitsch, Schutz, Sartre and Merleau-Ponty. My intention is not to advocate the overall philosophical position of any particular phenomenologist but to draw selectively from each of them and employ their various insights to aid reflection upon the structure of social life. One reason I appeal to phenomenology is that the FP literature is surprisingly bereft of detailed descriptions of social experience, understanding and interaction. Instead, it tends simply to describe every social scenario in terms of believing and desiring, failing to entertain the possibility of an alternative. Phenomenologists, in contrast, have offered a diversity of intricate descriptions. These can help bring to light aspects of interpersonal understanding that might otherwise be ignored, thus opening up the possibility of alternatives to FP. I also discuss some scientific work, including recent findings in neuroscience that relate to the perception of agency. My aim in so doing is not primarily to speculate about which mechanisms underlie interpersonal understanding but to show that certain phenomenological claims that conflict with FP are not at odds with scientific results or somehow mysterious. Phenomenological and scientific enquiry can interact and complement each other in various ways and the empirical case for FP does consist of scientific results but of scientific results that have already been interpreted through the lens of FP.

2
Where is the Commonsense in Commonsense Psychology?

What makes belief-desire psychology a 'commonsense' or 'folk' psychology? Part of the answer is that it is to be contrasted with a scientific psychology. The latter consists of a collection of evolving theories and hypotheses, formulated by professional scientists and tested via a range of explicit methods and experimental techniques. Knowledge of its various sub-disciplines, in conjunction with the relevant practical expertise, is acquired through a lengthy process of explicit training. FP, in contrast, is something that all typical people start employing at around the same early age, without any training. And it arises and persists in much the same form regardless of what one might know about scientific psychology. Hence it is not a 'pop science' acquired by educated non-scientists but an understanding that is possessed by educated and uneducated alike.

This alone is not enough to warrant the label 'commonsense'. People have numerous capabilities that do not originate in empirical science but are not ordinarily referred to as commonsense abilities. We do not have a commonsense heartbeat, commonsense pupil dilation or a commonsense ability to walk. So the term 'commonsense' implies more than just 'non-scientific'. Its application could be limited to conceptual abilities. However, this might be overly restrictive. 'Commonsense' could also refer to inarticulate but reliable intuitions and gut feelings, in addition to various practical skills incorporating non-conceptual elements. And it is likely that some such abilities will turn out to play a central role in interpersonal relations. Hence it would be premature to focus exclusively on possession and application of concepts when attempting to describe the abilities that underlie everyday interpersonal understanding and interaction. To further complicate matters, even if interpersonal understanding does depend upon a specialised set of inter-related concepts, it could well be that people do not, ordinarily at least, have an articulate appreciation of those concepts. A concept could be fundamental to our thinking about the world without being apparent to casual reflection. Hence, even if commonsense psychology is a primarily conceptual affair, the sense in which it is commonsense will need to be clarified. Are the relevant concepts (a) fundamental but non-obvious, (b) superficial and obvious or (c) fundamental and obvious?

As noted in Chapter 1, much the same description of FP is cited time and time again, with little if anything in the way of justification. So it might seem from much of the literature that the character of FP is plain obvious. In other words, that FP is the basis of social life is itself an item of commonsense; it is commonsensical. Of course, the processes that enable FP will not fall into this category. According to the theory theory, much of FP's structure is tacit. As Stich and Ravenscroft note, the claim that we possess a theory of mind is not intuitive; 'ordinary folk certainly don't take themselves to be invoking a theory when they use intentional terms to explain other people's behaviour' (1996, p. 117). However, in distancing the theory theory from what the 'folk' think, Stich and Ravenscroft seem to imply that 'ordinary folk' are at least aware of their reliance on intentional concepts. Botterill and Carruthers (1999, p. 31) draw a similar distinction, between a 'folksy list' and its 'underlying generative principles'. They acknowledge that unearthing the principles will be difficult but do not say the same about the list. Appeals to tacit simulation (Gordon, 1995a; Goldman, 1995) also make a distinction between the attribution of mental states and the mechanisms that underlie it. Hence it is important to distinguish FP from the abilities that make it possible. The former is taken to be commonsense, while the latter are not.

So is our reliance on FP something that is readily apparent to all of us? Many remarks would seem to support such an interpretation. For example, Fodor, while acknowledging that the full theoretical structure of folk psychology is difficult to articulate, states that 'the predictive adequacy of commonsense psychology is beyond rational dispute' (1987, p. 6) and later informs us of 'what common sense believes about the attitudes' (p. 15). Elsewhere he makes a number of assertions about 'how common sense has it' (1991, pp. 23–24). Likewise, Botterill and Carruthers (1999, p. 10) claim that 'we cannot help but think of each other in such terms' and later that 'common-sense psychology the world over recognises the difference between these two broad categories of intentional state [beliefs and desires]' (p. 35). Warren (1999, pp. 154–155) similarly tells us that 'the overall structure of everyday psychology is so familiar and ingrained that it seems counterintuitive to suppose that anything could be fundamentally wrong with the explanatory framework'. But what is meant by the claims that commonsense 'recognises' the belief-desire distinction, that we cannot help 'thinking' about others in this way, that commonsense 'has it' this way, that we have 'beliefs' about the attitudes and that FP is 'familiar and ingrained'?

An alternative interpretation of such claims is that the belief-desire distinction is engrained into commonsense thought, rather than being something that commonsense thought cannot help noticing. Belief-desire psychology could be part of commonsense without the belief that belief-desire psychology is part of commonsense also being part of commonsense. Nevertheless, it would seem that many proponents of FP do adopt the view that FP is not just commonsense but also commonsensical. After all, as already noted, FP is almost invariably accepted without argument. However, if it were to turn out that FP is not obvious to all, the question would arise as to how it was discovered. What methods and arguments were employed in order to make our reliance on belief-desire psychology explicit? In the remainder of this chapter, I will argue that FP is not intuitive to the so-called 'folk'. Hence it is not commonsensical. Having considered other options, I will suggest that it is in fact a contentious philosophical account of the structure of interpersonal understanding. Furthermore, it is an account for which adequate support, in the form of careful philosophical reflection upon various aspects of social life, has not been provided.

Natural born dualists?

Before turning to the relationship between FP and commonsense, I will take a slight detour in order to get a better idea of the kinds of problem that can arise when a particular view is claimed to be commonsense. Such problems are, I think, clearly illustrated by Bloom's recent claim that people are commonsense Cartesian dualists. As he puts it:

> We can explain much of what makes us human by recognizing that we are natural Cartesians – dualistic thinking comes naturally to us. We have two distinct ways of perceiving the world: as containing bodies and as containing souls.
>
> (2004, xii)

Bloom not only maintains that Cartesian dualism is something that people are generally well disposed towards. He also makes the stronger claim that it is hard-wired from birth and that behavioural dispositions indicative of substance dualism are evident even in pre-linguistic infants:

> . . . before they can speak or walk or control their bowels, babies see the world as containing both physical things, which are governed by principles such as solidity and gravity, and immaterial minds, which are driven by emotions and goals. Babies are natural-born dualists.
>
> (2004, xiii)

There is, he suggests, plenty of evidence in support of such claims. For example, it has been found that even young babies differentiate between people and inanimate objects. If a moving object in a baby's visual field ceases to move, she will rapidly lose interest in it. However, if a person she is observing suddenly freezes, she will become distressed (2004, pp. 14–15). The dualist tendencies of adults, Bloom indicates, do not need to be inferred from behavioural observations. Instead, we can reflect upon our intuitions and on our use of language. We do not identify ourselves with our bodies; we instead 'feel as if we *occupy* them' (p. 191) and 'our bodies are described as our possessions' (p. 195). He goes on to note that belief in an afterlife as a disembodied spirit is commonplace, a belief that would not make sense unless we were intuitive dualists, able to distinguish between the perishing of a physical organism and the continuation of a non-physical mind. Hence the behaviour of young children, everyday language and the pull of intuition all support the view that people are 'natural born dualists'.

How convincing is the evidence cited? Let us start with the claim that people generally believe in the possibility of a disembodied mind that can survive intact in the absence of a body. Consider the following questions:

> Would your disembodied mind have perceptual access to anything?
> Would it have a specific point of view?
> Would it have a spatial and temporal location?
> Would it be able to act and would there be any constraints on its ability to act?
> Would it be able to move and would there be any constraints on its ability to move?
> Could it communicate with other disembodied minds?

How do those who claim to believe in disembodied minds respond to such questions? I've asked several people. Some answer 'yes' to most, others 'no' and a common response is 'I don't know'.[1] What are the implications of a predominance of 'yes' answers? A disembodied mind that has a specific location, a point of view, structured perceptual access to things and constraints on its ability to act looks suspiciously like an embodied mind. So it is not clear that those in the 'yes' camp really do believe in disembodied minds. And those in the 'don't know' camp presumably aren't sure what they think. Their intuitions are hazy, rather than Cartesian. What about the 'no' camp? When it is suggested that a disembodied mind without location, mobility, perceptual inputs or communicative abilities would have an existence quite different from ours and a rather undesirable one at that, people tend to become more hesitant. Some protest 'well that's not really what I meant by a disembodied spirit', others reconsider their answers and the remainder just look confused.

What is the point of all this? It seems fair to assume that fundamental ontological commitments cannot be extracted from a few everyday utterances and that yes/no answers are not always indicative of clear metaphysical positions that people have explicitly or implicitly formulated. It is far more likely that most people do not have a concise metaphysical view of bodies and minds but, rather, a host of vague and perhaps conflicting intuitions. Of course, we generally do distinguish between people and inanimate objects. But this alone does not make us Cartesian substance dualists. Rather than considering the philosophical alternatives or the possibility that most people don't have consistent intuitions on the matter, Bloom seems to assume that the only alternative to treating people and inanimate objects alike is Cartesian substance dualism. He is not alone in this. For example, Wellman also claims that empirical evidence points to people being commonsense dualists:

> With regard to ontology, adults' knowledge of the mind is based on a basic and relevant ontological distinction: that between internal mental entities and processes on the one hand and physical objects and events on the other.
>
> (1990, p. 8)

However, the language employed by both Wellman and Bloom suggests that they are themselves unclear as to what folk dualism amounts to. Bloom states that we think of ourselves as 'occupying' our bodies, which we regard as our 'possessions'. However, I doubt that many people would insist that we 'possess' our bodies in the same way that we possess a pair of shoes or that we 'occupy' them in the same way that we occupy our homes. The meanings of 'possession' and 'occupation' in this context are unclear. Other terms employed by Bloom and Wellman are also unclear. For example, Wellman claims that there is an ontological distinction between 'internal' mental entities and physical objects. But why should there be an ontological contrast between the internal and the physical? Many entities are internal to my head and at the same time physical, like blood vessels, for example. So the peculiar 'internality' of the mental referred to here cannot be analogous to the internality of a marble in a box that distinguishes it from another unboxed marble. Wellman later contrasts the nature of mental entities with 'physical objects and real events' (1990, p. 50). But what does a contrast with 'real' events imply? Are mental states regarded as 'unreal'? Could it be that people have an intuitive conception of internal, non-physical, unreal entities that are distinct from physical entities? Furthermore, neither Bloom nor Wellman clearly distinguish an assortment of non-physical mental states from a unitary non-physical substance or mind. Are mental states taken to be non-physical in virtue of their being properties of a non-physical mind or is 'the mind' just a collective term for lots of different non-physical states? Many further questions, along similar lines, could be raised about the nature of our alleged dualist intuitions.

To be fair, Wellman does cite a considerable body of empirical evidence in support of the claim that children are able to distinguish between mental and physical states from a very young age, including the results of some quite ingenious experiments. Much of this research is concerned with children's utterances and Wellman states that

> . . . natural language research suggests that children understand some appropriate distinctions between mental and physical entities and events towards the end of the third year of life.
>
> (1990, p. 23)

However, he presupposes that adults are committed to a distinction between mental and physical entities and proceeds to interpret children's linguistic and non-linguistic behaviour through this presupposed distinction. Thus his discussion does not actually address the question of whether people are dualists. It instead explores the issue of when and how dualistic thinking develops, under the assumption that adults are commonsense dualists.

Furthermore, both Bloom and Wellman take it that behavioural responses in babies and the utterances of adults are symptomatic of the same underlying cognitive trait. Yet it could well be that differences in babies' responses to people and inanimate objects are a product of non-conceptual, affective dispositions, which have little or even no relationship to conceptual abilities that later develop. Or perhaps the relationship between conceptual and non-conceptual abilities is more complicated than this; the two could interact and come apart in various ways. What people do is not always what they say or think they will do and practical commonsense need not cohere with verbal commonsense (Dennett, 1991b; Greenwood, 1999). In addition, maybe adults and children only behave and speak in a manner that is consistent with Cartesian dualism in certain contexts.

There are also methodological problems concerning how one should go about testing people's everyday intuitions. Which utterances should be regarded as indicative of underlying metaphysical commitments and how should the sample be acquired? Does one solicit answers to questions about minds and bodies, restrict oneself to sophisticated auto-biographical reflections on the question 'what am I?' or listen to the random mutterings of several teenagers drinking cheap cider in a park and try to work out which metaphysical assumptions underlie the cacophony of expletives that comprise their conversation? The more 'everyday' a situation is, the less likely it is that one will find clear indi-cators of metaphysical commitments and, if one turns to cases of more sophisticated reflection, the views offered will look more like idiosyn-cratic philosophical positions than shared everyday intuitions.

Are there any plausible alternatives to a dualist interpretation of people's verbal and non-verbal behaviour? Developmental psychology certainly does not require or entail the view that people are dualists. Indeed, Hobson (1993a, p. 115, 1993b, p. 211) suggests that the patterns of interaction between parents and young children cohere better with Strawson's view that the concept 'person' is a basic element of our everyday conceptual scheme. As will become clear in Chapter 6, I am inclined to agree.

Strawson (1959, p. 9) distinguishes between descriptive and revision-ary metaphysics. The former involves charting 'the actual structure of our thought about the world', whereas the latter attempts to improve on that structure. He restricts his own enquiry to descriptive meta-physics. Hence his project looks to be the same as that of describing the 'folk' or 'commonsense' view; both descriptive metaphysics and FP claim to articulate conceptual structures that people ordinarily rely upon. However, Strawson acknowledges from the outset that descriptive metaphysics will be tough going. Unearthing our most fundamental commitments is no easy task and it is not likely to conclude with a time-less account that will be accepted by all. Any account will reflect both the 'climate of thought' at the time of writing and the philosopher's own idiosyncratic ways of thinking (pp. 10–11).

According to Strawson, substance dualism is not compatible with our actual conceptual scheme. Everyday language ascribes both psychological and bodily characteristics to the same entity; 'I' have arms, legs, thoughts and feelings (1959, p. 90). Bloom, in contrast, observes that we tend to describe our bodies as our possessions but neglects to mention that we speak in just the same way about our minds and mental states. Strawson argues that Cartesian dualism would require revision of our actual conceptual scheme. The 'I', 'you', 'he' or 'she' to which both psychological and physical characteristics are ascribed would turn out to be a 'linguistic illusion' (p. 94). If Cartesian dualism is true and 'I' am a Cartesian mind, then I do not have the properties of being six feet tall and having two arms. I have only psychological properties. So a different entity must be six feet tall, the body with which I am closely associated. There are two options then. It could be maintained that 'I' refers only to a mental substance and that, contrary to everyday language, I do not have physical characteristics at all. Alternatively, 'I' could have two different referents, a mental substance and a physical body. Neither solution, according to Strawson, would cohere with our actual conceptual scheme. He proposes that psychological and non-psychological characteristics are both ascribed to persons and that 'person' is a primitive, unanalysable element of our conceptual scheme, more fundamental than any distinction between mind and body. We do not take ourselves to be, first and foremost, embodied egos or animated bodies and a disembodied ego is not added to a body to make a person. It is instead a concept derived from that of a person. He does remark on the possibility of the ego surviving bodily death but suggests that a disembodied ego would have an extremely impoverished existence. It would perhaps be 'a former person' (p. 115), rather than a person without a body.

Strawson also avoids making a clear-cut distinction between psychological and physical predicates. Instead, he distinguishes between M- and P-predicates. The former can be ascribed both to material things and to persons, whereas the latter are ascribable only to persons. The set of P-predicates does not consist exclusively of internal mental characteristics. Strawson also includes embodied characteristics such as 'is smiling' and 'is going for a walk', in addition to more typically psychological predicaments such as 'is thinking hard' (p. 104). Smiling and walking are ascribable to persons, rather than being internal characteristics of brains or minds. Thus the distinction between mental and physical states starts to look decidedly unclear, as does that between the 'internal' states that allegedly distinguish people and the 'external' characteristics that are ascribable to entities more generally. If Strawson is right, the 'folk' conceptual scheme does not incorporate a clear-cut distinction between an internal mental realm on the one hand and everything impersonal on the other.[2]

All the evidence cited by Bloom and Wellman is equally compatible with the Strawsonian view that 'person', rather than 'mind', is fundamental to our conceptual scheme. Even if a category of 'internal mental states' is admitted, this does not entail that such states belong to minds. They could just as well belong to persons. But what lessons can we draw from the contrast between Strawson's view and that of Bloom and Wellman? The fact that they offer contrasting accounts of our conceptual scheme is sufficient to demonstrate that 'commonsense dualism' is a contentious account of 'the commonsense view', rather than just 'the commonsense view'. The contrast also serves to illustrate a more important point. Strawson reaches his conclusions via a number of sophisticated philosophical arguments. Our deepest commitments will not be the most obvious ones. Hence the task of making them explicit requires considerable philosophical work and the outcome is a contentious philosophical account of our conceptual scheme, rather than just a statement of commonsense. Bloom and Wellman do not do this work. In other words, their view amounts to a philosophical position but one that is asserted without philosophical argument. Given that Cartesian dualism is not a position that most people have explicitly formulated or assented to, the task of showing that they are indeed committed to it is not one of stating the obvious but of trying to make explicit something that is both deeply engrained and pre-reflective.

If 'commonsense' concepts are taken to be those that are most fundamental to our understanding of the world, they will most likely be hidden from casual reflection and very difficult to unearth. Alternatively, 'commonsense' concepts could be understood as those that are both possessed by people and readily accessible to most people. In the former sense, commonsense is of considerable philosophical interest. In the latter, it could well be a series of superficial intuitions, vague assertions and hunches, the description of which would contribute very little or nothing to the study of what is central to our understanding of world, self and each other. Thus, if 'commonsense psychology' amounts to the latter, it may tell us very little about the structure of interpersonal understanding. However, if it is intended in the former sense then, either (a) philosophical argument or some other form of justification is required in support of the claim that FP is an adequate description of what we do or (b) some account is required of how FP can be both fundamental and accessible without much intellectual effort.

Commonsense as taken-for-granted reality

Strawson's approach involves a specific subject matter, our conceptual scheme, and an explicit method for approaching it, conceptual analysis. Given such an approach, 'commonsense' could be taken to mean something like 'the core structure of our actual conceptual scheme'. As I mentioned earlier, this might prove too restrictive for studying the structure of everyday interpersonal understanding. It does not encompass non-conceptual feelings and practical abilities, which could well play a key role in our relations with each other and might also contribute to our ability to understand and apply certain concepts. So perhaps it would be better to begin by adopting a more liberal conception of commonsense. I will argue in later chapters that practical, affective, non-conceptual elements do have a significant role to play in our relations with others, as does a practical familiarity with shared social situations. In so doing, I will draw on the work of phenomenologists, such as Husserl, Scheler, Heidegger, Gurwitsch, Schutz, Merleau-Ponty and Sartre. One reason for doing so is that these authors have provided a range of insightful (although of course debatable) descriptions of interpersonal relations and of the shared social world. These, I suggest, can be selectively integrated into an account of what everyday interpersonal relations consist of without assenting to the more general methodological commitments or claims of any particular phenomenologist. A further reason for focusing on phenomenology is that phenomenological descriptions are more encompassing in scope than conceptual analyses, in emphasising the practical, perceptual and affective aspects of interpersonal relations.

Although phenomenology differs from descriptive metaphysics in many respects, it is worth noting for the purposes of this chapter that several phenomenologists have emphasised the philosophical difficulty involved in bringing to light what might be termed the structure of commonsense. In the remainder of this section, I will offer a sketch of some themes in Husserl's phenomenology, in order to further emphasise the complexities involved in exploring commonsense.

Some of the difficulties involved in articulating commonsense commitments are addressed by Husserl in his last and unfinished work, *The Crisis of European Sciences*. His method in this text departs from that of earlier works such as *Ideas* and *Cartesian Meditations*. One of the reasons for this departure is his increasing recognition of the difficulties involved in describing the structure of our everyday experience and understanding of the world. To appreciate Husserl's method in the *Crisis*, it is perhaps best to begin with a discussion of his approach in earlier works. Hence I'll briefly summarise the method he outlines at the beginning of *Cartesian Meditations*.[3] This text is premised on the view that science and philosophy have become disconnected from their foundations, the result being a confused and fragmented collection of doctrines. Husserl proposes to remedy the situation by adopting the Cartesian ideal of providing an 'apodictic' foundation for science, meaning a foundation the contrary of which is inconceivable. As the starting point for such a project, he emphasises the need to be free from the various prejudices that are ordinarily presupposed by philosophical and scientific enquiry. All that is to be retained is the regulative idea of a 'genuine science' built on apodictic foundations and acquired without the distorting influence of unacknowledged prejudices (1960, p. 9).

At this point, Husserl's method departs from that of Descartes. Like Descartes, he acknowledges that objects of experience and thought can be doubted; their non-being is at least conceivable. Indeed, the existence of the world as a whole is not something that is given to us in experience and thought as apodictic. Thus the assumption of its existence cannot serve as a secure foundation for knowledge. However, even though the existence of the world and its constituents can be doubted, what cannot be doubted is that the experience itself, through which certain things are presented as existent, is occurring. So it is possible that the structure of experience will have apodictic elements, which can serve as a foundation for philosophy and science. The method that Husserl adopts to investigate this possibility involves a kind of perspectival shift. One suspends one's everyday acceptance of the existence of things and instead scrutinises the structure of the experiences through which those things appear to us as present, remembered, anticipated, real, imagined and so forth. Husserl calls this methodological shift the 'epoché' and describes it as a putting out of play of the 'natural attitude' of believing in the existence of the world. The epoché, Husserl claims, need not distort the structure of the experiences that are being investigated. In the case of any experience that normally incorporates tacit acceptance of an experiential object's reality, the sense of that object's reality, which is part of the experience, is preserved. However the stance through which one examines the experience does not itself involve the same acceptance of the object or of the world more generally. The phenomenologist is no longer concerned with questions of what does and does not exist. She instead 'brackets' the experience and, in so doing, is able to study its structure, the manner in which things are experientially presented. As Husserl puts it

> . . . the world experienced in this reflectively grasped life goes on being for me (in a certain manner) 'experienced' as before, and with just the content it has at any particular time. It goes on appearing, as it appeared before; the only difference is that I, as reflecting philosophically, no longer keep in effect (no longer accept) the natural believing in existence involved in experiencing the world – though that believing too is still there and grasped by my noticing regard.
>
> (1960, pp. 19–20)

He goes on to claim that experience has a highly complicated structure and that aspects of this structure do not causally facilitate our comprehension of various entities but, rather, render those entities intelligible. Experience 'constitutes' or gives meaning to its objects. The aim of phenomenology is to offer rigorous descriptions of apodictic structures of experience that are presupposed by the possibility of our many and varied experiences of the relations between self, others and world. As Husserl puts it, the epoché reveals *'an infinite realm of being of a new kind*, as the sphere of a new kind of experience: transcendental experience' (1960, p. 27), which is not noticed by everyday, casual reflection upon one's experiences.

Both the method and what Husserl claims it to reveal are of course contentious in numerous respects. For example, it is arguable that a complete 'bracketing' of the natural attitude is just not possible. We will always take something for granted, hold on to certain prejudices or retain some degree of rootedness in the natural attitude. And, if it turns out that a complete epoché or 'phenomenological reduction' is a stance that is impossible to adopt, any conclusions about apodictic experiential structures arrived at through the epoché are likely to be unreliable.[4]

Despite concerns about the reliability of his method and the 'discoveries' made through it, Husserl's emphasis on a radical and difficult methodological shift at least suggests that commonsense or casual reflection, if employed as a method, will not go very deep at all. The most fundamental commitments that structure our experience and thought are not themselves objects of everyday experience or thought.

Is the structure of experience that Husserl claims to describe 'commonsense', in any sense of the term? If commonsense is taken to be something phenomenologically accessible that underlies the intelligibility of everyday experience and thought, rather than something readily available to casual reflection, then perhaps Husserlian phenomenology does amount to an investigation of our most engrained commonsense. Alternatively, it could be maintained that Husserl is attempting to articulate the underlying structure of commonsense, rather than merely provide a description of its superficial form. Hence his task is perhaps analogous to that of articulating a theory of mind that underlies FP, rather than that of articulating FP. His project is far more ambitious than a surface description of commonsense, which is why it is so difficult. Perhaps commonsense is instead integral to what Husserl calls the 'natural attitude', the everyday way in which we take things for granted in experience and thought. And this, surely, is much easier to describe than the structures that underlie it.

However, what Husserl acknowledges in the *Crisis* is that his earlier Cartesian approach was flawed in its assumptions that the natural attitude itself is easy to describe and that the starting point from which one performs the epoché can be readily understood. He argues that describing the everyday manner in which we find ourselves in the world is itself a difficult task, as our thoughts about the world and our relationship with it are shaped by layers of historically entrenched conceptual systems that themselves take for granted the operation of the natural attitude. Husserl suggests that the problem stems largely from a historical build up or 'sedimentation' of scientific concepts and methods. Scientific methods and associated concepts start off as useful devices with which to navigate the 'life world' that we inhabit. However, over time, conceptual systems become so familiar to us that we forget their methodological role and start interpreting our everyday relationship with the world in terms of them. Further methodological innovations then accumulate, all starting off as tools with which we navigate the everyday world but ending up as entrenched conceptual frameworks through which we think. Over time, these frameworks come to quietly take the place of the world that they were originally devised to help us cope with. Hence reflection on our everyday relationship with the world is progressively obscured by a reliance on conceptual systems the origins of which lie in pragmatic concerns. As Husserl puts it, starting with Galileo, we have:

> . . . the surreptitious substitution of the mathematically substructed world of idealities for the only real world, the one that is actually given through perception, that is ever experienced and experienceable – our everyday life-world.

> (pp. 48–49)

So how are we to recover an appreciation of the 'life world', the everyday manner in which we find ourselves in the world, from the conceptual systems that cover it up? To unearth the manner in which the world is taken to be in the course of day-to-day life, Husserl proposes what he calls an epoché of objective science (1970, p. 135). The aim of this new epoché is to suspend acceptance of conceptual systems that have their origins in scientific and technological innovations, in order to arrive at the proper starting point for the kind of phenomenological enquiry that is attempted in *Cartesian Meditations*. Hence preparatory work is required to reach a proper appreciation of the natural attitude. The epoché of objective science does not take the form of a sudden perspectival shift. Instead, Husserl suggests that it requires historical work, a lengthy process of charting the various historically sedimented conceptual systems whose acceptance is to be bracketed. The culmination of this process is, according to Husserl, a description of the structure of our everyday acceptance of the world. And the sense in which we take the world as given is, he maintains, quite different from that of taking it as an object of thought. The everyday life world is instead a kind of possibility space that we inhabit, which is presupposed by specific acts and objects of explicit thought:

> It belongs to what is taken for granted, prior to all scientific thought and all philosophical questioning, that the world is – always is in advance – and that every correction of an opinion, whether an experiential or other opinion, presupposes the already existing world, namely as a horizon of what in the given case is indubitably valid as existing, and presupposes within this horizon something familiar and doubtlessly certain with which that which is perhaps cancelled out as invalid came into conflict.
>
> (1970, p. 110)[5]

Husserl's method and his description of the life world are, of course, not without problems. For example, it is arguable that scientific innovations do not just build upon the life world but also reshape it in quite fundamental ways. This being so, the project of unearthing an uncorrupted life world from beneath the conceptualisations that we have imposed upon it may turn out to be a futile one. Another troubling aspect of the account is Husserl's adoption of a contentious instrumentalist view of scientific concepts, which many will find unacceptable. Nevertheless, for the purposes of this chapter, it is possible to draw some important lessons from his approach and from his conclusions. Our most basic understanding of the world and of our relationship with it could well be far removed from the objects of explicit thought. Its articulation may require an explicit philosophical method and a lengthy process of investigation. In addition, it is quite possible that descriptions of commonsense, construed as something that underlies everyday experience and thought, will be obfuscated by the surreptitious imposition of inappropriate concepts from science and elsewhere. Indeed, I will argue later in this book that descriptions of interpersonal understanding tend to be structured by the misleading assumption that it is a variant of mechanistic understanding, the latter being pervasive in certain areas of science and philosophy but very different from our everyday ways of understanding and interacting with people. But can Husserl's description of the life world be regarded as an attempt to articulate our 'commonsense'? I see no reason why not, if we think of commonsense as a deeply engrained background of commitment that structures all practice and thought.[6]

The question of which method to adopt in order to describe commonsense is a difficult one. It could well be that the epoché itself is founded on some kind of unhelpful prejudice, impossible in practice to adopt or perhaps just too obscure in nature to adequately comprehend, let alone employ. But, regardless of what we think about Husserl's method, it is still possible that many of the intricate descriptions he offers on the basis of phenomenological reflection will be able to illuminate various areas of philosophical and scientific enquiry. For instance, Petitot, Varela, Pachoud and Roy (1999) argue that Husserl's work can serve as a useful starting point for cognitive science's attempt to provide naturalistic accounts of experience. They note that descriptions of consciousness, intentionality and so forth in mainstream Anglophone philosophy of mind are rather cursory when compared to Husserl's detailed descriptions of the manner in which things appear to us. At the very least, Husserl's recognition of the sheer complexity of experience and thought, and of the difficulties involved in attempting to adequately describe it, amounts to an important lesson about the hazards involved in offering simple descriptions on the basis of undisciplined reflection.

Similar lessons can be drawn from the work of other phenomenologists. For example, in *Being and Time*, Heidegger offers an elaborate account of the manner in which we find ourselves in the world. His method departs from the epoché, as he takes it that we are entangled with the world to such an extent that a complete suspension of its acceptance is impossible. In place of the epoché, he proposes to interpret our predicament from within, through a progressive unravelling of presupposed structure. Despite this difference in approach, Heidegger, like Husserl, emphasises the contrast between what is readily apparent to explicit thought and what is most fundamental to our understanding of the world. As he puts it, what is 'ontically closest' is 'ontologically furthest' (1962, p. 36), meaning that what is most familiar to us does not ordinarily appear as an object of thought. So, despite the many differences between Strawson, Husserl and Heidegger, all point to the conclusion that commonsense, if it is to be interesting, will most likely be something that is not easy to articulate. This can be applied more specifically to commonsense concerning people, to our most engrained ways of experiencing and understanding others. What is most basic to interpersonal understanding is likely to be far removed from casual reflection.

The origins of 'folk psychology'

To summarise the ground covered so far, 'commonsense' has various different meanings. In its more philosophically interesting senses, it is likely to be something that is difficult to articulate. And there is the question of which method to adopt in order to investigate it. So what kind of commonsense is FP claimed to be and which methods were employed to discover it? To address these questions, I will briefly outline the intellectual origins of FP. The term 'commonsense psychology' has been around for some time. For example, Heider refers to a 'commonsense psychology', which he compares to a naïve physics (1956, p. 5). However, his description of commonsense psychology differs markedly from more recent formulations of FP:

> . . . the ordinary person has a great and profound understanding of himself and of other people which, though unformulated or only vaguely conceived, enables him to interact with others in more or less adaptive ways.
>
> (1956, p. 2)

Heider thus acknowledges that our everyday understanding of people is not something that is explicitly thought out or clear. He also assumes from the outset that the 'person' is the 'basic unit to be investigated', rather than a mind that contains propositional attitudes (1956, p. 1). So how did FP, in its more familiar sense, emerge? I am not sure who first used the term 'folk psychology'. The earliest reference I can find is to Wundt's 'Völkerpsychologie', a term that he first employed around 1900 (Greenwood, 1991, p. 90). However, I am not sure how strong a historical connection there is between this and more recent Anglophone use of the term 'folk psychology'. The latter only became firmly established in philosophical circles at the beginning of the 1980s. However, appeals to what the everyday folk think have been around for a lot longer. To give two fairly recent examples, Sellars (1956/1963, p. 135) discusses the language of the 'plain man' and Austin (1962, p. 7) similarly refers to the 'ordinary man' but cautions against caricaturing such a figure. In so doing, they both take issue with earlier contrasts made by Ayer (1940) between what the philosopher and the everyday person think about perception.

What about the alleged core ingredient of FP, the attribution of internal propositional attitude states in order to predict and explain behaviour? FP owes a lot to Sellars (1956/1963), who sets out to dispense with the view that we have incorrigible first person access to certain kinds of mental state. He concocts a fictional historical narrative to illustrate how attribution of mental states to others and to oneself could arise through the adoption and progressive refinement of a theory. The story begins with a society of behaviourists, our 'Rylean ancestors', who have acquired a sophisticated language and can characterise verbal behaviour semantically (1963, p. 179). These people eventually work out that certain kinds of observable event are best explained and predicted by the postulation of unobservable causes of observed behaviour. In other words, they learn to theorise. Then along comes a genius called Jones, who applies this ability to people, postulating that unobservable episodes of inner speech are responsible for both overt utterances and non-linguistic behaviours. He calls these 'thoughts' (pp. 186–187). Jones proceeds to teach others how to offer such descriptions and eventually everyone starts using this new language to report on their own inner states too. From this, a further theory develops about 'immediate experiences', 'impressions' and the like. Hence the story is intended to show how intuitions concerning privileged first-person access to mental states could originate in intersubjectively grounded competence with a theory. Sellars is generally credited as the originator of what became known as the theory theory of FP.[7] For example, Churchland (1998a, p. 4) begins his account of FP's origins with a discussion of Sellars, as do Stich and Ravenscroft (1996, pp. 117–121).

Another landmark in the development of FP is the arrival of functionalism. Functionalists, such as Lewis (e.g. 1972/1980), claim that mental states are definable as the occupants of certain causal roles. Given this, it is only a short step to theory of mind. If mental states are internal states with characteristic causal roles, then successfully predicting and explaining behaviour is plausibly a matter of having a sufficiently accurate theory of the kinds of internal state involved and of the ways in which they interact so as to cause observed behaviours. As Lewis puts it, 'think of commonsense psychology as a term-introducing scientific theory, though one invented long before there was any such institution as a professional science' (1980, p. 213).[8] This view is further supported by the acknowledgement of tacit knowledge, which allows for the possibility that certain mental states and a large part of the theory we employ to attribute them are hidden from reflection (Fodor, 1968/1980). In conjunction with all this, as noted by Stich and Ravenscroft (1996, p. 121), there is the rise of a complementary cognitive science, with its emphasis on internal, systematically organised knowledge structures.

The association between theory of mind and functionalism is explicit throughout much of the literature. For example, Heal (1995a, p. 45) describes theory of mind as the 'functionalist' strategy. Its central assumption is that we are all tacit functionalists who understand others on the basis that 'people are just complex objects in our environment whose behaviour we wish to anticipate but whose causal innards we cannot perceive'. Botterill and Carruthers (1999, p. 11) also describe the theory theory as a variant of functionalism.

The term 'theory of mind' was coined in 1978 by Premack and Woodruff, whose primary concern was to address whether chimpanzees had one. They employed the term 'theory' in a fairly liberal way. However, it was subsequently applied to humans as a synonym for FP and also, more specifically, for the view that FP rests upon a theory in the literal sense of 'theory'. The term 'theory theory' then appeared in 1980, courtesy of Morton. With Wimmer and Perner's false belief task (1983) and its later application to autism (Baron-Cohen, Leslie and Frith, 1985), disciplines including philosophy of mind, cognitive science, developmental psychology and primatology came together to form something of a consensus regarding the centrality of FP, construed as a theory, to human social life.

Then, in 1986, an explicit challenge to the theory theory arose in the form of simulation. Some proponents of simulation acknowledge the influence of the *Verstehen* tradition and, more specifically, figures such as Schutz (Gordon, 1995a). They also appeal to the everyday intuition that we sometimes imaginatively enter into the predicaments of others (Heal, 1995b). However, simulation theory is not a radical historical departure. It simply inherits FP from the view that the 'folk' are functionalists, while at the same time challenging the claim that we need to be functionalists in order to apply it. So FP, the common explanandum for both theory and simulation, seems to have originated in functionalism and the work of Sellars, although it undoubtedly owes something to earlier philosophers and philosophies. The basic rationale for FP seems to be fairly simple; if mental states are internal causes of behaviour, successfully understanding and predicting people's behaviour will most likely be a matter of postulating internal states with the right causal roles. Causal roles can be divided into information gatherers and motivators, which fit in very nicely with the everyday terms 'belief' and 'desire'. Hence FP emerged from quite specific philosophical concerns and is closely associated with a particular philosophical account of what mental states are.

Regardless of the precise historical details, what I have not found anywhere in the literature is an account that begins by looking at the varied tapestry of interpersonal interactions that we participate in every day in order to offer a detailed description of how it is that we understand and interact with people in different contexts. FP just seems to have been imposed upon everyday life, having emerged from a context of philosophical theorising and been declared as commonsense, although what is meant by 'commonsense' remains unclear. It is arguable that FP's emphasis on internal propositional attitude states owes much to its philosophical origins and little to what people actually think and do. Goldman expresses this concern succinctly with specific reference to the theory theory:

> A skeptic is entitled to suspect [. . .] that what goes on when philosophers proffer mentalistic platitudes is not the extraction of pre-existing representations in the minds of the 'folk', but the fresh creation of laws designed to accommodate philosophical preconceptions about the character of 'theoretical' terms.
>
> (Goldman, 1995, p. 80)

Indeed, Sellars himself, though supportive of the view that philosophy and science are continuous, warns that an outcome of philosophy-science interaction has often been:

> . . . a confusion of the task of philosophy and the task of science, and almost equally often a projection of the framework of the latest scientific speculations into the common sense picture of the world.
>
> (1963, p. 171)

Could FP be a theoretical imposition upon everyday life, rather than 'what the folk think'? Proponents of FP do offer numerous examples of everyday life, dressed up in FP terms, but nothing remotely resembling a detailed discussion of the many ways in which we encounter and interact with others. However, perhaps it will turn out that FP is, after all, obvious to us all. As I have suggested, this would run the risk of rendering it superficial and perhaps misleading when it comes to exploring the deeper structure of interpersonal understanding. Nevertheless, it is a possibility that needs to be considered.

What do the folk have to say?

That we attribute internal propositional attitudes in order to predict and explain behaviour might seem like an item of commonsense, if one has been taught FP as an undergraduate by Jones the philosopher, been immersed in relevant philosophical debates for several years and long ago familiarised oneself with the ways in which the terms 'belief' and 'desire' operate in these debates. However, what one takes to be commonsense after several years of studying philosophy or cognitive science may be a far cry from the explicit pronouncements made by people who have not been immersed in the same kinds of academic environment. What do people more generally think that interpersonal understanding consists of? I presented the question to a group of philosophy undergraduate students in 2003 but was met with silence. Having restated the question in several different forms, I was finally offered a couple of vague comments about consciousness and a few remarks along the lines of 'they're like me'. The following year, I decided to investigate the matter in more depth. The students in question had a significant head start over most 'folk'. They were in the middle of a second-year Philosophy of Mind course and had already been introduced to the terms 'propositional attitude', 'representation' and 'intentionality'. However, the term 'folk psychology' had not yet arisen. I asked for written answers, so as to give them time to think about the question and respond without the intimidating prospect of communicating their view in front of several peers. Answers could, if they wished, remain anonymous. But how should such a question be phrased? Suppose I had asked the following:

> Actions are caused by entities inside people's heads called beliefs and desires. Different combinations of beliefs and desires cause different actions. Given this, what do you have to do in order to predict which action another person will perform?

This would of course stack the odds very heavily in favour of FP. There was a need to present the question in a less leading way, while retaining sufficient clarity to ensure that students understand what was being asked of them. I settled on the following:

> What is central to your understanding of others? To put it another way, understanding or interacting with another person is very different from understanding or interacting with a rock. What does that difference consist of? Please state your intuitive or commonsense view rather than stating philosophical positions or engaging in philosophical argument. Write up to half a side of A4 and return it to me at next week's tutorial.

As a brief aside, I put the question in this way having re-read the preface to Fodor's *Psychosemantics* shortly before the lecture in which questionnaires were distributed. In his preface, Fodor discusses how he goes about interpreting his pet cat, the point being that the behaviour of 'Greycat' is rendered intelligible via the attribution of beliefs and desires. He states that what makes Greycat different from 'rocks and the like' is that a 'commonsense belief/desire psychology' is applicable to him (1987, x). Of course, Fodor claims that belief-desire talk plays an even more conspicuous role when we interpret each other. Hence a contrast between understanding people and understanding rocks seemed appropriate. I added the term 'interaction' because a restriction of interpersonal understanding to contexts of observation would be premature. Indeed, many of our interpretations of others occur in contexts of interaction, rather than through a standpoint of detached observation. Fodor, I assume, interacts with pussycats and attributes propositional attitude states to them in contexts such as feeding, stroking or retrieving injured birds from their jaws.

How did the students respond to this exercise? They mentioned a diverse range of factors, many of which had little in common. Here is a selection of comments:

> 'Can understand me in conversation.'
> 'Can detect their emotions through facial expression and body language.'
> 'Can relate to my plight.'
> 'An understanding of why we do certain things in certain situations.'
> 'Difficult to say exactly [. . .] lots of things.'
> 'Empathy.'
> 'Knowledge of the individual.'
> 'Their relationship to ourselves.'

'The soul knows itself, and it knows others, for all souls come from the one.'

'You can interact with others and see the way people react to things.'

'They act similarly to us.'

'How they respond to me.'

'Being able to care for their well-being.'

'It's when you're in Kingsgate bar [the student union bar at Durham] with some friends, having a drink, when Franz Ferdinand comes on the radio and you notice that everyone in the bar has started nodding along to it . . . and so have you.'

'Reactions and engagement – able to interact in the world.'

'The same type of thing – the same species of entity – as myself.'

'Others have the same facial movements as me and show emotion via the same route.'

'We don't understand everyone! e.g. psychos, scientists.'[9]

I received 25 responses. The term 'belief' appeared twice in total and 'desire' only appeared once, as did 'prediction'. 'Explanation' was not mentioned at all.[10] I ran the exercise again in 2005 and received a similarly mixed bag of answers. Of the 25 responses received that year, three superficially resembled versions of simulation theory:

'I assume that other people are essentially the same as me.'

'The difference consists in the assumption that a person is similar to myself, whereas a rock is not.'

'That they think in a similar way.'

There was no mention of 'desire' or 'explanation', and 'prediction' appeared once. The word 'believe' did appear four times but in all cases it referred to 'my' believing things about others, rather than my figuring out their beliefs. In all 50 responses gathered over the two years, there was no mention of anything resembling an ability to attribute internal mental states or any emphasis on figuring out beliefs and desires.

It might be objected that all sorts of everyday terms can play the roles that 'belief' and 'desire' do in descriptions of FP and that the frequent references I found to emotions and feelings could also be interpreted in terms of an ability to attribute internal affective states. However, even if everyday discourse can, at a stretch, be translated into FP terms, there are no grounds for just assuming that it should be. (Indeed, I will argue in Chapter 7 that everyday descriptions and explanations of action bear little resemblance to FP.) Now a group of philosophy students is hardly a representative sample of 'the folk'. However, students who have already been introduced to various relevant debates, concepts and terms (although not the term 'folk psychology' itself) are surely as likely or more likely than most people to volunteer descriptions along the lines of FP. That none of them came up with anything closely resembling FP is, I think, sufficient to show that it is not a commonsensical description of interpersonal understanding, which can be easily extracted from the kinds of things that people say.

Despite the broad range of responses offered by the students, there was a common thread running through several of them, an emphasis on mutuality. Out of 50 descriptions in total, 10 in 2004 and 15 in 2005 emphasised the centrality of mutual relatedness and suggested that interpersonal understanding was something that people achieve together, by responding to each other in certain ways. The view that understanding is a task shared between participants differs from the emphasis on a detached observer attributing states to an observed person that is typical of FP. This is something that will be addressed in Chapter 6, where I will suggest that these students were on the right track. Interpersonal understanding is principally a matter of mutual responsiveness, rather than the detached deployment of internal cognitive abilities by A in the service of predicting B.

One might object that an alternative approach could demonstrate that FP is, after all, intuitive to the 'folk'. Suppose that, rather than asking the students what they thought, I had offered them a description of FP and asked whether they found it intuitive. If most of them answered 'yes', then it could be argued that FP is indeed commonsensical. It is something that people recognise easily but do not recall so readily. I investigated this possibility by explaining to a tutorial group that philosophers tend to regard the attribution of internal states called beliefs and desires as central to social life and asking them if they agreed. Sure enough, everyone nodded and happily agreed that belief-desire attribution played a central role. But there is the worry that claims made by an appropriate authority figure will be uncritically accepted. Such concerns are, I think, of particular relevance to FP, which is usually introduced as 'what the folk do' or 'what commonsense believes'. Philosophical questions are of course raised concerning whether 'the folk' have it right and how they manage to do what they do. However, FP itself is seldom introduced as a debatable philosophical position but, rather, as something to be accepted as a premise for philosophical discussion. So here's one possibility: Eager trainees are taught by Jones-like mentors how to talk about FP in the institutionally established way but not to ask whether FP is something that people actually employ. It is difficult to question whether we actually do something when all the emphasis is on whether neuroscience will ultimately usurp it and whether that would amount to the greatest intellectual tragedy in humanity's history: 'If that's the structure of the debate, then of course we must do it; otherwise all these clever people would be talking about nothing.' After a few years of this, once one has accepted the parameters of debates and learned the various argumentative strategies, perhaps a reliance on FP does seem obvious. After all, it is now operating as a key premise of one's intellectual enquiries, without which those enquiries would have no object.

So, do students accept FP because it is indeed an intuitive account of social life or because of other factors, such as its coming from an authority figure or its being the only option offered to them? In order to address this question, I distributed a questionnaire:

Which of the following claims best describes how you understand other people? It might be that you think several of the following are important or that none of them gets it quite right. Please place a tick next to the one answer that *best* expresses what you think is *most* central to interpersonal understanding. This is not a test. I really do just want your opinion. The reason for this questionnaire will be explained to you once you've chosen your answer.

Options: Please tick just one.

1. Perception of people's feelings, which are displayed in their gestures, expressions and activities, coupled with an ability to respond to these feelings in a complementary way.
2. Understanding people as acting in accordance with their various social roles, such as 'teacher', 'fire fighter', 'taxi driver', 'waiter' and 'cashier'.
3. Understanding that people's actions arise from different character traits, personality traits and moral outlooks, such as being oversensitive, level-headed, moody, selfish, kind, considerate, reliable and so forth.
4. Getting to know people by sharing thoughts with them through informal conversations, with mutual understanding progressing as conversation develops and as the number of conversations you have with them increases.

5. There is no single way in which we understand other people. All sorts of very different things are involved and we only really 'understand' those whom we get to know well through long-term exposure, such as friends, family and lovers.
6. Understanding the internal mental states, principally beliefs and desires, that cause a person's observable behaviour, such as the belief that it will rain or the desire for an ice cream.
7. Understanding others is dependent on the extent to which we share a common cultural background with them.
8. It is difficult to articulate how one understands other people. One is just struck by the sense that one is in the presence of another animate agent, who has experiences and thoughts that are like one's own.

This presented students with FP, rather than asking them to describe it themselves. Hence the concern that people do find it intuitive but do not generally articulate it very well does not apply here. However, as FP is presented alongside seven other possibilities, the problem of steering students towards FP by presenting it as the intuitive view or as the only view on offer is also avoided.

The questionnaire was completed by 40 first-year logic students in February 2006 and responses were as follows: (1). Five. (2). None. (3). Three. (4). Five. (5). Twenty one. (6). One. (7). One. (8). Four.[11] Although student questionnaires do not amount to a rigorous scientific study, that only one person picked FP (Option 6) is, I think, enough to show that FP is not something that people generally regard as central to social life. Furthermore, the fact that the majority of students picked Option 5 suggests that there may be no such thing as a 'commonsense psychology', in the sense of a distinctive way of understanding people that is generally acknowledged as central to much or all of social life. It might be objected that one of more of the other options presuppose FP, while dressing it up in a more alluring way. However, the following chapters will hopefully show that this is not the case.

As already noted, FP is claimed to be a conceptual ability. It is 'the pre-scientific, commonsense conceptual framework that all normally socialized human beings deploy' (Churchland, 1998a, p. 3). Furthermore, it cannot be wholly tacit if FP concepts are explicitly incorporated into explanations of behaviour. Hence FP must be something that we routinely employ but which does not easily spring to mind when we reflect upon what we do. And so we return to the points that thinking about thinking is difficult and that any account offered of our social common-sense will be a philosophical position, rather than a pre-philosophical account that is intuitive to all. However, given that FP originates in functionalism and a host of related philosophical concerns, rather than in philosophical reflection upon the structure of social life, it is unclear how FP relates to what people actually do and to what people think they do, assuming that functionalism is not itself an item of commonsense.

Science and folk psychology

Given that FP is neither obvious nor grounded in a philosophical analysis of social life, there is a further option to be explored. Perhaps our everyday practice of attributing internal propositional attitudes is something that has been discovered through scientific studies of intersubjectivity, rather than via philosophical or commonsense reflection. However, almost all scientific studies that refer to FP also *presuppose* that FP is an adequate description of how we go about understanding each other. The questions they address instead concern the abilities that underlie FP and how they develop. For example, Bartsch and Wellman offer an account of how children think about minds, based upon careful analysis of numerous records of children's everyday talk about mental states. They begin by stating at length, but not arguing, that adults understand each other by attributing unobservable, internal propositional attitude states on the basis of behavioural observations (1995, Chapter 1). Hence FP is taken for granted as the endpoint of intersubjective development. The question they address is how its development unfolds. Given the premise of FP, Bartsch and Wellman restrict their enquiry to how children use terms that are allegedly indicative of FP, such as 'belief', 'desire' and 'thought' (p. 11). So FP is not discovered through such studies. Rather, it is written into them from the start as a framework that influences the selection and interpretation of data.

FP is also presupposed by the experimental paradigm that is most often appealed to in the FP literature, the false belief task, which is frequently described as a 'litmus test' for FP ability (see, for example, Frith and Happé, 1999, p. 3). The task was devised by Wimmer and Perner (1983) as a means of ascertaining the age at which children are first able to attribute mistaken beliefs to others, the emphasis being on the detection of specific false beliefs, rather than detection of a lack of knowledge. As Wimmer and Perner put it, 'understanding of another person's wrong belief requires explicit representation of the wrongness of this person's belief in relation to one's own knowledge' (1983, p. 103). The

original false belief task involves children watching a social performance. A character, Maxi, puts chocolate in cupboard x. Maxi's mother
then removes the chocolate in Maxi's absence and puts it in cupboard y.
Children are asked to indicate where Maxi will look for the chocolate.
Mentalistic verbs such as 'belief' are not included in the task and children are asked to point, rather than to respond verbally, thus distinguishing an ability to detect false beliefs from an ability to describe
one's doing so.

Wimmer and Perner (1983) employ several variants, including scenarios that involve deceit and cooperation. They also add conditions to
rule out other explanations for poor performance, such as forgetfulness
and impulsive response. They report that most 6-to-9-year-olds pass the
test and suggest that the reasons for failure in younger children fall into
two categories. Memory prompts and asking children to think about
their answers, rather than just point impulsively, both significantly
improve the performance of 4-to–5-year-olds, indicating that they have
the relevant abilities but often fail to complete the task due to the interference of other factors. However, these modifications have no positive
effect on the performance of 3-to-4-years-olds, suggesting that the task
is just too complicated for the latter age group and that their failure may
or may not be attributable to an inability to attribute beliefs.

Wimmer and Perner's original experimental design involves a number
of questionable assumptions. For example, Maxi and her mother are not
played by people; they are 15 cm tall paper cut-outs. The cupboards are
painted cassette containers and matchboxes, glued to a polyester wall.
Hence, in order to even comprehend the task, children must already be
able to recognise that a puppet can stand in for a person and to play
along with a context of pretence. The performance also incorporates a
lengthy narrative, which children need to follow in order to interpret
the activities of the two participants. In addition, they must be able to
understand what is asked of them by the experimenter (Gallagher,
2001a, p. 99). One might wonder how they interpret the experimenter's
own requests for information. Do they recognise something of his epistemic predicament or just respond as prompted, without thinking anything at all about the experimenter?

Given the considerable social abilities that children must already have
in order to even comprehend the task, it is questionable how central a
role the further ability to attribute false beliefs has in social life.
However, Wimmer and Perner's paper does not include any discussion
of the scope of false belief attribution. Furthermore, there is some ambiguity as to just what it is that children are detecting. They are not

required to articulate their knowledge in the form 'B thinks/believes that the chocolate is in x'. All they need do is point. One could have some success in tracking entities of type x by tracking entities of type y that are usually associated with x. Hence there is a difference between being able to reliably detect beliefs and having an understanding of what it is that one is detecting. Indeed, the original task does not seem to rule out the possibility of children supposing that B will take x to be where B last saw x. There is also the possibility of various intermediate states.

The task also incorporates a number of debatable assumptions concerning the structure of interpersonal understanding, which are symptomatic of the presupposition of FP. For example, there is the assumption that an ability to detect mental states can be measured via a paradigm that involves a child observing a narrative unfold, rather than more familiar situations that involve structured interaction with caregivers. It is possible that an ability to detect what others are thinking first arises in structured contexts of interaction and is supported by the shared environment. Take away that familiar context and you may be taking away something that is partly constitutive of the relevant ability. By analogy, if you take away my lecture notes and other props, it is likely that I will give a very poor lecture. However, this does not entail that I am unable to lecture but, rather, that I have been denied the environmental props that enable me to deploy that ability. Similarly, it may well be that interpersonal understanding is not simply a matter of deploying an internalised ability to attribute mental states, as assumed by FP, but a matter of interacting with the environment in certain ways that are partly constitutive of the ability, a point I will return to in Chapters 4 and 6.

In addition, interpretations of children's behaviour *presuppose* that a central intersubjective achievement is best described in terms of the attribution of a type of internal mental state, called a 'belief', to another person on the basis of behavioural observation. And, in assuming that a puppet show is a fair substitute for real people, the task suggests that understanding mental states is a matter of inferring internal states from rather crude behaviour patterns, accompanied by narratives. What is not addressed is the possibility of perception of subtleties in gaze, expression and action, in addition to one's affective responsiveness to real people, playing a crucial role in understanding people.[12]

Since Wimmer and Perner's experiments, the false belief task has become something of an industry and it has been modified in a variety of ways. The original task makes considerable demands on children's verbal and non-verbal abilities (Frith and Happé, 1999) and subsequent versions have simplified it in certain respects. Wellman, Cross and Watson (2001) analyse the results obtained through numerous different experimental conditions and conclude that these results point to a fairly robust phenomenon. An ability to attribute false beliefs emerges at between 3 and 4 years of age in almost all children, the same age at which the ability is apparent from their everyday conversations.

However, even if such tests do succeed in detecting a distinctive achievement, this does not entail that the achievement in question should be interpreted as an ability to detect internal propositional attitudes. Empirical results need not be disputed in order to challenge the theoretical framework through which those results are routinely interpreted. FP was not discovered through studies of children's intersubjective development. The assumption that adults understand each other by attributing internal propositional attitudes was written into these studies from the start. It motivates them, influences their experimental design and operates as a framework for the interpretation of results. In the following chapters, I will argue that FP is not a good account of what adults do. In the absence of this presupposition, the results of false belief tasks do not themselves provide adequate grounds for interpreting what children do at various developmental stages in FP terms. The point can be couched in terms of a distinction made by Dennett between folk psychology as craft and as ideology. A craft is what people do, whereas an ideology is what people think they do:

> I want to distinguish between craft and ideology, between what we learn to do and what our mothers and others have actually *told* us the craft was all about when they enunciated the lore, for what the anthropologists tell us is that craft and ideology are often quite distinct.
>
> (1991b, p. 137)

Hence we can distinguish between how children respond from how practitioners of a certain ideology interpret their activities. However, the practitioners of this ideology may not be 'the folk' and so further distinctions need to be made:

(i) What people do.
(ii) What people think they do.
(iii) What philosophers and cognitive scientists think people do.
(iv) What philosophers and cognitive scientists think that people think that they do.

FP is, I suggest, an ambiguous blend of (iii) and (iv), whereas what the false belief task measures is (i), which neither presupposes nor implies (iii) or (iv), given the scope for alternative interpretations. The view I will be arguing for in what follows is that FP, construed as (iii) and/or (iv) has little in common with (i) and (ii). Results of the false belief task relate to (i) and some variants also relate to aspects of (ii). It is important to be cautious of couching its results in terms of an account of (iii) and (iv) that is not itself a product of careful reflection upon social life.

That FP is not a product of scientific enquiry is, I think, made especially clear by Fodor, who claims that it is so indispensable to us all that a transcendental argument, in the style of Kant, could even be offered on its behalf (1987, pp. 9–10). This implies that it is intuitively compelling, regardless of what science might tell us. Indeed, such remarks suggest that it could be an item of 'commonsense', in the sense discussed by Moore (1959). Moore takes commonsense to be a set of shared propositions that we all know to be true even if we do not know how we know that they are true. He argues that, even though philosophers frequently deny such propositions, they do so only in the form of unwitting self-contradictions. Could such an argument be formulated on behalf of FP? Despite alluding to the possibility, Fodor does not offer one and neither does he indicate which aspects of FP might be secured by it. An undeniability argument might look tempting when applied to propositions such as 'people have beliefs'. However, as I will argue in Chapter 7, such propositions need not be denied in order to challenge FP. And several of the assumptions underlying the claim that we have 'an ability to attribute internal propositional attitude states on the basis of behavioural observations', which I outlined in Chapter 1, are certainly not beyond rational doubt.

So my conclusion is that FP is a debatable philosophical position, which is generally not acknowledged as such. One person who seems to approve of such a view is Dennett (2005). He describes the task of working out the axioms of folk psychology as a 'sophisticated aprioristic anthropology of folk (naïve) psychology' and goes on to remark that

> It is tempting to interpret the field of philosophy of mind as just this endeavour: an attempt at a rigorous unification and formalization of the fundamental intuitions the folk manifest in both their daily affairs and in reflective interaction with the questioning anthropologists.
>
> (p. 33)

Dennett makes these remarks in contrasting a philosophy that proceeds independently of science and relies on intuition with an approach that takes its lead from science and draws counter-intuitive conclusions. His point is that science quite rightly prizes counter-intuitive conclusions. Thus a philosophy that respects intuition above all else will be a poor guide to truth. Philosophical accounts of mental phenomena, arrived at without due attention to the sciences of mind, are just folk views. There is no distinction to be drawn between unscientific philosophy and folk theorising. However, it is unclear whether Dennett is worried that FP is itself an outcome of aprioristic philosophical enquiry or whether his claims are restricted to the issue of how we should go about studying FP's underlying structure. I suspect the latter.

It is doubtful that a strict contrast can be drawn between folkish and scientifically based philosophising. If the aim is to study how we understand each other in everyday life, at least some pre-scientific assumptions concerning interpersonal understanding need to be made. Otherwise there would be no account of what it is that the science is required to explain. Of course, an account of intersubjectivity could be progressively clarified and revised through the input of empirical science and this is, I think, the kind of approach that Dennett wants to support. Nevertheless, one has to start somewhere, with a description of what it is that people do. And this is the role that FP has been playing. It is not something arrived at via science but something that operates as a starting point for most scientific studies of intersubjectivity. However, it is not at all clear why this starting point is so widespread and recalcitrant to revision, given that it certainly is not obvious to those who have not been taught that it is obvious and it does not originate in an explicit philosophical investigation of social life.

In what follows, I will explore the structure of interpersonal understanding without assuming that it is easy to articulate or 'commonsensical'. I will not restrict my enquiry to conceptual understanding, given the possibility that non-conceptual practical skills, affective responsiveness and such may turn out to be central to the ability to interact and coordinate with other people. Thus, if my subject matter is 'commonsense', it is commonsense construed as a range of conceptual and nonconceptual abilities that we depend upon in everyday life, which are accessible to careful reflection but by no means obvious. By the time I conclude, I hope to have shown that FP is not a part of everyday interpersonal understanding at all but, rather, a theoretically motivated and misleading abstraction that has been imposed upon it. Thus FP is not 'commonsense' in any sense of the term.

3
The World We Live in

Let us assume for now that we at least sometimes interpret, explain and predict one another's behaviour by employing something like FP. We do not attribute beliefs and desires to other people in a vacuum. When we do so, we take for granted not only that the other person is already in a world but that we are both in the same world. Furthermore, it is not simply a matter of assuming the same shared context in every instance. Aspects of an interpreter's situation will be shared with that of the interpreted to varying degrees and interpersonal understanding may be aided considerably by an appreciation of what both parties have in common. This need not take the form of an analogy between self and other, which starts with 'I take the world to have a certain character' and moves from this to 'he takes the world to have the same character'. Instead, as I will show, it can take the form 'the world has this character' and 'we are both in it'. In other words, an understanding that at least some aspects of a situation are shared is not assigned to others in the form of a belief system but presupposed. For example, when trying to pass a person in a busy shop, one might think 'he wants to get to the checkout' but one would not ordinarily think 'he believes he is in a shop'. That *we* are in a shop is not a belief that each party attributes to the other. It is an appreciation of how things are that both assume each other to share in advance of attributing any mental states. In considering the scope of FP, it is important to ascertain how much, if anything, of the burden of social understanding, interaction and coordination can be taken up by an understanding of shared situations.

The aim of this chapter is to offer preliminary descriptions of (a) the manner in which we take the world for granted when interpreting others, (b) how we understand more specific situations in which people are encountered, prior to our deploying anything like FP, and (c) some of the different ways in which people are experienced and understood in the context of various situations. To do so, I will focus on phenomenological descriptions offered by Heidegger, Gurwitsch and Schutz. It is these descriptions that originally kindled my reservations about FP. I will begin with a discussion of Heidegger's account of our 'Being-in-the-world', from which I will extract some key features of (a). I will then consider Gurwitsch's account of situations and roles, thus addressing (b). Finally, I will turn to (c) and outline some distinctions that Schutz makes between different ways of understanding and relating to other people. The points I draw from these three phenomenologists will be further developed in Chapters 4 to 6, where I will also appeal to complementary scientific findings.

The commonsense world

It might seem that the world, as ordinarily understood, is trivially easy to describe. It is a realm of objects located in space and time, most of which are inanimate. In this world, there is a sub-class of entities that have propositional attitudes. Hence we have FP, an ability that is distinct from our more general understanding of the world and dedicated to dealing with these entities. Of course, FP can only be successfully applied if it operates in conjunction with a more general ability to navigate the world, given that minded agents are also spatiotemporally located objects and subject to the same causal influences as inanimate objects. Thus an understanding of the physical world is required in order to predict and explain their behaviour. However, FP is still a discrete and more specifically applicable ability, rather than something that is inextricable from an appreciation of the world more generally. Predicting people is a matter of applying FP *plus* a more general understanding of things.

But is it really the case that the world, as we ordinarily understand it, is just a realm of causally interacting entities residing in space and time? If this sounds too simplistic, the question can be rephrased: Is the world, as taken for granted in everyday life, something that is comprehensively described by the physical sciences? Some suggest not. For example, Baker (1999) argues that such a view is highly misleading. She claims that 'commonsense psychology', construed in FP terms, is not a discrete ability that we apply to only a sub-class of entities within the world. Rather, it is inextricable from an appreciation of the 'commonsense world' more generally; it is 'part and parcel of the comprehensive commonsense framework of persons and medium-sized objects in terms of which we make our way in the world' (1999, p. 5). The world of commonsense is not, according to Baker, the world as described by physics but a world of norms and conventions. These are not accommodated by physical, causal descriptions and are not, she maintains, reducible to physics (p. 8). So the distinction between FP ability and an ability to negotiate the world more generally is premised on the false assumption that the world of commonsense is the world of physics. Although the 'physical world' frequently operates as a background assumption for philosophical thought, it is not an adequate description of the world that we actually experience and think about in our daily lives:

> The Physicalist Picture is so engrained in us that we hardly even notice it. Even so, it is just that: a picture. It is not dictated by reason or experience. (Certainly not experience!)[. . .] The commonsense conception is riddled with intentionality and normativity through and through. Commonsense psychology cannot be extricated from the total commonsense conception, leaving the rest of the commonsense conception intact.[1]
>
> (1999, p. 13)

Baker uses the term 'commonsense' to refer to the world and other people as they are ordinarily understood but she does not assume that this understanding is 'commonsensical' or easily articulated. Indeed, the difficulties involved in describing our everyday or commonsense understanding of things are exemplified by the shortcomings of FP. The problem with FP, according to Baker, is that it considers our commonsense psychology against the backdrop of a scientifically described rather than commonsense world, where it looks decidedly out of place. Everyday and scientific conceptions are thrown together, the result being a misleading picture of how commonsense psychology is integrated into a more general understanding of the world. Once commonsense psychology is considered in the context of a commonsense world, it becomes clear that the two are inseparable. In addition, Baker claims that scientific practice and thought do not transcend but instead presuppose the commonsense world. She advocates, in place of physicalism, a metaphysical position that she calls 'practical realism' (1999, p. 15), which acknowledges that the world is not just a realm of physical laws but also of norms and rules.

One response to this argument is to point out that, even if the world is indeed 'riddled with normativity', ascribing a belief is quite different from following a social norm or acting in accordance with convention. Hence some account is still required of how, if at all, the ability to attribute specific mental states relates to the ability to engage in other norm-governed practices. Baker's account also includes a controversial metaphysical position; her 'practical realism' is unlikely to persuade hardened physicalists. However, even if such objections are conceded, Baker still manages to make an important point about commonsense psychology: If one offers a description of commonsense psychology, one also owes a description of the commonsense world and an account of how the two relate. And the world of physics is not the world that we take for granted in our everyday activities. This point relates to the task of describing how people ordinarily take the world to be, rather than to that of describing how it actually is. It therefore applies regardless of whether one ultimately opts for physicalism, practical realism or some other metaphysical position.

I think Baker is quite right to stress that the everyday world incorporates normativity. It is a world of standardised norms, roles, functions and so forth, which involve a sense of what 'should be the case', 'what ought to be done', 'what one does in a given context', 'how a tool is supposed to perform' and so forth. In support of this view, I will consider some phenomenological claims made by Heidegger and Gurwitsch, both of whom seek to describe the nature of our understanding of the world and of more specific situations within the world.

The manner in which we understand the world in our practical and theoretical activities need not be identified with the way in which it is explicitly conceptualised by scientific or even by everyday thought. The world as ordinarily understood is, I will suggest, a background to explicit thought, rather than an object of thought. Describing the structure of this understanding requires a kind of enquiry that seeks to articulate what is taken for granted prior to reflection, rather than one that starts by assuming the world to be an intentional object, revealed through a reflective stance. As noted in Chapter 2, Husserl embarks on just such an enquiry in the *Crisis*, where he seeks to recover the life-world via a methodological shift, an epoché, which suspends acceptance of those conceptual systems that presuppose our background familiarity with the world. Heidegger's description of 'Being-in-the-world' in Division I of *Being and Time* and in *Basic Problems of Phenomenology* is similar in many respects to the Husserlian life world. However, Heidegger has more to say about how an everyday understanding of people relates to an everyday understanding of the world more generally. Hence I take his discussion as a starting point for my enquiry.

Heidegger's world

My aim in this section is to outline certain themes in Heidegger's early work, rather than to offer a comprehensive overview of his philosophy. The key theme I will focus on is the manner in which we ordinarily find ourselves in a 'world'. Regarding the world as a collection of entities, whose behaviour is to be observed, explained and predicted, involves the adoption of a somewhat detached, observational stance. However, Heidegger emphasises that everyday understanding does not ordinarily proceed in this way. Instead, it is embedded in our practical dealings with the world. Entities, as encountered through our practical concerns, are not understood in the same way as objects that are theoretically contemplated by a detached viewer. And the presupposed world that underlies our various practices is quite different in character from the world revealed as an object to detached reflection.

In order to understand Heidegger's account of how we find ourselves in a world, it is important to have some appreciation of his overall project, which is to articulate our ordinarily tacit understanding of 'Being'.[2] Being, for Heidegger, is not itself a being or a kind of being, such as a duck, a gold bar or a human being. Rather, it is a meaning-giving background that is presupposed by the intelligibility of all the beings that we encounter and think about:

> In the end something is given which *must* be given if we are to be able to make beings accessible to us as beings and comport ourselves toward them, something which, to be sure, is not but which must be given if we are to experience and understand any beings at all.
>
> (1982, p. 10)

Being is a structure that makes an understanding of beings possible and, given that we do understand beings, it follows that we also have an understanding of Being. This understanding is not something that we can effortlessly reflect upon and is, Heidegger claims, largely tacit. It is a background of sense through which we think, rather than an object of thought. He maintains that our understanding of Being has been progressively obscured and forgotten due to the cumulative historical acceptance of all manner of questionable philosophical presuppositions, which dispose us to misinterpret it in various ways. Being is not at all clear to us; it is 'the darkest of all' our concepts (1962, p. 23). Heidegger's aim in *Being and Time* is to wriggle free of obfuscatory philosophical assumptions and, in so doing, progressively articulate our understanding of Being.

In order to explore what is presupposed by our everyday understanding of beings, one needs to start with an adequate characterisation of that understanding. The obvious starting point for such an enquiry might seem to be entities that appear to us as *objects* of experience and thought; chairs, tables, mountains, trees, human beings and so forth. Surely such things, as contemplated by a subject, comprise an inventory of beings to serve as a convenient starting point. There is also the subject itself. Hence one could begin with our understanding of subjects and objects. Indeed, Heidegger observes that intentionality is routinely construed as a relation between two discrete entities, an object and the subject to whom the object appears (1982, p. 60). However, he suggests that this would be a bad place from which to begin. Understanding is not, ordinarily at least, a matter of connecting one's subjective inside with an objective outside. Hence a characterisation of beings as understood should not begin by documenting how things are revealed through a voyeuristic subject-object stance. This would incorporate an artificial and misleading detachment from the world, construing us as strangely removed from the objects of our understanding. To describe the world as a collection of entities, grouped into kinds, which appear to a contemplative spectator, would, he claims, be a superficial endeavour that failed to capture the manner in which we already find ourselves *in* the world before we embark on such intellectual pursuits:

> To accomplish this task seems easy and so trivial as to make one keep taking for granted that it may be dispensed with. What can be meant by describing 'the world' as a phenomenon? It means to let us see what shows itself in 'entities' within the world. Here the first step is to enumerate the things that are 'in' the world: houses, trees, people, mountains, stars. We can *depict* the way such entities 'look', and we can give an *account* of occurrences in them and with them. This however, is obviously a pre-phenomenological 'business' which cannot be at all relevant phenomenologically.
>
> (1962, p. 91)

Heidegger emphasises the extent to which, in our everyday lives, we are participants in the world, rather than detached spectators. In place of the contemplative subject, he uses the term 'Dasein' to refer to the human way of being in the world. Use of this term (translated as 'here being' or 'there being') serves to indicate that we are usually to be found caught up in a world, rather than looking upon it from afar. Heidegger takes Dasein as the being from which to begin his enquiry. As

Dasein is the being that has an understanding of Being, a description of the manner in which it finds itself in the world, of its 'Being-in-the-world', is a first step on the way to articulating that understanding. With an adequate description of how we ordinarily understand our relationship with the world, an enquiry into what that understanding presupposes can then proceed. Heidegger maintains that 'Being-in-the-world' is a unitary structure, which cannot be broken down into discrete parts. However, he does distinguish two inextricable aspects of it, 'the world' and the sense in which we are 'in' it. It is these that I will focus on here, given the aim of exploring our everyday understanding of the world, and I will not be returning to the question of Being.

Heidegger (1962, p. 93) lists four different senses of 'world':

1. The totality of 'present-at-hand entities' [*Vorhanden*], meaning all the entities that appear to us as objects of experience and thought.
2. The Being of those entities. Heidegger offers, as an example, the world of the mathematician, which is understood as the space of intelligible mathematical objects.
3. The everyday world in which we live.
4. 'Worldhood', meaning the general character of 'world', which is had by all worlds, where 'world' is understood in the sense of the 'world' of mathematics, motor racing or football.

He begins by addressing the world that we inhabit during the course of our daily lives, the surrounding world or *Umwelt* that operates as a background to our various theoretical and practical activities. How is the nature of this pre-understood world to be articulated? Heidegger proposes to take the way in which certain entities are encountered as a clue from which to work back to the way in which the world as a whole is understood. He suggests that we should start with the kind of understanding that is most commonplace in our daily lives and thus asks 'how do the beings with which we dwell show themselves to us primarily and for the most part?' (1982, pp. 162–163). The answer, he says, is that we do not ordinarily come across things from a standpoint of detached contemplation but instead within the context of our dealings. They are understood not as objects divorced from our various concerns but instead as things to be used, assembled, manipulated and so forth:

> In the domain of the present analysis, the entities we shall take as our preliminary theme are those which show themselves in our concern with the environment. Such entities are not thereby objects for

knowing the world theoretically; they are simply what gets used, what gets produced, and so forth.

(1962, p. 95)

What is distinctive about our appreciation of such entities? Heidegger notes that they are not first of all encountered in a removed fashion as *objects* but, rather, in terms of their equipmental character:

> In our dealings, we come across equipment for writing, sewing, working, transportation, measurement. The kind of Being which equipment possesses must be exhibited. The clue for doing this lies in our first defining what makes an item of equipment – namely, its equipmentality.

(1962, p. 97)

He draws a distinction between entities as they appear to theoretical knowing, as 'present-at-hand' [*Vorhanden*], and as they appear through our practical dealings, as 'ready-to-hand' or useable [*Zuhanden*]. A practical appreciation of a piece of equipment is quite different from theoretical contemplation of an object and, according to Heidegger, does not presuppose it. Given that entities are, for the most part, encountered in the context of our practical dealings, he takes the characteristic of readiness-to-hand [*Zuhandenheit*] as his preliminary focus.

How does an appreciation of equipment differ from a spectatorial understanding? As I type these words, I encounter the keyboard as something to be used in the context of a given project. It disappears seamlessly into my activities and, when the writing proceeds smoothly, I do not draw a firm boundary between myself and it. My relationship with the keyboard does not, while I am practically engaged with it, incorporate an explicit distinction between the subject (me) and the object (keyboard). It does not simply appear before me as an object but is integrated into my activity. Heidegger suggests that our dealings with equipment more generally do not respect traditional subject-object distinctions; user and used are bound up together in contexts of activity. These practical relationships can, however, break down in various ways. For example, suppose the coffee cup that I am drinking from suddenly falls on the floor, pouring coffee all over the carpet. I turn round startled and do not encounter the cup in the manner that I did the keyboard but as an entity that has disrupted the project I was previously absorbed in. The cup stands before me as an object of experience and thought, as 'present-at-hand' [*Vorhanden*].

A sharp division between presence-at-hand and readiness-to-hand might seem rather implausible. While I am typing, the keyboard does not usually 'disappear wholly' and become fused with my practical activity. And as I reach for a sip of coffee, it seems to me that I am aware of the cup both as a distinct object and, at the same time, as something usable. Furthermore, the cup that lies on the floor retains a sense of its functionality and my consideration of it does not involve the same theoretical stance as that of a scientist attempting to ascertain its molecular constitution, at least not to the same degree. So it is arguable that we encounter entities along a continuum between objects of contemplation and ingredients of our activities (Wheeler, 2005, p. 141). This is something that Heidegger acknowledges, stating that 'there are many intermediate gradations' (1962, p. 201). Hence the distinction between presence-at-hand and readiness-to-hand should not be interpreted as implying that tools invariably 'disappear' into our activities. However, what Heidegger does want to claim is that equipment is individuated by its purposive character; its functionality makes it what it is (1982, p. 292, 1962, p. 164). A hammer is only a hammer in virtue of its ability to perform a particular role in the context of certain projects. An understanding of equipment is thus inseparable from an understanding of salient practical activities.

Heidegger suggests that present-at-hand understanding is not established prior to an appreciation of readiness-to-hand. It is something that emerges out of practical understanding. An understanding of functionality is not projected onto an understanding of present-at-hand objects. Rather, the revelation of presence-at-hand involves a privation of readiness-to-hand, a stripping away of practical character to reveal bare presence as an abstraction from a richer, practical appreciation of a thing. However, one of the most conspicuous examples he employs to illustrate this point is somewhat suspect:

> 'Nature' is not to be understood as that which is just present-at-hand, nor as the *power of Nature*. The wood is a forest of timber, the mountain a quarry of rock; the river is water-power, the wind is wind 'in the sails'. As the 'environment' is discovered, the 'Nature' thus discovered is encountered too. If its kind of Being as ready-to-hand is disregarded, this 'Nature' itself can be discovered and defined simply in its pure presence-at-hand. But when this happens, the Nature which 'stirs and strives', which assails us and enthrals us as landscape, remains hidden. The botanist's plants are not the flowers of

the hedgerow; the 'source' which the geographer establishes for a river is not the 'springhead in the dale'.

(1962, p. 100)

Nature, understood as present-at-hand, is stripped of the ready-to-hand meaning with which it was previously imbued. However, the nature that 'stirs and strives' and 'enthrals us' is arguably not nature construed as equipment to be employed in the context of some project. Instead, this looks like a kind of aesthetic appreciation, different in character from both the detached mode of presence-at-hand and the practical absorption that characterises readiness-to-hand.[3] So, even allowing that readiness-to-hand and presence-at-hand form a continuum, it is arguable that the distinction fails to accommodate various other ways in which we encounter entities.

But let us assume that Heidegger is at least right in maintaining that we understand *many* entities as equipment and that we ordinarily encounter them as such in relation to our practical activities. This much, at least, seems plausible, given the extent to which most of our everyday activities involve a reliance on inter-related tools. Even a walk through the countryside, although far removed from a technologised office environment, usually involves an appreciation of trails, signs and maps. Regardless of whether or not readiness-to-hand adequately accommodates all of the ways in which we encounter nature, it is still an extremely pervasive way of relating to things. The point I want to draw from Heidegger is that the 'commonsense world' is, among other things, a context in which entities are understood through our practical concerns. They are encountered as functionally individuated items of equipment, rather than as objects with no relationship to our activities, which are only *subsequently* understood in terms of their utility. This observation will prove important when it comes to considering our relations with other people.

The sense in which Heidegger takes presence-at-hand to be a privation of readiness-to-hand is not entirely clear. He states that Descartes construed the world in terms of 'permanent presence-at-hand' and, in so doing, neglected to recognise the 'founded character of all sensory and intellective awareness' (1962, pp. 130–131). This seems to indicate that the intelligibility of theoretically contemplated objects always presupposes a more fundamental practical familiarity with things. But in what sense is present-at-hand understanding 'founded'? Is the meaningfulness of presence-at-hand always bound up in our dealings or do we somehow manage to pass through readiness to get at unadulterated presence, the way the world really is independent of our concerns?

Sometimes it looks as though Heidegger is erring towards the latter. For example, in the passage I quoted he claims that, 'if its kind of Being as ready-to-hand is disregarded, this "Nature" itself can be discovered and defined simply in its pure presence-at-hand'. However, he also assumes throughout *Being and Time* that all the ways in which entities are encountered presuppose an understanding of Being. Thus, even if some account, perhaps a scientific one, could transcend readiness-to-hand and expose the way things are, an appreciation of 'how things are' would still depend on an understanding of Being for its intelligibility, even if not on readiness-to-hand.

Such issues have considerable implications with regard to how the relationship between the everyday world and the theoretical, scientifically described world should be construed. However, my own enquiry can proceed without taking a stand here (although I will say something about the relationship between phenomenology and science in Chapter 8). Even if present-at-hand understanding ultimately trumps readiness-to-hand in an account of how the world actually *is*, this will not have any implications for a description of how the world is *taken to be* in everyday life and the latter is my concern. Hence Heidegger's emphasis on a practical appreciation of things may well prove valuable, regardless of how his account of the relationship between the world of everyday practice and that of theoretical cognition is interpreted.[4]

Heidegger makes a number of further points about our understanding of equipment. Central to the argument I will develop in Chapter 4 is his observation that pieces of equipment are understood in terms of their relations to other pieces of equipment. The function of an item of equipment is something that it has in virtue of these relations and its individuation thus requires them. As Heidegger puts it,

> Taken strictly, there is no such thing as an equipment. To the Being of any equipment there always belongs a totality of equipment, in which it can be this equipment it is. Equipment is essentially 'something in-order-to'. A totality of equipment is constituted in various ways of the 'in-order-to', such as serviceability, conduciveness, usability, manipulability.
>
> (1962, p. 97)

The keyboard that I use to type is functionally interconnected with the computer, the monitor, the printer and the paper in the printer. But why stop there? The chair I am sitting on, the desk in front of it, the papers and notes that surround me, the pen, the office as a whole and a host of other items constitute a functional whole that is bound up with my current project. The same can be said of equipment more generally. Signs, road markings, traffic lights, car parks, streets, shops, cash dispensers, advertisements and so forth together comprise an integrated structure that one inhabits during the course of one's weekly shopping trip. And an understanding of the project of shopping incorporates references to a host of other projects, like cooking dinner tonight, which are themselves tied up with other equipmental configurations, such as kitchens.

With an appreciation of the character of equipmental understanding, Heidegger claims that we can gain insight into how the everyday world, the context in which we use equipment, is itself understood. He thinks that this understanding is illuminated by those instances where equipment breaks down, where we experience the transition from readiness-to-hand to presence-at-hand. Presence-at-hand reveals itself when equipment is damaged, missing, getting in the way of things or is unsuited to the job at hand. In such cases, it becomes conspicuous. Even so, it is still interpreted through a context of dealings. An unusable hammer is understood as unusable against the backdrop of a project that involves hammering. Nevertheless, its conspicuousness is a first step on the way to characterising it as pure presence-at-hand, to fully extricating it from a context of concern. As Heidegger puts it, 'the modes of conspicuousness, obtrusiveness, and obstinacy all have the function of bringing to the fore the characteristic of presence-at-hand in what is ready-to-hand' (1962, p. 104). However, the transition from readiness to presence also involves something else. As the hammerhead suddenly flies off, one not only becomes aware of the broken hammer as present-at-hand. In that moment of unanticipated disruption, something else happens too. The purposive structure, which one was previously absorbed in, flickers into view. When equipment breaks down, one briefly glimpses the whole teleological framework of which that equipment was a part, a web of relations between the 'in order to', 'towards' and 'for the sake of', which one previously inhabited and did not reflect upon:

> When an assignment to some particular 'towards-this' has been thus circumspectively aroused, we catch sight of the 'towards-this' itself, and along with it everything connected with the work – the whole 'work-shop' – as that wherein concern always dwells. The context of equipment is lit up, not as something never seen before, but as a totality constantly sighted beforehand in circumspection. With this totality however, the world announces itself.
>
> (1962, p. 105)

This teleological structure is the taken-for-granted world of everyday life. 'Worldhood', the characteristic common to all instances of worldly understanding, takes the form of a presupposed web of teleological relations. Different teleological frameworks are inhabited at different times, such as kitchens, offices, shopping centres and football pitches. However, all of them have the same kind of purposive structure and, according to Heidegger, this characteristic best captures the nature of our everyday relationship with the world. The world is not a present-at-hand object or a collection of tools but a teleologically organised possibility space, which can be configured in various concrete ways by different assemblies of equipment. We are not *in* the world in the way that a marble is in a box but, rather, in the way that we might be *in* a football match or *in* a profession:

> Being-in-the-world, according to our Interpretation hitherto, amounts to a non-thematic circumspective absorption in references or assignments constitutive for the readiness-to-hand of a totality of equipment. Any concern is already as it is, because of some familiarity with the world.
>
> (1962, p. 107)

But what has all this got to do with our understanding of other people? As Heidegger's discussion of interpersonal relations makes clear, he thinks that our practical dealings with equipment and our appreciation of people are intimately interconnected.

Heidegger on other people

If we follow Heidegger in emphasising the extent to which understanding is embedded in our practical dealings, the detached, spectatorial understanding of people that characterises FP starts to look rather misplaced. For the most part, we understand people in the midst of our dealings too, suggesting that they are not usually interpreted as complicated present-at-hand entities. Consider a piece of equipment, such as a tennis racket. Everyday understanding of tennis rackets is associated with familiar contexts of activity. Tennis racket understanding, on the part of the player at least, is not usually a matter of detached contemplation of a racket that has been extricated from its role in the context of tennis playing. Similarly, it is arguable that spectatorial accounts of interpersonal understanding artificially remove it from the practical contexts in which we encounter other people. Heidegger suggests something along just such lines. He claims that people are not ordinarily understood as objects revealed to a detached voyeur; they are understood in the midst of the world of work. Most of our activities are structured by frameworks of equipmental relations and other people, he says, are not posited as add-ons to these frameworks. An understanding of equipment already includes references to others, as designers, co-operators, co-users or recipients of a finished product:

> . . . along with the equipment to be found when one is at work [in Arbeit], those Others for whom the 'work' [Werk] is destined are 'encountered too' [. . .] Similarly, when material is put to use, we encounter its producer or 'supplier' as one who 'serves' well or badly.
> (1962, p. 153)

The world of work is always a shared world and other people are implicated in the intelligibility of our projects. We do not need to reach out to them from a pre-understood, non-social world as they are already integrated into an understanding of the world. This point can be illustrated by a consideration of functionality. The function of an item of equipment is not something that it has solely in virtue of its relationship to a set of purely personal concerns. Instead, the function of a standardised tool is what 'one' does with it, regardless of who 'one' is. Equipment is understood as something that is *supposed* to be used in a certain way. This prescription is intrinsic to the sense of what a tool is, regardless of whether we are talking about coffee cups, shoes or chairs. Norms of use are applicable to everyone or at least to those people who use the tool or are supposed to be using it. We do not generally encounter an item of equipment as something 'I can use for x' and then afterwards as something that 'you can use for x' but as something that is 'to be used for x' by some 'we'. A wider system of equipment includes a host of interrelated references to 'what one does' and so the world, as understood through our practical dealings, is always a shared world. As Heidegger puts it, 'the world of Dasein is a *with-world* [*Mitwelt*]' (1962, p. 155). Given that we often understand equipment in terms of what 'one' does with it, regardless of who one is, he suggests that practical understanding often involves a largely undifferentiated 'we', rather than the recognition of a group of distinct individuals. Other people are, he says, 'those from whom, for the most part, one does *not* distinguish oneself – those among whom one is too' (1962, p. 154).

Heidegger claims that a practical grasp of the shared world is more fundamental to our appreciation of people than the understanding that is obtained through a subject-object perspective. If enquiry is restricted to the latter, the result is a misleading abstraction from the shared world, where interpersonal understanding is misconstrued as a matter of one subject contemplating a distinct object and somehow inferring that it too is a subject. He warns that

> Theoretically concocted 'explanations' of the Being-present-at-hand of Others urge themselves upon us all too easily; but over against such explanations we must hold fast to the phenomenal facts of the case which we have pointed out, namely, that Others are encountered *environmentally*.
>
> (1962, p. 155)

People do not ordinarily encounter each other through a theoretical stance. And an enquiry that unwittingly assumes that we do will misconstrue the structure of interpersonal understanding from the beginning. When studying the manner in which we understand each other, it is important not to quietly impose the theoretical form of one's own enquiry upon that understanding.

Although Heidegger maintains that people are not ordinarily understood as present-at-hand entities, he does not claim that they are understood as equipment. Of course, one might, while absorbed in a project, treat someone else as nothing more than a tool to be used so as to achieve a certain end, such as 'to buy a loaf of bread from' or 'to mend the washing machine'. However, according to Heidegger, this is not a recognition of others as Dasein but a failure to acknowledge them as such. He claims that we appreciate the distinctive character of people through a specific kind of concern, which he calls 'solicitude' [*Fürsorge*]. This differs from the kind of concern [*Besorgen*] through which we encounter equipment. Solicitude involves receptiveness to the fact that another is not just an entity to be used but also a locus of projects. Heidegger suggests that solicitude can manifest itself in two principal ways; there are authentic [*eigentlich*] and inauthentic [*uneigentlich*] relations between people. The latter can be exemplified by what he calls 'leaping in', where one responds to another's project by completing some part of it for them, rather than by nurturing the conditions that enable them to do it for themselves. Think about wading in when someone is just about to finish a crossword puzzle and writing down the last answer for them. Authentic intervention, in contrast, involves acting so as to enhance a person's own ability to seize hold of certain possibilities and actualise their aims. Imagine two climbers trying to scale a cliff face, both helping each other to realise their goals but without either one of them compromising the other's active engagement with the project (1962, pp. 158–159). In both cases, interaction and mutual interpretation are constrained by the space of possible projects afforded by shared equipmental configurations. But in neither case is the other person understood as a mere thing or instrument. Rather, she is a locus of agency and possibility, which one can respond to in different ways and respect to varying degrees. So, for Heidegger, other people are integral to the world of work and are interpreted through it. But they are encountered in a distinctive way and are not ultimately reducible to present-at-hand entities or ready-to-hand equipment.

Of particular relevance to the argument I will develop in Chapter 4 is Heidegger's description of what happens when one settles into an inauthentic interpretation of self and other. We increasingly live in a world of standardised equipment, which embodies a specification of 'what one is supposed to do' that is applicable to all. This, according to Heidegger, allows Dasein to disappear into public ways of doing things and just drift along doing what one does. He calls this predicament 'Das Man' (1962, p. 164), a way of being in the world where one just does what 'they do', 'what everyone does', 'what's done' or 'what one does'. One drives on the left because that is what one does, goes to the parking meter, gets a ticket, walks into town, stares in shop windows and makes a few purchases, all because that is what one does, regardless of who one is. Situations regulate activities and Dasein is thus 'disburdened' of any responsibility for taking hold of the possibilities afforded by its situation and integrating them into its own project (1962, p. 165). Instead it 'falls' into the world, responding to behaviour-prescribing equipmental frameworks in the way that everyone does and interpreting them as doing just the same (1962, p. 213). In the extreme case, Dasein becomes a total situationist, letting the world of shared norms do all the work and just drifting along. An authentic attitude towards one's activities, in contrast, involves seizing hold of various possibilities offered by the shared world and actualising them in the context of projects that are actively pursued. Heidegger is not making a point about different kinds of activity that people engage in. His concern is not *what we do* but *how we understand what we do*; a mundane shopping trip could be authentically or inauthentically carried out. He does not take authenticity to be a more fundamental way of interpreting self and others than inauthenticity. Both are, he thinks, equally basic; authenticity involves a 'modification' of Das Man, a different way of responding to the possibilities offered by the world (1962, p. 168).[5]

According to Heidegger, inauthentic ways of being in the world and with others predominate in everyday life. Leaving aside the seemingly negative connotations of 'inauthenticity', which are I think misleading, we can extract an important observation from his discussion. Shared norms are embedded in the everyday world, serving to specify what one does in certain situations. Those who share a common environment of standardised equipment already have a situational understanding of what they and others are doing, which can do much of the work of facilitating interpersonal interaction and interpretation. The assumption that people will do 'what one does', in the context of a framework of shared norms that are partly embodied in assemblies of equipment, serves as a basis for shared conduct. If Heidegger is right, much of our everyday understanding of others is also an understanding of the world, given that an understanding of equipment is an understanding of public norms of conduct. There is no need to assign mental states in cases where people's activities are in line with a shared normative context.

Two further points, drawn from Heidegger's account, will also be of relevance to my argument. First, our understanding of people and the world more generally does not proceed from a detached standpoint and is quite different from the observer-observed relation typical of FP. So it is important to consider whether an account that emphasises 'observer' and 'observed' can also accommodate the ways in which we understand people in practical contexts. In Chapter 4, I will argue that it cannot. Second, Heidegger claims that there is a tendency to miscast certain practical achievements as theoretical achievements. In adopting a theoretical stance towards a human activity, one should be wary of inadvertently misinterpreting that activity as itself a theoretical pastime, a concern that will be addressed in Chapters 6 and 8.

Gurwitsch on situations and roles

Heidegger's description of the shared world, and the interplay that it involves between equipmental functions and shared norms, can be supplemented by Gurwitsch's largely complementary discussion in *Human Encounters in the Social World*. Gurwitsch emphasises a practical appreciation of differentiated *social roles* in the context of shared situations. His aim is to offer an account of how people experience and understand each other in everyday life and, in formulating this account, he draws on the work of other phenomenologists, including Husserl, Heidegger and Scheler. He begins by discussing the view that we understand the mental states of others through an analogy between our behaviour and theirs, on the basis of which we then infer similar behavioural causes in the guise of internal mental states. Gurwitsch notes that such a view is counterintuitive, given that the mental lives of other people seem to be perceptually accessible in their expressions and gestures:

> . . . we immediately and openly witness his joy, see it directly in his face. In daily life the idea never arises that we do not have in perception what itself occurs in our fellow human being.
>
> (1979, p. 3)

However, even if it is admitted that this kind of appreciation is acquired perceptually (and I will argue in Chapter 5 that it is), Gurwitsch maintains that perception of expressive phenomena is not the primary route by which we understand each other in everyday life (1979, p. 33). Like Heidegger, he claims that understanding a person is not a matter of interpreting the behaviour of a complex object and that, rather than encountering each other through spectatorial standpoints, we do so in the course of our 'natural living' (p. 35). He goes on to distinguish personal encounters with a 'you' from unthinking social relations between anonymous participants in shared social situations and argues that the latter play a more basic role in social understanding. Gurwitsch, like Heidegger, claims that we do not, in everyday life, act and interpret activity against the backdrop of an objective, physical world. Instead, we practically inhabit various concrete situations, which are understood as configurations of interconnected utensils that are bound up with appropriate and expected patterns of activity. Other people, he argues, are included in the meaning of a situation from the start, not as wholly undifferentiated users of tools but as the occupiers of distinct social roles:

> . . . situations become visible in the horizons in which sellers, anonymous buyers, purveyors, employers, listeners, readers, masters, servants, etc., act out their roles. *As bearers of these roles in the 'co-included' situations (and only in these roles of theirs), those who belong to the world of fellow human beings appear in the references mentioned.*
>
> (p. 98)

Gurwitsch thus supplements Heideggerian 'being-with' by suggesting that we understand the world in terms of situation types that incorporate a range of differentiated, inter-related roles. We understand people's activities as the performances of these roles. As with universally applicable

norms, roles are integrated into an understanding of the kind of situation we are in. Roles are not ordinarily understood in a standoffish,
detached fashion. It is through active participation in a certain kind of
situation that we encounter each other. We do so through the performance of our respective and interactive roles, as teachers, pupils, shop
attendants, customers and so forth. A person might be understood as
someone to give the money to, forward an invoice to, direct a customer
to and so on.

According to Gurwitsch, awareness of a 'personal presence', as manifested in gestures or expressions, is insufficient for interpersonal
understanding in the absence of a shared context. Without a common
situation, two people may inhabit physical spaces in close proximity
to each other but they will not be *with* each other. He claims that
the shared situations, through which we encounter each other in our
respective roles, operate as contexts that enable us to interpret each
other's expressive behaviour and to interact. Even though another person might be understood as more than *just* a role, her activities are still
interpreted through the situation in which both participants' activities
are embedded:

> When I ask someone for something, I then experience the way in
> which the person asked listens to me, enters into the request, offers
> resistance, avoids the request, sets conditions, gives in, etc.; I do not
> experience something like an alien or autonomous will simpliciter.
> Rather a human being encounters me who comports himself in a cer-
> tain way in the situation in question, who is unfriendly or compli-
> ant, who allows this or that purpose to clearly appear or even be
> explicitly expressed, who lets a certain position toward the affair be
> known, etc. Even the one asked to do something does not experience
> anything like the 'claim of the Thou' simpliciter.
>
> (p. 113)

In some parts of his discussion, it seems as though Gurwitsch takes
the appreciation of another person to consist of nothing more than an
understanding of his current place in a shared situation. Indeed he
remarks that individual role-bearers can be substituted for each other
without any disruption to an understanding of the situation; 'only in
this role do I have something to do with him. In this situation, his being
is exhausted in the role whose bearer he is' (p. 108). Perhaps this is so
in some cases, such as walking off the train every day and handing over
a ticket, oblivious to *who* the person is that collects it. However, given

that we frequently do comprehend each other as more than just our social roles, how does Gurwitsch distinguish an understanding of people from an understanding of utensils, which are also understood in terms of standardised roles?

Situations begin and end; people drift from one situation to the next, occupying different roles at different times. A police officer goes home and takes off her uniform, whereas a police car remains fixed in its role. According to Gurwitsch, that people phase in and out of a situation indicates that they are somehow more than just their roles. Situations regulate exchanges but do not constitute the full sense of who someone is. People can, as he puts it, 'appear in their freedom', unconstrained by the situation and relieved of a situational partnership that one had with them for a time (p. 116). However, this aspect of his discussion is a bit vague. For example, it is unclear why someone would appear 'in their freedom', rather than simply as 'an occupier of several different social roles'. Gurwitsch's emphasis on social roles also plays down other aspects of human relations, such as emotional contact, friendship and the kind of unconstrained, free flowing conversation that takes place between people when all the uniforms are off. He does at least acknowledge such features of interpersonal relations, contrasting affective social relations with the absence of personal feeling that can characterise interaction between bearers of social roles:

> The cool and internal distance of societal being-together stands in contra-distinction to the human warmth, the feeling of belonging together and of commonality, to the sentiments of benevolence, of solidarity and mutual demands, etc., that is, to everything which can be comprised by the expressions 'being close' and 'feeling close'.
>
> (p. 120)

Nevertheless, he claims that emotional connections between people rest upon an appreciation of shared situations. Role-based understanding comes first and only once this has been established can a more personal understanding be pursued. The kind of societal understanding that precedes it does not just involve a grasp of specific situations but also a broader familiarity with traditions and customs, much of which is taken for granted as a backdrop for interpersonal interpretation, a 'life-context' to which one belongs, which is variably shared by others (p. 125).

Gallagher (2005b) suggests that Gurwitsch's account of presupposed situations can be developed into an effective critique of FP, in showing how a practical appreciation of shared situations does most or all of the work of interpersonal understanding in many cases. Thus the role of intentional state attribution is overstated and, even in those cases where FP is employed, interpretations are constrained by situations. However, he also raises the concern that Gurwitsch risks implausibly construing interpersonal understanding as a practical appreciation of tools.[6] As will become clear in Chapter 4, I agree with Gallagher about the relevance of Gurwitsch's account to the issue of FP's scope. However, I do not think that Gurwitsch fails to accommodate the personal; he does leave space for a properly personal understanding within the context of an already established situational understanding. Nevertheless, in Chapter 6, I will reject Gurwitsch's claim that situational understandings have priority over affective relations between people. I will argue that, although the latter do rely upon the former, they can also shape and reshape the normative structure of situations. Thus there is a dynamic between the two, in which neither has clear priority.

Even though Gurwitsch does underplay the personal, the kind of role-based social understanding he describes has quite considerable scope. If we combine the insights of Gurwitsch and Heidegger, we get an account of worldly situations as intricate frameworks of equipmental functions, general norms of conduct and more specific roles, which together make a substantial contribution to an understanding of people's activities. As I will argue in Chapter 4, there may be many cases where norms, functions and roles do most or even all of the work. It would seem, phenomenologically at least, that an appreciation of shared situations is already in place before anything like FP is employed to understand behaviour. In Chapter 4, I will suggest that there are no good grounds for claiming that phenomenology has been misled here; an appreciation of norms, roles and functions does not presuppose FP ability.

Encountering others

Gurwitsch (1979, p. 126) claims that emotionally rich face-to-face interactions, involving anything more than participants' role-specified activities, are the exception rather than the norm. However, even if this is so, it could still be that such interactions are most fundamental to an appreciation of what people are. The deepest understanding we have of people may not play a role in all or even most of our interactions and relations with them. Just such a view is proposed by Schutz in his *Phenomenology of the Social World*. Schutz does not dispute the view that many social relations are a matter of situational understanding.

However, he offers descriptions of other kinds of social understanding and emphasises, in the process, the fundamentality of a distinctively personal form of relatedness.

Descriptions of FP tend to emphasise those instances where an observer attributes mental states to an observed entity. Claims for its ubiquity rest, in part, on the assumption that abilities implicated in such cases will be employed more generally. Something that Schutz's work makes clear is the heterogeneity of interpersonal understanding; there are many different ways in which we understand and relate to other people. In order to assess the scope of FP, it is important to differentiate these and assess which, if any of them, accord with FP. I will outline some of Schutz's distinctions here. My aim in so doing is (a) to draw attention to some of the different kinds of interpersonal and social relations and (b) to provide a preliminary characterisation of a kind of interpersonal relatedness that will be further explored in Chapters 5 and 6.

Schutz's work is strongly influenced by both Husserl and Weber. It is more individualistic than that of Gurwitsch and takes a sense of the 'personal' to be the foundation of social life. Schutz aims to describe social relations as they arise in what Husserl calls the 'natural attitude'; he is offering an account of the everyday ways in which we experience and understand others. Hence much of his discussion can be construed as a philosophical exploration of 'commonsense psychology', in a non-superficial sense of the term. He begins by emphasising four different kinds of interpersonal relation (1967, xxvii):

(a) A and B observe each other.
(b) A observes B and B is unaware of A.
(c) A affects B while B observes A.
(d) A and B affect each other.

Already, this serves to illustrate the potential limitations of FP descriptions, which often take the form of (a) or (b) but fail to consider whether the two might make different cognitive demands or whether they might both be importantly different from (c) and (d). Schutz then makes several further distinctions that are relevant to an investigation of the scope of FP. For example, he claims that there is a big difference between how we understand people during face-to-face interactions and how we do so when we resort to a theoretical, reflective stance. In the latter case, he suggests that we sometimes try to figure out the motives behind someone's actions by resorting to a procedure that looks like what has more recently been referred to as a simulation routine:

> . . . we imaginatively project the in-order-to motive of the other person as if it were our own and then use the fancied carrying-out of such an action as a scheme in which to interpret his lived experiences.
>
> (p. 115)

This kind of imaginative procedure is, he suggests, only applied when one has withdrawn from social activity. Hence it does not underlie most social relations. In everyday social life, regardless of whether we interact with somebody or observe her, that person's experiences are somehow perceptually available to us. Hence there is no need to resort to simulation (p. 115). What we can perceive in another's gestures, expressions and activities is of course limited in scope. Schutz grants that we can perceive the meanings of actions, such as 'pleading' or 'begging' but adds that we cannot perceive the reason why a person might be pleading or begging (pp. 23–24). However, he suggests that, when we experience others, we are ordinarily preoccupied with the actions that are occurring rather than with a search for reasons:

> In everyday life we directly experience the acts of another. [. . .] Observational understanding is then focused on the action as it takes place, and we, as beings living alongside the actor and sharing his present, participate experientially in the very course of his action.
>
> (p. 30)

Although further interpretation is required to work out the motives behind an activity, Schutz suggests that perception of action is often all we need to get by in everyday life and that we seldom engage in further interpretation or in a consideration of likely reasons and motives (pp. 30–31). Although he claims that observation of people and interaction with them both involve perception of experience, Schutz argues that there is a 'radical difference' between the two (pp. 204–205). He distinguishes between our consociates, our contemporaries and our predecessors. Consociates are those we interact with on a frequent basis, often through face-to-face contact. Our predecessors are those with whom we can never interact. Although we do interact with our contemporaries in certain ways, our relations with them differ from those we have with consociates. The latter are those whom we encounter personally, whereas the former are often appreciated only as impersonal role-bearers or anonymous others. According to Schutz, it is consociate encounters that involve our most basic sense of the personal. We never think of a predecessor, contemporary or consociate as merely an 'it'. In all three cases, he claims that we adopt an 'Other orientation', meaning a stance that recognises the other as a locus of experience, rather than a mere thing (p. 146). However, in face-to-face interactions with consociates, we not only recognise an 'other' as opposed to an 'it'; we address a 'Thou'. The distinction between 'thou' and 'other' is respected in every-day discourse by the distinction between second- and third-person pro-nouns. Addressing a 'you' is distinguished from contemplating a 'he' or 'she' and both are distinguished from looking upon a mere 'it'. Schutz claims that we do not come to appreciate a 'Thou' through theorising or reflecting upon experience. A 'Thou orientation' is something that strikes us with a kind of immediacy; it is integral to the experience. As he puts it, it is not a 'conscious judgment' but a 'prepredicative experi-ence' (p. 164). Schutz is quite clear that a Thou-orientation is not a mat-ter of being aware of another as the possessor of internal mental states. It is instead a way of experiencing, which incorporates a sense of the other as a locus of experience:

> The concept of the Thou-orientation does not imply awareness of what is going on in the Other's mind. In its 'pure' form the Thou-orientation consists merely of being intentionally directed toward the pure being-there of another alive and conscious human being.
>
> (p. 164)

Experiencing a Thou is not a matter of encountering something from a detached perspective. Intrinsic to the experience is a sense of related-ness. Schutz emphasises a sense of mutual openness and permeability that characterises the interactions between I and Thou:

> In the living intentionality of the direct social relationship, the two partners are face to face, their streams of consciousness are synchro-nized and geared into each other, each immediately affects the other, and the in-order-to motive of the one becomes the because-motive of the other, the two complementing and validating each other as objects of reciprocal attention
>
> (p. 162)

He suggests that such face-to-face relationships involve a 'we' that can-not be analysed in terms of two wholly separate participants, and that the ability to participate in an I-Thou relation is foundational to social life (p. 171). However, the structure of the relation is not something that we entertain as an object of experience or thought while immersed in it. So, in order to articulate the manner in which one experiences a Thou, one has to step out of the relation and adopt a reflective standpoint towards it (p. 168). Nevertheless, Schutz stresses that the way in which others are experienced in the course of everyday life should not be confused with the perspective that is adopted to reflect on social experience; 'lived experience' is not 'systematising scrutiny' (p. 10).

How might such claims contribute to an exploration of the nature and scope of FP? Schutz distinguishes encounters with Thou, Other and It, taking the former to be fundamental, but such distinctions have not been drawn by proponents of FP. Some, such as Dennett (1987), assume that an intentional stance is just a matter of interpreting a very complicated 'it'. Others take FP to be a matter of third-person interpretation but seldom attempt to characterise the difference between a 'third-person' and an 'it', perhaps assuming that the proper applicability of FP to only one of them is constitutive of the distinction between people and inanimate objects. None draw a distinction between interpreting a 'he' or she' and relating to another person as 'you'. Furthermore, FP assumes that interpersonal interpretation is a matter of A ascribing mental states to B from afar and does not include an account of how interaction between A and B might itself structure their appreciation of each other. It makes no reference to mutual permeability, openness to others or inter-mingling and sharing of experiences. There is also the concern that FP fails to distinguish what is involved in everyday social relations from what is involved in folkish or philosophical reflection upon everyday social relations. They could be quite different in character.

It might be objected that the claim that some standpoint or stance discloses a 'Thou' is vague to say the least and does not amount to a clear alternative, let alone an objection, to FP. This may well be so. However, Schutz's descriptions do at least draw attention to the possibility of a distinctive kind of personal stance that has not been explored by FP. According to Schutz, our sense of others as people, in contrast to mere objects, is dependent on the ability to adopt a particular stance. This stance is not, like Dennett's intentional stance, a detached, theoretical affair. It is instead a kind of practical, bodily openness between people, which is constitutive of the possibility of experiencing the personal. The claim that there is some such 'orientation', and thus a substantial difference between what can be revealed through participant and observational stances, is at least worthy of further investigation.

The same applies to Schutz's claim that a spectatorial Other orientation, although not as 'personal' as a Thou orientation, is also quite different in character from the adoption of an observational stance towards a complex object.

Schutz does of course acknowledge that social life is not just a matter of relating to people as 'Thou' and as 'Other'. He maintains that it is multi-layered and highly complicated. However, he does argue that all the various strata of social meaning are founded on experience of the Thou. An I-Thou relation involves an experience of sharing, which underlies comprehension of the possibility of a shared social world. Schutz (p. 180) divides social relations into various levels of remoteness from face to face I-Thou relations, the remoter being less personal in nature:

1. Those I've met face to face and may do again.
2. Those encountered by the person I'm talking to.
3. Those I am to meet.
4. Those I know according to their social function.
5. Collective entities like a Parliament, whose members I cannot name.
6. Anonymous collective entities like nations.
7. Meaning configurations of the world of my contemporaries, like the rules of grammar or the Highway Code.
8. Artefacts which refer to the meaning-contexts of unknown people.

It would seem that the social relations emphasised by Gurwitsch rank as 4 and also 8 on the list. Schutz describes understanding others in terms of functional roles as involving a kind of 'abstraction, generalization, formalization, or idealization' that should not be confused with lived experience (p. 187). Social roles are indeed an important element in our interpretive practices and we do construe the actions of individuals as stemming from 'personal ideal types' meaning kinds of role, such as banker, teacher and factory worker. However, this alone gives us what Schutz calls a mere 'shadow person', which should not be confused with how people are experienced as *people* (p. 190). He offers the example of a card game. One can encounter a person as a *card player* or one can face a *person* in a game of cards. Only the latter, he maintains, involves a truly personal stance, even though the former has a role to play in reflective interpretations when one withdraws from the flow of social experience (p. 186).

In the next three chapters, I will further develop some of the themes I have outlined here, in order to investigate first of all whether there are cases of social understanding that do not require FP and then whether FP adequately characterises any aspect of interpersonal understanding and interaction. In Chapter 4, I will suggest that Heidegger and Gurwitsch are quite right to emphasise norms, roles and functions. They allow many instances of social understanding, interaction and coordination to proceed quite happily without any help from FP. Then, in Chapter 5, I will address the question of whether, as Gurwitsch and Schutz indicate, we can, in our everyday experiences of others, perceive rather than infer agency, gesture and expression. In Chapter 6, I will suggest that a kind of 'personal stance' similar to what Schutz terms a Thou-orientation is fundamental to our sense of others as people and to our ability to understand and interact with them. This stance is not something that has been acknowledged by FP.

4
Letting the World do the Work

It is often claimed that FP is fundamental to human social life. As Currie and Sterelny (2000, pp. 145–146), put it, much of our social understanding is 'deeply and almost exclusively mentalistic'. Some proponents of FP do acknowledge that other factors are important and also that such factors might facilitate some instances of social understanding and interaction without the aid of FP. For example, Botterill and Carruthers (1999), having discussed the nature and role of FP, go on to note that some predictions of behaviour may 'owe more to social rules and cultural order than they do to the application of folk psychology'. They suggest that the 'intentional stance' of FP is complemented by a 'social-role stance' (p. 45). However, they have little more to say about what this additional stance involves, where it is employed and how it relates to FP. Other proponents of FP are less willing to concede that social understanding sometimes proceeds without FP. Fodor, as discussed in Chapter 1, seems to think that FP underlies all our social achievements. Indeed, there is a tendency throughout the FP literature to describe all manner of social interactions in terms of FP or to assert that it is what makes them possible. Consider the following passage from Fodor:

> Someone I don't know phones me at my office in New York from – as it might be – Arizona. 'Would you like to lecture here next Tuesday?' are the words he utters. 'Yes, thank you. I'll be at your airport on the 3 p.m. flight' are the words that I reply. That's *all* that happens, but it's more than enough; the rest of the burden of predicting behaviour – of bridging the gap between utterances and actions – is routinely taken up by the theory. [. . .] the theory from which we get this extraordinary predictive power is just good old commonsense belief/desire psychology.
> (1987, p. 3)

Although Fodor asserts that belief-desire psychology is what facilitates the arrangement, he neglects to explain how it does so or to distinguish its role from other factors that might be aiding interpretation, interaction and coordination. It is arguable that much of the interpretive work is done by an appreciation of shared professional norms, codes of conduct, commonplace procedures pertaining to visiting speakers and the assumption that people generally do what they say they will do.[1] It also seems reasonable to assume that Fodor would have exchanged further communications with the host institution and received detailed information and instructions from them. (I have never boarded a plane on the basis of a single e-mail or phone call from an academic in another institution.) When we take such additional factors into account, it is unclear what role, if any, an ability to ascribe beliefs and desires is playing here.

In this chapter, I will begin by arguing that abilities other than FP frequently shoulder much or all of the burden of interpersonal interpretation. I will then deal with the objection that instances of social understanding that do not involve the attribution of specific propositional attitudes still presuppose an appreciation of others as possessors of propositional attitudes and thus presuppose FP. Finally, I will argue that the kind of social understanding I describe is not a matter of deploying an internal cognitive ability to apply concepts from a detached, observational standpoint. Rather, it is a form of what is often called 'situated', 'embodied, embedded' or 'extended' cognition. Social understanding is inextricable from *interaction* with the social world. Interpretations of others usually presuppose a shared context of social activity and, in so far as interpretation is enabled by this context, accounts that emphasise the deployment of wholly internalised cognitive abilities are misleading.

Norms, roles and functions

Consider an example from Dennett (1987). In order to emphasise the predictive power of FP or, as he calls it, application of the *intentional stance*, Dennett asks us to entertain the possibility of otherwise superintelligent Martians who lack the capacity for intentional psychology. In the absence of an ability to interpret each other in terms of a systematically organised framework of propositional attitudes, the everyday scenario described below would, Dennett claims, seem miraculous to them:

> From the Earthling's point of view, this is what is observed. The telephone rings in Mrs. Gardner's kitchen. She answers, and this is what

she says: 'Oh, hello dear. You're coming home early? Within the hour? And bringing the boss to dinner? Pick up a bottle of wine on the way home, then, and drive carefully.' On the basis of this observation, our Earthling predicts that a large metallic vehicle with rubber tires will come to a stop in the drive within one hour, disgorging two human beings, one of whom will be holding a paper bag containing a bottle containing an alcoholic fluid.

(1987, p. 26)

Dennett offers this as an example of the predictive power of propositional attitude psychology. However, as with Fodor's example, it is clear that a lot more is at work in driving interpretation and prediction. Consider the following background assumptions, which must be made in order to understand Dennett's social exchange:

- Telephones are for communicating with.
- 'Employee' and 'boss' are different social roles.
- Social interaction between employers and employees is commonplace and conforms to certain socially accepted standards.
- Dinners can, if appropriately orchestrated, be social events.
- Dinners can be prepared in rooms that are functionally organised for food preparation (kitchens).
- Wine is an appropriate accompaniment to a dinner.
- Wine can be acquired via standardised monetary transfers that conform to certain rules.
- One pays for wine, rather than steals it.
- There are good and bad ways to drive.
- There are long-term normative commitments between people, which take the form of 'marriage'.

The list of such assumptions is near endless and all of them involve one or more of the categories discussed in Chapter 3:

1. Artefact functions. Telephones, kitchens and off-licenses have specific roles. They are 'for' certain things, regardless of which individual uses them.
2. Social norms. One does certain things and does not do others, regardless of who 'one' is. Social norms are general codes of conduct, which people are expected to abide by, such as 'one pays for the things one acquires in shops'.

3. Social roles. People have different social roles in a given context, such as 'host', 'boss' or 'wine merchant'. Some norms apply only to those in certain social roles.

All three categories are normative; artefacts are *supposed* to be used in certain ways, people are *supposed* to behave in accordance with various social roles and all of us are *supposed* to conform to certain norms. Hence an appreciation of interconnected norms, roles and functions specifies not just how one is expected to behave in a certain situation but how one ought to behave. Norms, roles and artefact functions most likely incorporate a number of subcategories. This is especially apparent in the case of norms. Some norms take the form of moral prescriptions concerning what is and is not the right thing to do in certain kinds of situation or in all situations. Others are procedural and have no ethical connotations. For example, if someone uses a screwdriver as a chisel or discards an instruction booklet and consequently assembles a table wrongly, his behaviour has failed to accord with procedural norms but not in a way that is ordinarily viewed as morally wrong. There are also norms of conduct that are perhaps not moral in nature but still invite disapproval, anger or disgust when violated. For example, one does not pick one's nose in full view of others while attending a public lecture or eat one's dinner while everyone else is still waiting to start. Some of these norms are tied to quite specific contexts, while others are more generally applicable. One never picks one's nose in public but one does wolf down the takeaway cheeseburger outside the late night fast food stall while one's friends are still queuing for theirs. Although there may be several different kinds of norm, all of them take the general form 'one is supposed to do p in context x', where x is a type of situation, partly comprised of other norms. It is this general form, rather than distinctions between more specific kinds of norm, that I will be addressing here.

Norms are grasped in various ways. Some are understood explicitly, such as when one wonders where to queue and sees a sign that says 'please queue on the left' or when one lights a cigarette, only to be swiftly informed that smoking is prohibited in the building. However, the vast majority of the norms that regulate our conduct are, I suggest, taken for granted by our everyday thought and activity, rather than explicitly considered. Some of these will once have been objects of thought and may well have been explicitly taught. Others may have become embedded in our practical dealings without ever having been explicitly entertained. However, even if it is the case that all the norms regulating our conduct were first learned explicitly (and I think this is highly unlikely), most of the norms that apply in a given situation will operate as a presupposed background to our practical and theoretical activities, rather than as objects of thought. And, even if all norms can be explicitly entertained, it is still the case that most norms are not explicitly entertained in most of the situations where they play a role in regulating behaviour. (As Heidegger observes, norms are embedded in the world as it is understood in the context of our practical activities.) As with norms, many roles and functions are taken for granted, rather than explicitly pondered over on every social occasion.

In what follows, I will focus primarily on the way in which norms, roles and functions operate as a background for interpretation, rather than on those cases where one ponders over a norm, considers one's role or tinkers with a device in order to ascertain how it works or even what it is. Following Gurwitsch and Heidegger, I will argue that interrelated norms, roles and functions comprise kinds of 'situation' and that an understanding of situations is, at the same time, an understanding of what is to be done by oneself and others.

Many examples offered on behalf of FP actually serve to illustrate that situations, as understood in Chapter 3, play a considerable role in social understanding. Even when mental states do feature in interpretations of behaviour, these interpretations are usually massively constrained by shared context. Consider the game of chess, which Gordon (1995a, p. 63) offers as an example of how we predict each other's behaviour:

> The task is to answer the question, 'What would I do in *that* person's situation?' For example, chess players report that, playing against a human opponent or even against a computer, they visualize the board from the other side, taking the opposing pieces for their own and vice versa.

It is clear that interpretation in such cases is aided by shared norms, some being specific to the game of chess and others more generally applicable. When anticipating B during a chess game, A does not ordinarily need to assign propositional attitudes such as 'B believes that a Knight can be moved in the following ways' or 'B desires victory and intends to abide by the same rules as A in order to achieve it'. Rather, A can usually assume that B is playing chess and knows how to play chess properly. It is not just an understanding of an opponent's psychology that is required to decide on the right move to make but an understanding of the game itself. One can think through strategies that an opponent might deploy by thinking about the situation, involving a particular board configuration, rather than that opponent's mental states. Gordon's example emphasises visualising the board from the other side, rather than seeing the world from another person's egocentric perspective. The first question asked is perhaps not 'what will she do?' but 'what is to be done when one is in that position?' One can then go on to consider whether *that* person will do what should be done or which one of two or more sensible moves she is likely to make. This might not be a matter of attributing specific mental states but of making judgements about an opponent's level of expertise and whether she has certain dispositions, such as cautiousness or impulsiveness. Even when there is a role for belief assignment, it is clear that an understanding of how the game is played, regardless of who plays it, has a significant and perhaps primary role in anticipating the behaviour of an opponent. It is not a case of 'what would I do in that position?' followed by 'what will she do?', but of 'what should *one* do?' accompanied by 'is she likely to do it?'

In contrast to the chess game, imagine being in the commercial district of a major city, which has been largely demolished by some disastrous event a few hours beforehand. Much of the normal social order has broken down and chaos reigns. You see an unfamiliar person approaching you from across the ruined street. Without the usual background of shared norms in place, the task of understanding what she is doing and why is rendered much more difficult. Of course, such a scenario, although very different from the highly constrained environment of the chess game, does not amount to a complete eradication of the shared situation. One might still be able to rely on norms of gesture and expression, in addition to verbal communication. Interpretation will also be made easier if she is heading for a certain item of equipment, carrying a tool, wearing a uniform that indicates a role or just doing what several hundred other people are doing. Other non-social information, such as whether the person is limping, wounded or being chased by a tiger is of course relevant too. Without such information, perhaps one would just fail to understand why she does what she does, rather than achieving an understanding by employing an unsupported FP. When few shared norms are in place, the ability to 'read' others is, at the very least, significantly impaired.

How does the assumption that others share a common situation do much of the work of interpretation, explanation and prediction, without falling back on FP? As noted in Chapter 3, it is already written into the concept of a tool, such as a pen or a toaster, that it is 'to be used' in a certain way, regardless of the psychological states of specific individuals.

To use a term coined by Gibson (1979), artefacts *afford* certain kinds of action and the opportunities for action that they offer are integral to a sense of what they are. Artefacts have shared affordances; they reflect patterns of activity in a way that is not person-specific. Furthermore, they are not conceived of in isolation from each other but are what they are in virtue of wider frameworks of equipmental relations. These frameworks serve to partly specify *what is to be done* in a given situation.[2]

An additional appreciation of psychological states is, I suggest, not required in many cases. This is most apparent in situations where equipment has standardised uses and is tightly locked together in arrangements that are to be navigated in the same fashion by everyone. Consider a routine, daily trip down the escalator to the ticket machine and onto the subway system of a familiar city, where one waits with others on the platform until the train pulls up. As one co-ordinates one's activities with others, one need not attribute intentional states but can instead work on the implicit assumption that they will do 'what people are supposed to do' in that kind of environment. The assumption that they inhabit the same world of interrelated equipment and routines is sufficient to anticipate the majority of behaviours in situations where routines are there for *all* to follow. Simultaneously attributing beliefs and desires to several hundred people would require considerable cognitive effort, with little if any reward.

Now, when it comes to actually boarding the train, things can get a bit more tricky. Perhaps one finds oneself part of a disorganised horde, all scrambling for a seat. But does FP play a role in this scenario? It is not clear that it does. When faced with such a situation for the first time, one might refrain from interpreting the thoughts of specific others and instead just 'go with the flow' or 'take a step back' and see whether any norms of conduct prevailed. Once it becomes clear that it is indeed just a scramble for the nearest seat, it is not a matter of attributing 'B believes that seat x is free and desires to get it' but of looking for free seats, assuming that everybody else is going for a seat and that any unseated person nearer to a seat than oneself will most likely get it first. That said, such conduct is still usually regulated by many norms, such as letting people off the train before attempting to board, prioritising disabled or elderly people, not forcibly pushing people out of the way and not diving in front of somebody to swipe the seat that they are aiming for. And, to the extent that such norms fail to apply, the result is unpredictability, rather than an elaborate process of anticipation, achieved by attributing different beliefs and desires to dozens of interacting people all at the same time. When one participates in such situations on a routine basis, one might learn where best to stand, which carriage is likely to be least crowded and which seats tend to be taken last but this is a matter of induction, rather than FP.

Many other instances of social interaction have a similar structure to this. For example, driving a car, like navigating a subway, involves interacting with many other people at the same time. The norms of conduct for drivers are also quite rigidly prescribed and embodied in the form of signs, road markings, crossings, traffic lights, the Highway Code and so on. In cases where such prescriptions do not do all the work, norms such as flashing one's lights to let someone pass first or turning on the hazard lights when one's car breaks down can come into play. When people disregard all such conventions, the result is often a hazardous and unpredictable situation, rather than one where FP can be hastily deployed to work out what somebody is up to. Again, the assumption that others will ordinarily do 'what one does' or 'what one is supposed to do' can do most of the work of coordinating interaction. In such situations, we are, of course, still aware of others as agents and of their actions having a certain purposive direction, such as 'heading for that seat'. However, as I will argue in Chapters 5 and 6, this kind of minimal appreciation of actions and their target objects does not require FP either.

The role of presupposed situations is recognised to some extent by Gordon (1995a,b,c), who observes that the amount of cognitive work involved in projecting oneself onto another's predicament is a reflection of the extent to which a situation is shared:

> Within a close-knit community, where people have a vast common fund of 'facts' as well as shared norms and values, only a minimum of pretending would be called for.
>
> (1995a, p. 65)

The greater the extent to which norms and values are shared, the less need there is to make adjustments to one's own psychology in order to grasp how things are for another person. Gordon suggests that, in contexts where much of the social environment is common to both parties, straight projection of one's own experiential world may serve as an adequate guide to the other person's psychology and behaviour. He also claims that undifferentiating projection is not an occasional cognitive activity, carried out only in the few contexts that demand it. Instead, 'when we are aware of others – that is, aware of them *as* others – we are constantly, automatically projecting onto them our own beliefs about the environment' (1995c, p. 105). In fact, for Gordon, the starting point for interpersonal understanding is 'total projection' (1995c, p. 108), which is supplemented by varying degrees of differentiation in certain cases, achieved by making imagined adjustments to one's own psychology.

Although Gordon describes the process as 'projection', I suggest that it is better interpreted simply as the assumption that others inhabit the same world. Consider the intricate framework of road signs, markings, crossings, roundabouts and traffic lights through which drivers navigate. The default assumption is that 'we participate in this', rather than 'the world appears like this to me', accompanied by tacit attribution of the same situational appreciation to you. Similarly, I interpret you on the basis that *we* are playing chess. A situation is not *attributed* to others, even tacitly. It is already given that 'we do x', 'we are x', 'we are doing what one does in x', or 'one does x with tool M'. Before any mental states are assigned to other people, it is presupposed that they and we inhabit the same world. And, in most if not all cases, the world that is assumed as a backdrop for interpretation is not simply a shared space and time, within which everything else is attributed in the form of psychological states. It is usually assumed that a great deal more is given to all parties, in the form of a common situation.

Gordon seems to think that projection is required, rather than an understanding of shared norms, because mechanical application of norms in the form 'A always does p in x' is too insensitive to context and does not include an appreciation of how actions are influenced by variations in a situation. He offers the example of A always throwing his coat on the chair when he enters B's home and asks how this norm can accommodate the difference in A's behaviour when he enters B's home, not as a guest but as a burglar who is trying to burgle the house next door but has entered B's house by mistake (1995c, p. 105). However, norms are not rigid, mechanical descriptions of what people do. They are prescriptions as to what people are supposed to do, which are interpreted in the context of other norms that together comprise a situation. Norms of conduct and related expectations that apply to guests do not apply to burglars. So a normative understanding of the situation does seem capable of accommodating such differences in behaviour.

Gordon (1995a, p. 65) also claims that, due to differing norms and values, a lot more pretending will be required to simulate someone from an alien culture. However, it is not clear how a series of adjustments to one's own psychology could disclose a set of norms that one was not already aware of. To make the relevant adjustments, one would need to know the relevant norms and, if one was already familiar with the norms and thus recognised the situation, even as one that differed from one's own, there would be no need to simulate. The kinds of adjustments that he postulates would seem to be more effective when it comes to taking in considerations such as the information available to a person. No doubt we do adjust our interpretations by supposing that certain aspects of a normatively configured situation are not understood by another or that she lacks certain information. However, this is not refinement of a projection but partial suspension of a context that would otherwise be taken as 'ours', rather than 'mine' and also 'yours'. It alerts us to a lack of common ground, rather than supplying new information about norms that were unfamiliar prior to the adjustment.

The issue arises as to how we do manage to appreciate new norms and I will suggest in Chapter 6 that coming to understand, share, create and reshape norms is something that we usually accomplish via verbal and non-verbal interaction with others, rather than by theorising about them or simulating them. However, obtaining bodies of explicit information about norms and codes of conduct can also serve as a source, as any good travel guide illustrates.

Features of a situation not only serve as an undifferentiating guide to what 'one does'. They can also contribute to an understanding of how the actions of another person are likely to differ from one's own. They can do so because, as Gurwitsch notes, situations incorporate distinctions between different social roles. One can often predict what a particular person will do, rather than what everyone or anyone will do, without attributing internal mental states to that person or imaginatively adjusting one's own psychology. Bermúdez (2003) considers the role 'waiter'. When one knows what waiters do and assigns this role to someone in a restaurant, one knows just about everything one needs to know in order to understand his behaviour. There is no need to postulate internal states in order to make sense of what he is doing and anticipate his actions:

> We don't need to have any thoughts about what is going on in their minds at all. The social interaction takes care of itself once the social roles have been identified [. . .] Identifying someone as a waiter is not a matter of understanding them in folk psychological terms at all. It is understanding him as someone who typically behaves in certain ways within a network of social practices that typically unfold in certain ways.
>
> (2003, p. 44).[3]

There are many such cases where interpreting, predicting and explaining a person's actions do not fall back on FP. For example, if one observes somebody running towards a burning house with a hose and is asked to explain her behaviour, 'she's a fire fighter; it's her job' is an adequate response, while 'she believes that there is a fire and she desires to extinguish it' is not. Such explanations are commonplace. For example:

'Why did she get so annoyed by this morning's news broadcast?' 'Because she's a teacher.'
'What's he doing standing out in the cold?' 'He's a security guard!'

Explanations of one person's actions often include reference to the social roles of another person or to relations between people's social roles:

'Why did she leave work early?' 'She has a dentist's appointment.'
'Why is he sitting under his desk?' 'He hasn't done his work and is hiding from his boss.'

Other explanations make indirect reference to social roles, by referring to activities that are characteristic of them and that only make sense in terms of them:

'Why did he grab that man?' 'He's arresting him.'
'Why did she suddenly disappear?' 'She's been called out to a medical emergency.'
'Why's he not doing this morning's service?' 'Oh, he's been asked to do an important wedding.'

Social role explanations can be more complicated than this. For example, I might say 'I was required to do p in my role as A but, if I had the choice, I would have done q instead'. This attributes an action to a role but also implies that factors other than roles can be responsible for actions and that the various factors can come into conflict. Sometimes, these other factors take the form of norms. For example, 'I know that p is not ordinarily acceptable but my role as A required it in context x'. In other cases, psychological states, such as preferences, moral convictions and emotions are also appealed to.

In many instances, designation of roles, accompanied by norms and functions, will not be *sufficient* for understanding and explanation. For example, if a student comes to see me with a troubled expression and is reluctant to talk about the nature of his problem, I might hypothesise as to what that problem is. My deliberations are of course already significantly constrained by shared norms and the differentiated social roles of 'student' and 'teacher'. But such constraints are not enough.

However, even when they do not supply everything I need, it is not clear that FP alone is what fills the gap. Knowledge of person-specific traits and dispositions, such as character and temperament, arguably make just as significant a contribution, if not more so, to the ability to interpret (Goldie, 2000, Chapter 6). Indeed, knowledge of a wide range of idiosyncratic factors can aid understanding. These include hobbies, long-term projects, religious and political commitments, phobias, social background, upbringing, political orientation and so on. Hence, even if the shared world cannot do all the work, acquaintance with certain variably specific dispositions and circumstances of an individual can do much of the rest. This is especially so with friends, family and long-term colleagues. What often drives the ability to interpret, predict and explain is person-specific knowledge embedded in a shared situation, rather than an ability to attribute propositional attitudes.

Situations are reasons

Proponents of FP, especially theory theorists, claim that its predictive power is largely due to its picking up on systematic connections between intentional states. Given a certain set of beliefs and desires, one can reliably infer various other beliefs and desires, all of which stand in systematic relations to each other and to behaviour. However, it is worth noting that the relations between the roles, norms and functions that together comprise a situation also have an intricate, systematic structure. Indeed, many norms, roles and functions only make sense if one presupposes a host of additional norms, roles and functions. As Heidegger notes, tools such as hammers are individuated by their relations to other tools, such as nails. Similarly, to understand the role of a professional teacher, one also needs to appreciate that there are pupils or students. And to understand norms of conduct applicable to a cashier, one needs to understand a broader context of norms that apply to customers, financial transfers, acquisition of goods and so forth. Hence social situations can play a similar role to that which FP is alleged to perform, in comprising a complex, systematically organised, normative framework through which to interpret behaviour.

Davidson, Dennett and others emphasise the indispensability of a presumption of rationality when it comes to interpreting action. It is claimed that the rational organisation of intentional states binds them together into a coherent whole and allows us to draw inferences concerning the relationships between particular beliefs, desires and actions. As Davidson (2001, p. 211) puts it, 'successful interpretation necessarily invests the person interpreted with basic rationality'.[4] However, a principle of rationality alone cannot encompass all the norms that guide behaviour and interpretations of behaviour. As McGeer notes, there are norms of dress, communication and conduct, which are not accommodated by the core rationality claimed by some to be integral to FP (2001, p. 117). This broader background of norms, she adds, operates as a shared framework for mutual interpretation, allowing much of the work of interpersonal understanding to be 'carried by the world, embedded in the norms and routines that structure [day to day] interactions' (p. 119).⁵ Hence many of the norms that regulate our activities are ingredients of presupposed situations. It thus seems that much of the work supposedly done by a general principle of rationality, incorporated into an intentional stance that we adopt towards each other, is instead done by the worldly situations that we usually take for granted as a backdrop for interpersonal interpretation. It is questionable whether a more abstract principle of rationality could do anything at all, unless embedded in a more general appreciation of norms. As Morton points out, 'there is no simple pattern connecting beliefs, desires and actions, alone, which we can use to explain and predict what people will do' (2003, p. 35).

The claim that many of the norms that guide behaviour are embedded in the shared world is supported by the observation that the reasons people offer for actions often take the form of simple assertions about features of a situation. For example:

'Why did she turn left?' 'The road to the right is one-way.'
'Why is he in a hurry?' 'His bus is about to leave.'
'Why did he leave the pub?' 'To go to the cash dispenser.'
'Why isn't she coming with us?' 'The VIP entrance is over there.'

References to aspects of a situation can pick out the norms that guide action and make it appropriate. In such cases, there is no need to appeal to mental states. The question 'what is going on here?' is often the way in which we attempt to understand instances of aberrant or unexpected individual or group behaviour. Appropriate responses include 'it's B's birthday', 'we're on strike', 'the plane has been cancelled', 'the electricity's off', 'it's a fire drill', 'they've heard that Madonna's coming out through that door in the next five minutes' and so forth. What is often expected is a description of a situation that makes clear the relevant norms of activity, rather than an account of people's psychological predicaments. FP and situational explanations have a similar structure. Just as one can say 'if B believes p and desires q, all things being equal, B ought to do r', one can say 'if p is the case and q is the case, all things being equal, B ought to do r'. Norms are integral to the relationships that comprise situations, just as many proponents of FP claim that they are integral to the relationships between beliefs, desires and actions. The systematic structure we require in order to interpret people is out there in the shared world. So the burden need not be carried by a complicated understanding of the relationships between mental states.

One might object that the physical world, the world as described by the natural sciences, does not incorporate norms. Hence the claim that norms are embodied in shared situations looks downright mysterious. However, I am discussing the world as we take it to be in everyday life. As discussed in Chapter 3, to describe everyday psychology against the backdrop of the scientifically described world would be misleading. Even if the scientifically described world is bereft of normativity (and this is, of course, debatable), the world that is taken for granted as a context for action and thought is not.

In suggesting that situations play a considerable role in facilitating interpersonal interpretation, I do not want to claim that all norms and roles take the form of rigid prescriptions that everyone abides by. This may be the case with a 'no smoking' sign but there are many norms that apply only if one chooses a particular course of action and others that make fairly loose prescriptions that allow for a range of appropriate behaviours. Many norms of politeness and conversation are neither strict nor universal. Not everyone accepts them all and people have quite different ideas as to what constitutes a transgression. Furthermore, situations are not inflexible. There is room for discussion, criticism, revision or abandonment of norms and for the establishment of new norms, which can serve to reshape the situation as a whole, as I will discuss further in Chapter 6. The point is that *some* norms (regardless of which ones) will almost always be presupposed in a given situation. Norms, roles and functions can do a considerable amount of work, even if a situation is open to many different kinds of activity, rather than being a rigid specification of what one does. That conduct is *guided* by norms does not imply that it is wholly *determined* by norms. As Rouse (2002, Chapter 5) makes clear, normative accountability is not the same as unbroken regularity. It is the former that I am interested in.[6]

The development of social ability

It could be objected that, although FP is not explicitly present in our appreciation of social situations, it still *underlies* that appreciation. Assignment of specific propositional attitudes might be constrained by

situational assumptions and it could well be that, in many circumstances, propositional attitude assignment is not required. However,
this does not rule out the possibility that FP *ability* is presupposed by an
understanding of situations; all social understanding could have its
source in a largely implicit FP ability. One could even make the stronger
claim that all situational understanding can be convincingly re-described
in FP terms, with the result that FP is ubiquitous after all.

Let us start with the stronger claim. I am not sure that anyone explicitly holds such a view but the surreptitious translation of just about all
social activity into the language of FP is a feature of some recent discussions. Blackburn (1995) raises this concern with regard to theory theories
of FP, which, he argues, need to do more than just describe an activity in
FP terms, if they are to convince. However, any position maintaining that
all situational understanding can be wholly or largely re-interpreted in
terms of tacit intentional state attribution can be swiftly dismissed. When
applied to a shared understanding of equipment (A believes that B believes
that cups are for drinking from, and so forth), this is phenomenologically
implausible and also far more cognitively demanding than required.
Furthermore, understanding or explaining A's ability to interact with B by
appealing solely to the intentional states that A takes B to hold would
lead to an infinite regress, a point argued by Searle (1992, Chapter 8),
among others.[7] Trying to account for any action, whether one's own or
someone else's, in terms of an exhaustive list of beliefs and desires would
be a never-ending and futile task. Every belief listed would presuppose
further beliefs. These would presuppose yet further beliefs and so forth.
In order to break this regress, Searle postulates a pre-intentional realm of
background practices, which fix the content of intentional states.[8]

Given that an exhaustive understanding of action in terms of a complete catalogue of intentional states is not an option, it must be conceded
that social understanding does not consist wholly of propositional
attitude attribution. It will of course be trivially easy to describe most
behaviour in terms of propositional attitudes. But it is not clear why a
particular behaviour that we do not ordinarily interpret as the outcome
of beliefs and desires *should* be re-described in those terms. The mere possibility of doing so does not itself support the move.

However, one could concede that social understanding is not just a
matter of attributing propositional attitudes and still maintain that FP
is more fundamental to social life than situational understanding. It
might be that an ability to interpret people in FP terms is a prerequisite
for the ability to navigate social situations competently, even if no
specific intentional states are assigned in some situations. So FP is not a

description of every aspect of social life; it is instead an enabling condition for social life. This claim has certainly been made by some proponents of FP. For example, Currie and Sterelny remark that

> Mind-reading [FP] and the capacity to negotiate the social world are not the same thing, but the former seems to be necessary for the latter [. . .] our basic grip on the social world depends on our being able to see our fellows as motivated by beliefs and desires we sometimes share and sometimes do not.
>
> (2000, p. 145)

Such assertions either are developmental claims or imply developmental claims. If the ability to cope with social situations arises before FP, FP cannot be a prerequisite for navigating the world. Hence claims for the primacy of FP over situational understanding are empirically testable. If situational understanding appears first, then they are false. If FP appears first, then they may or may not be true, depending on whether or not situational understanding and FP are developmentally connected.

What does the developmental evidence suggest? As noted in Chapter 2, the false belief task is generally regarded as a 'litmus test' for FP ability. Typical children respond correctly to at least some versions of the task at around 3 to 4 years of age (Wellman, Cross and Watson, 2001), suggesting that they are unable to deploy FP before that age. However, it is also clear that younger children possess considerable intersubjective ability. For example, Meltzoff (1995) presented eighteen-month-olds with two different scenarios. In the first, an adult tried but failed to perform a certain action. In the second, an inanimate object made the same movements as the adult. He found that the children could appreciate the nature of the intended act in the first case and also re-enact it but did neither in the second case. Meltzoff remarks that

> Eighteen-month-olds situate people within a psychological framework that differentiates between the surface behaviour of people and a deeper level involving goals and intentions. They have already adopted a fundamental aspect of folk psychology – persons (but not inanimate objects) are understood within a framework involving goals and intentions.
>
> (1995, p. 838)

Various other social competences have been observed in young infants. For instance, Papafragou (2002, p. 58) reports studies demonstrating that two-year olds are responsive to the epistemic states of others, noting that they 'are more likely to name the object, name its location and gesture to its location when the addressee has not seen where the object was hidden than when he/she has'. And Bloom and German (2000, p. 29) note that young infants can participate in and understand pretence, associate gaze with attention and imitate action.

It is arguable that an appreciation of goals, intentions, gestures, perspectives and of the communicative possibilities that others afford, which is present before children are able to identify false beliefs and thus to apply a fully fledged FP, is itself sufficient to facilitate enculturation into contexts of norms, roles and functions (Gallagher, 2001a; Bermúdez, 2003). In addition, it may be that interaction with others in social situations is not only prior to FP but also an enabling condition for the development of FP. As Garfield, Peterson and Perry put it:

> It is not the case that mind-reading is a necessary condition for social negotiation. Rather, the learning of the basic skills for interacting with others that enable the social world to be negotiated is a necessary condition of learning to mind-read, together with the acquisition of language.
>
> (2001, p. 525)

So they suggest that Currie and Sterelny (2000) have got things the wrong way round. Participation in the social world is a prerequisite for the development of FP, as opposed to vice versa. Before children are able to pass false belief tasks, they are already 'able to perceive a wide variety of socially meaningful objects and properties in their social environments' (p. 532). Garfield, Peterson and Perry also apply their view more specifically to studies of autism. Empirical findings concerning the behaviour of autistic people, usually children, are frequently cited in support of the claim that FP lies as the heart of social ability. Autistic children are both profoundly lacking in social ability and, it turns out, have a specific problem detecting false beliefs, even though they can often handle non-social tasks that seem to involve greater complexity. Hence it is arguable that evidence from autism, suggesting a specific FP deficit and associated social impairment, points to the primacy of FP. However, autistic children demonstrate social impairments long before they reach the age at which other children generally pass the false belief task. Garfield, Peterson and Perry suggest that problems with FP arise as a consequence of these earlier impairments. In typical children, early abilities facilitate interaction with the social world and this interaction comprises the developmental framework through which FP is acquired. Such abilities, they claim, are impaired in autism. Gerrans (2002, p. 317) offers a similar account of autism, suggesting that early abnormalities in 'sensory, affective, perceptual and motor systems' result in a lack of ability or motivation to interact with the social world and a consequent privation of the early social interactions that enable later development of an ability to attribute intentional states.

Although there are many other explanations of autism on offer, there does at least seem to be a consensus that various early impairments are involved and that these lead to later FP impairments. For example, Baron-Cohen and Swettenham (1996, p. 167) suggest that, in typical children, a shared attention mechanism develops at around 9 to 14 months of age and that this is impaired in autism. The mechanism is an important precursor to the development of FP and, they suggest, if it is damaged, FP will also be affected. The developmental trajectory involved could turn out to be very complicated indeed and may not be the same in every case.[9] However, what is clear is that autism involves impairment of abilities that normally arise before both FP and situational understanding. It would also seem that an inability to participate in social situations, or perhaps a lack of interest in social situations, is apparent before a failure to appreciate propositional attitudes.

There is, however, an obvious objection to the view that situational understanding precedes FP. Early sensitivity to intentions, goals, perspectives and communicative affordances, it could be argued, just amounts to an immature stage of FP. And it is to this early stage that proponents of FP refer when they claim that an appreciation of social situations depends upon FP. For example, Bloom (2002) argues that children's learning of new words depends on 'what has variously been called naïve psychology, theory of mind, and mindreading' (p. 38). But the ability Bloom actually cites is that of 'inferring the referential intentions of other people' in contexts of interaction with them (p. 38). This alone does not amount to 'theory of mind' or FP, in the usual sense of the term. One can be receptive to and co-ordinate with communicative gestures, without being able to conceptualise underlying mental states. So such abilities could be thought of as earlier stages of FP.

But this response simply presupposes that FP has pride of place in intersubjective development. The developmental precursors to both situational understanding and an ability to detect false beliefs will only be interpreted as stepping stones en route to a mature ability to attribute internal propositional attitude states, rather than to situational understanding, if it is already assumed that FP ability is more central to

social life. There is the risk of over-inflating the role of FP by construing it as the end-point of a developmental trajectory, rather than just
one among many social achievements that has no special status.
Associated with this, there is the worry that various early abilities risk
being misinterpreted, if it is assumed from the outset that they comprise a proto-FP. Lord (1993) makes this point in relation to studies of
autism, remarking that autism involves deficits in gaze, gesture, and
verbal and non-verbal communication. Thus it does not appear to be a
specific cognitive deficit. Despite this, she notes that an impaired ability to perform on false belief tasks is often taken not just to confirm the
presence of autism but to exemplify the central underlying deficit
(impaired FP). She suggests that this may amount to a self-fulfilling
prophesy:

> It is not surprising that cognitive explanations have seemed so attrac-
> tive, when what has been studied has for the most part been cogni-
> tive tasks that are set up in surroundings quite different from those
> of naturally occurring, affect-laden settings.
>
> (p. 310)

It is because of such concerns that Bruner and Feldman (1993, p. 269)
refer to passing the false belief task as the awarding of a 'False Belief
Diploma' on an arbitrary 'Graduation Day' during development. On
behalf of FP, one might respond that appreciating the perspectival
nature of other people is absolutely essential to most social encounters
and that this is precisely what detecting a false belief involves; early
receptivity to perspectives is just a less refined version of the ability to
attribute specific internal mental states. However, it would be a mistake
to jump to such a conclusion. Appreciating that another person is a
locus of experience and action is not the same as being able to attribute
states to them of the form 'B believes that p' and 'B desires that q'.
Furthermore, it might well be that an appreciation of others as having
perspectives that differ from one's own involves a kind of understanding that differs markedly from FP. So such abilities need not be interpreted as early stages of FP. Indeed, I will argue in Chapters 5 and 6 that
a sense of others as loci of experience and agency is perceptual in nature
and does not involve the positing of internal, unobservable states.
Furthermore, an appreciation of the perspectival nature of others is
essentially affective and bodily. It is therefore quite different from the
detached inference that many accounts of FP take to be characteristic of
interpersonal understanding.

Another possible objection to my view is that recent experiments show FP to arise earlier than was previously thought. So it may arrive before situational understanding after all. Although an understanding that others can have false beliefs was originally thought to appear at around four years of age, recent findings show that even younger children display such an understanding when the problem is presented in a different way, in the context of more familiar social surroundings. For example, Bloom and German (2000, p. 27) observe that three-year-olds often pass more 'pragmatically natural' variants of the task, with simpler or more specific questions. Whiten (1997, p. 145) similarly remarks on how a 'second wave' of studies has revealed an ability to detect false beliefs in younger children, abilities that were 'masked by various aspects of the earlier methodologies that do not fully engage the abilities of fledgling 3 year old mindreaders'. He notes an analogous contrast between the results of laboratory and ecological studies of primates. When animals are studied in their natural, social environments, rather than out of context, they often appear to display abilities that are not evident under laboratory conditions.

However, although the developmental achievement required to pass such tests *could* be described in terms of a distinctive cognitive ability to 'attribute an internal propositional attitude state that differs from one's own', this by no means implies that it *should* be. I will argue in Chapter 7 that there is considerable ambiguity surrounding use of terms such as 'belief' and even 'propositional attitude'. It might well be that early abilities are interpreted in terms of propositional attitudes or proto-propositional attitudes simply because the centrality of FP has already been assumed. In addition, as Bloom and German note, modifications to the task only lower the age at which children tend to pass it by six months to a year (2000, p. 27). Children younger than three years of age already have social abilities which, I have suggested, facilitate a considerable appreciation of normatively configured social situations.

It is interesting to note that younger children have more success with 'pragmatically natural' versions of the task. One explanation for this is that performance in more familiar social environments is aided by situational understanding. Accounts of FP tend not to acknowledge such situational factors, assuming instead a rather socially removed, spectatorial standpoint on the part of the interpreter. This assumption is integrated into many versions of the false belief task. For example, Wimmer and Perner (1983) ask children to *watch* a social performance, rather than *participate* in it, and to point to a location in response to a verbal request, rather than to do so within a context of shared social activity, where not all the relevant cues need be verbal in nature. One need not have a comprehensive linguistic appreciation of a social situation in order to be a competent participant. Nevertheless, as Greenwood (1999) observes, developmental studies tend to emphasise children's verbal understanding of what they or others are doing, whereas everyday social life requires successful interaction. Fixation on linguistic knowledge risks eclipsing practical social skills. It amounts to a bias in favour of explanations that emphasise an ability to conceptualise and report on behaviour and its causes, rather than an ability to engage in complex social performances. Of course, false belief tasks generally require children to point to where A will look for x, as opposed to verbally reporting on where A thinks x is. However, they are still asked to point in response to a verbal prompt, in a situation where neither they nor the questioner are participants in the relevant social scenario.

An emphasis on detached, linguistic comprehension is symptomatic of the more general assumption that social skills can be adequately studied by examining the behaviour of non-participant observers. And I suggest that this assumption serves to obscure the nature of early intersubjective abilities and also the intersubjective abilities of adults. Most discussions of FP assume that interpersonal understanding is a matter of deploying an internalised cognitive ability, perhaps in the form of a 'module' for theorising or simulating, in order to interpret, predict and explain the behaviour of others from a spectatorial stance. This is quite peculiar, given that most of our everyday social understanding takes place in participant, rather than non-participant situations. Furthermore, differences in how one understands something as a participant and as a non-participant might be quite considerable. Hence it is not clear that false belief tasks even require the same *kind* of cognitive performance as most interpersonal understanding and interaction. One important difference, which will be my focus in the remainder of this chapter, is that a participant understanding need not rely wholly on internalised cognitive resources to regulate interaction, given that

(a) One can acquire information concerning what is to be done next by manipulating the social environment so as to access the relevant information, rather than by working things out from a spectatorial standpoint.

(b) Much of the structure that regulates social interaction is embedded in the shared social environment. It is the world that guides us, rather than an internalised FP.

Understanding social behaviour through the lens of an observational FP thus serves to obscure the extent to which social understanding, interaction and coordination are achieved by active, embodied agents, embedded in intricate, shared environments, rather than by passive observers of social life with wholly internalised interpretive abilities.

The claim that infants' social and more general cognitive abilities are partly constituted by their interaction with structured environments was made by Vygotsky in the 1930s. According to Vygotsky, social props and internal cognitive processes together form a system that regulates children's social activities and contributes to their ongoing development. So the environment is not just a context in which social abilities are deployed but also 'scaffolding' for the operation and further development of those abilities. According to Vygotsky, internalised social skills do not come first. Instead, social behaviour is regulated by patterns of interaction with a structured cultural environment and certain processes that start off as inter-personal are later internalised and become intra-personal (1978, Chapter 4). Several recent studies of children's social ability have taken a Vygotskian line, emphasising the roles of social interaction and enculturation. For example, Garfield, Peterson and Perry's account is explicitly Vygotskian in its claim that 'it is [. . .] only in the context of a social matrix [. . .] that we can make sense of cognitive development' (2001, p. 532).[10] Hobson (1993a,b, 2002) likewise claims that interaction with a social environment and, most centrally, patterned relations between children and care-givers, structure social development. If, as such work suggests, an ability to understand others is bound up with structured interaction in a shared social context, the standard false belief task is an inappropriate test of that ability, given that an emphasis on decontextualised observation serves to strip away patterns of interaction that may well be partly constitutive of social understanding.

It could be maintained, along with Vygotsky, that development involves a gradual process of internalisation. This is the route that Garfield, Peterson and Perry take. Acquisition of FP, they claim, involves the internalisation of abilities that were originally embedded in interaction with the social learning environment and, in their earlier stages of development, undifferentiated from a broader range of ecologically embedded abilities (2001, p. 532).[11] Thus, as children develop, external social scaffolding is progressively replaced by an internalised FP. In adopting such a position, a proponent of FP would have to concede that engagement with structured social situations has developmental priority over FP. However, she could then propose an alternative formulation of the claim that FP is the basis of social life. The following are compatible:

1. Capacity x (FP) of person A develops through interaction with y (social situation) during development.
2. y is itself sustained by capacity x of mature individuals in A's environment.

Hence a weaker claim for the primacy of FP can be made, even if one accepts that situational understanding comes first. It can be maintained that fully developed, sophisticated adult social interaction requires the internalisation of FP, which comes to play a central role in regulating all social understanding and structuring the social development of others. However, it is, I will now suggest, much more likely that an ability to respond to social situations is never wholly internalised. Even in adults, a great deal of the work of social understanding, interaction and coordination is embedded in our interactions with the shared environment.

Social interaction as embodied, embedded cognition

Much recent work on FP assumes that interpersonal understanding is achieved by deploying internal cognitive abilities to solve a problem posed by the external environment, that of predicting what others are likely to do. However, I suggest that the ability to understand and anticipate others has a very different structure. It is partly embedded in the social environment and is more often a matter of interacting with that environment than of detached contemplation. Rather than attempting to assign internal causes of behaviour in order to predict otherwise unpredictable behaviours, we use the shared environment to regulate our behaviour, thus making ourselves predictable to each other.

So far, I have appealed to phenomenology and certain examples from the FP literature in order to describe how situations contribute to the ability to interpret, predict and explain actions. However, the view I am proposing also complements a fast-growing body of work in cognitive science, which goes by various names, including 'extended cognition' (Clark, 1997, 2001, 2003; Clark and Chalmers, 1998), 'embodied, embedded cognition' (Haugeland, 1998; Rowlands, 1999; Wheeler, 2005), 'enactive cognition' (Varela, Thompson and Rosch, 1991) and 'situated cognition' (Strum, Forster and Hutchins, 1997).[12]

All of these labels are employed to refer to (a) or to both (a) and (b) below:

(a) Proprioception, bodily activity and manipulation of certain kinds of structured environment are integral to cognition.
(b) Structures of the environment that we interact with are often not just cognitive aids or accompaniments to cognition but full participants in cognitive processes.

As Haugeland (1998, p. 208) puts it, there is a 'commingling or integralness' between body and mind and between body and world that undermines 'their very distinctness'. Getting things done through bodily interactions with a structured environment, rather than relying wholly on internal cognitive resources to solve problems and regulate activities, has a simple evolutionary rationale: Why develop a complicated internal capacity when the environment can do the job for you? Integration of environmental structures into cognition and behaviour patterns is commonplace throughout the Animal Kingdom. Rowlands (1999, p. 91) cites the case of beaver dams. The beaver manipulates the environment in order to produce a complex physical structure, which then serves to regulate beaver behaviour. This offloads work onto the environment that would otherwise demand more complex internal cognitive resources and greater behavioural exertion. It also changes the nature of the tasks that internal cognitive resources are required to perform. The task of building and interacting with complex artefacts is quite different in character from that of coping in an environment without the aid of such artefacts. Other familiar examples include webs, burrows, nests and termite mounds. It would seem that the point has far greater scope when applied to humans, given the extent to which we rely upon complicated technological environments and upon each other to accomplish our goals (Haugeland, 1998, p. 223).

I want to suggest that research on embodied, embedded cognition complements and further supports the phenomenological claims I made earlier. One need not reflect upon the nature of our social *experience* in order to make the point that social understanding, interaction and coordination owe much to the structure of the social world. A similar point can also be made if one starts with the world as scientifically described. It might be argued that the embeddedness of norms and roles in the world looks rather odd, if we start with the scientifically described world rather than that of everyday experience. However, I have claimed that social understanding owes much to configurations of equipment, an appreciation of which is intertwined with an appreciation of norms and roles. For example, high tables and thrones are closely associated with certain norms and roles. Although a fully enriched interpretation of equipment is not part of physics, a scientific perspective can still acknowledge the extent to which the world is physically shaped into complex configurations by humans and also that patterns of human behaviour are constrained and regulated by these configurations. Hence artefacts, I suggest, comprise a bridge between a phenomenology of situations and a scientific approach to human cognition. A bridge is, of course, not a full-blown union and the question remains as to how phenomenological and scientific perspectives can be more generally brought together. One option is to attempt to assimilate the phenomenology into an objective, physical, scientific view of the world. In other words, the aim is to naturalise it.[13] However, I will suggest in Chapter 8 that this is too one-sided and that the interaction between phenomenology and cognitive science should be thought of in a more metaphysically open and even-handed way.

Before discussing the specific issue of how embodied, embedded approaches in cognitive science can complement and perhaps further support the phenomenological claim that social life is structured by shared situations, I will provide a more general outline of what such approaches involve. The embodied, embedded view has been worked out in some detail by Clark (1997, 2001, 2003), among others. He argues at length that our cognitive abilities more generally are indissociable from our interactions with socially and technologically structured environments. For example, in writing a book chapter, I do not simply spill out the internal contents of my mind onto a computer's hard drive via a keyboard. As Clark puts it:

> As I (literally, physically) move these things about, interacting first with one and then another and making new notes, annotations, and plans, the intellectual shape of the chapter grows and solidifies. It is a shape that does not spring fully developed from inner cogitations. Instead, it is the product of a sustained and iterated sequence of interactions between my brain and a variety of external props.
>
> (1997, p. 207)

This does seem to be a fair description. To produce the final draft of this chapter, I used external resources in a variety of ways. Many of the ideas were generated by engaging with others' work and discussing ideas with them. I did not retain these ideas 'in my head' but took detailed notes of references, quotations, claims, arguments and a range of my own semi-developed views. I then sat in front of a computer, surrounded by a nest of notes, sketched a rough plan, added in some key quotations, elaborated some points, wrote a few successive drafts, used a computer spell checker, printed out the finished product, marked certain passages and made critical notes, typed out a revised draft, read the book as a whole and then further fine-tuned this chapter. During the process of writing and rewriting, ideas came to me that I had not thought of before, as though the act of writing itself were partly responsible for their genesis. Furthermore, while reading through a printed draft chapter, I found myself able to see ambiguities and weaknesses in the argument that I had not been aware of before writing it or while writing it. The specific form that the process took was shaped by recent technological innovations. However, the general point about reliance on external props is just as applicable in the absence of modern computer software.

In such cases, cognition involves body and environment in a variety of inter-related ways. For example, bodily movement can make an important contribution to cognition, especially when it comes to accessing information. It is possible to move one's body so as to reveal new information, rather than relying on internal processes to obtain the same information via inference or by recalling it from some vast memory archive. Indeed, Gibson (1979, p. 126) famously suggests that perception of one's posture and movement is, at the same time, perception of the environment:

> Information about the self accompanies information about the environment, and the two are inseparable. Egoreception accompanies exteroception, like the other side of a coin. Perception has two poles, the subjective and the objective, and information is available to specify both. One perceives the environment and coperceives oneself.

In the case of vision, bodily movements change what is perceived. Proprioceptive awareness of how one has moved, coupled with changes in the pattern of ambient light, can serve to specify properties of the environment, such as distance, depth, gradient and so forth.[14]

We not only use our bodies to move about in the world but also to manipulate it. The ability to manipulate the problems that we face, so as to simplify them, is a pervasive feature of human cognition. Clark offers the example of a jigsaw puzzle:

> Completing a jigsaw puzzle [. . .] involves an intricate and iterated dance in which 'pure thought' leads to actions which in turn change or simplify the problems confronting 'pure thought'.
>
> (1997, p. 36)

The ability to complete the puzzle is inextricable from the ability to move and reposition pieces, to perceive the results and further manipulate them. It is not that some wholly internalised cognitive capacity is *manifested* during interaction with the environment. The ability to complete the puzzle is indissociable from an ability to interact with and reconfigure the environment. Clark and Chalmers (1998, p. 8) refer to actions that alter the environment so as to change the problems that cognition has to deal with as 'epistemic actions'. In some cases, epistemic actions might simplify tasks without changing their nature. For instance, in the case of the jigsaw puzzle, it is arguable that one still faces the same kind of cognitive task but that the accompanying manipulation of pieces lessens the burden somewhat. However, there are other cases where environmental manipulation enables us to perform a task, not just by lessening the burden on internal resources but by changing the nature of the task. Clark offers the example of an artist who works by using a sketchpad:

> The sketch-pad is not just a convenience for the artist, nor simply a kind of external memory or durable medium for the storage of particular ideas. Instead, the iterated process of externalizing and re-perceiving is integral to the process of artistic cognition itself.
>
> (2001, p. 133)

There is a difference between using mental imagery and visually perceiving something. Whatever the former consists of, Clark suggests that it is not simply internal replication of the latter. If one draws a Necker cube or a duck-rabbit, one can look at it and undergo a perceptual gestalt switch. However, for most people at least, mental imagery does not accommodate this kind of experience. So externalising something enables us to perceive it and consequently think about it in ways that would not be possible with internal resources alone.

In addition to moving around in and manipulating the environment, it is arguable that we incorporate certain environmental structures into our cognitive processes. Clark and Chalmers (1998) offer a thought experiment involving two people, one with an excellent memory and the other with a poor memory but a very well organised diary. They suggest that internal memory plus the external diary together facilitate the same behavioural performances as internal memory alone. Hence the diary should be conceived of not as a memory aid but as an external memory store with the same cognitive status as an internal memory. The idea that we use external memory was, I think, first proposed by Vygotsky (1978), who, writing in the 1930s, contrasts 'natural memory' with use of external aids, like knots and notches on sticks. He remarks that 'even such comparatively simple operations as tying a knot or marking a stick as a reminder change the psychological structure of the memory process' (p. 39). The task of memory need not be that of accessing a vast body of data from an internal store. It can instead involve remembering how to access external structures in such a way as to make the relevant data available. We can remember to follow the red crosses on the trees, rather than remembering every twist and turn in the path.

Strategies for offloading cognitive work onto the environment are perhaps most conspicuous in social organisms, which distribute the work among themselves. Tasks that no organism could manage alone can be achieved by dividing them among a group, all of whose behaviour is regulated and coordinated by shared environmental structures that they may themselves have constructed. This, Clark proposes, is one of the functions performed by human culture:

> The idea, in short, is that advanced cognition depends crucially on our abilities to *dissipate* reasoning: to diffuse achieved knowledge and practical wisdom through complex social structures, and to reduce the loads on individual brains by locating those brains in complex webs of linguistic, social, political, and institutional constraints.
>
> (Clark, 1997, p. 180)

This kind of view is also suggested by Griffiths and Stotz (2000), who draw together recent work on development, extended cognition and culture, to argue that environmental structures that operate as scaffolding for developmental processes are not always eventually internalised. Organisms continue to employ features of the environment as an ingredient of mature cognitive processes, offloading much of the cognitive burden. This is especially apparent in our own case; the cultural environment includes a unique wealth of sophisticated regularities and patterns that we can utilise, build upon and transform, changing and reducing the demands on our internal cognitive resources in the process. Indeed, Griffiths and Stotz suggest that our reliance on environmental and, more specifically, cultural resources is so pronounced that the project of studying internal cognitive processes in isolation from the contexts in which they operate could be deeply misleading, analogous to investigating 'the true nature of an ant by removing the distorting influence of the nest' (p. 45).

In what ways does the cultural and more specifically technological environment contribute to social understanding, interaction and coordination? So, far, I have distinguished four closely related aspects of embodied, embedded cognition:

(a) Acquiring information by moving one's body in appropriate ways.
(b) Manipulating the environment so as to make tasks easier, often by changing their nature.
(c) Off-loading cognitive tasks onto environmental structures, such as external memory stores.
(d) Diffusing tasks among members of a population.

When it comes to the role of the social environment in regulating interpersonal interaction, I suggest that all four are evident. Starting with (d), consider the division of labour among people with different roles in an organisation. A supermarket, for example, is a very complicated social structure, which prescribes patterns of conduct for cashiers, line managers, shelf stackers, store managers and so forth. Many of these roles are rigidly constrained by configurations of equipment. For instance, being a cashier nowadays requires interfacing with the checkout in a way that allows little flexibility. (c) is equally apparent throughout social life, in the form of books, the Internet, signs and so forth. Consider the case of signs. Just about any modern environment is littered with signs, which take the form of directions, rules, prohibitions, advertisements and instructions as to 'what one does if one wants or needs some x'. These signs can cue actions without one's having to memorise a complicated social arrangement. The example of signs also makes clear the relevance of (a) to social cognition. By simply moving around and changing what we perceive, we can reveal previously unnoticed features of the technological environment that specify what to do next. Consider tasks such as finding out the way to a well-known landmark, where a train is due to leave from and at what time, where to check in for a flight to Paris, where to go if you have a ticket for a seat in the circle and so forth. In such cases, we can often just follow the signs. Furthermore, the shared assumption that all of us will do much the same makes us predictable to each other. Our interaction with equipment also involves (b). We do not simply observe signs and equipment but manipulate them so as to simplify and change the social tasks we face. For example, pressing a button at a pedestrian crossing and waiting for the green man to light up modifies the task that pedestrians and drivers face when it comes to judging when to cross and when to expect someone to cross. Rather than attempting to predict an individual's psychology, both parties can, to some extent, move the burden of coordination onto the manipulation of shared technologies that embody norms.

Bermúdez (2003, p. 45) notes that much social understanding involves matching perceived situations to 'prototypical social situations' that operate as guides for conduct. However, I suggest that, in many cases, the script that guides our conduct is not something that we have knowledge of before entering into the situation. Instead, with the right kind of behaviour in the right kind of environment, a script can be assembled as we go along. No prototype is required, if the environment is configured so as to make the steps involved in a social situation predictable as the participants proceed. In other words, the environment itself amounts to a dynamic script of sorts and 'what is to be done next' by oneself and others is revealed through one's on-going interactions with them in a structured but open-ended social environment. Signs point the way, one tool points to the next tool and one's own behaviour changes what one perceives in such a way as to constrain or even specify the next course of action. Consider installing a piece of software; actions are followed by prompts, which guide the next action. Others' behaviours also guide us in contexts of interaction, in a manner that can make clear what is to be done next. As you approach the check-in desk at an airport or some other place, someone might look at you and tell you to go to the queue on the left. Or everyone else might go to the left and so you do too. In such mundane scenarios, social understanding is facilitated by a coupling between internal cognitive capacities and structures of the social environment, which takes shape through interaction. One need not wholly internalise these structures; they are out there in the social world.

The extent to which an understanding of norms can depend upon bodily interaction in a situation is perhaps most evident from sporting examples, where a grasp of what ought to be done often seems to be embedded in the practical activity, rather than being something that is thought about independently of that activity. Consider a well-known example from football (soccer). In the 1996 European Championships, Paul Gascoigne, playing for England, scored the second goal against Scotland by sprinting forward without support, lobbing the ball over the head of Scottish defender Colin Hendry, running round him and then kicking it into the corner of the net past goalkeeper Andy Goran. His ability to anticipate complicated behaviours on the part of others and interact with them in a sophisticated and open-ended fashion was very much in evidence. However, it is implausible to suggest that this display of genius was an instance of particularly good FP thinking. Gascoigne is not an all-round Machiavellian social genius (no disrespect intended). His remarkable feat was the product of skills specific to the pitch. Furthermore, the speed of his responses indicates that he had no time to think about what was going on. If neurobiological findings reported by Libet (2004) are accepted, there would not have been sufficient time between stimulus and response for him to have even been aware of his response before it happened. This should come as no surprise. As Libet observes:

> Great athletes, in general, are those who can let their unconscious mind take over without interference from the conscious mind. Athletes tell us that if they try 'to think' (become aware) of immediate responses, they become less successful.
>
> (2004, p. 111)

Expert sportspeople and game players, when asked why they responded in a particular way to the actions of others, will often report that they 'just saw it' or 'did it', rather than offering a complicated narrative about their ability to detect the relevant internal mental states. Gascoigne reports 'I just knew where he'd be, when he'd commit himself, so I knew what to do' (2004, p. 214). Many strategic interactions in sport involve a practical, situation-specific grasp of 'what is to be done', partly embedded in the situation at hand. One need not rely on an internalised script, a complex process of deliberation or the assignment of internal mental states to opponents. As Dreyfus and Dreyfus argue, expertise involves attuning oneself to a situation in such a way that the situation itself drives and structures one's action; 'once one has a skill one is solicited to act without needing to have in mind any goal at all' (1999, p. 111). Wheeler describes this in the context of sport:

> Sport, in particular, provides a rich source of intuitively compelling examples in which the neural contribution may be more a matter

of nudges and triggers than specification and control, with real intelligence residing in the bodily (e.g. muscular) adaptations and dynamics.

(2005, p. 229)

The example of Gascoigne's goal involves competitive interaction, embedded in a framework of shared norms (the game). However, footballers and others also have to make themselves predictable to teammates and I suggest that this need to make oneself and others predictable, rather than unpredictable, is evident in many, if not most, situations. Rather than attempting to predict someone on the basis of a hypothesised set of internal psychological states, we can make our behaviour predictable to each other by participating in a shared regulatory framework. There will be many cases where we do not need to assign psychological states at all, given that shared situations will rigidly specify activities or make certain activities highly likely. In other cases, where psychological factors are appealed to, the range of factors to be considered can be substantially constrained by the assumption of a shared situation.

Clark (1997, pp. 181–182) makes an analogous point concerning rational choice theory. The description of a 'rational agent' at the heart of this theory maps roughly onto the systematically ordered framework of beliefs, desires, intentions, goals and actions that comprises FP. Rational choice theory can thus be regarded as utilising a simple conception of FP (see Morton, 1995). Clark notes that the predictions of rational choice are variably successful in different contexts. They are ineffective in weakly constrained scenarios, where social norms are not very standardised. However, in cases such as economic systems, where norms are highly constraining and systematically related, prediction of others on the basis of rational choice models is much more successful. Hence social prediction depends not just on the assignment of mental states but on that assignment taking place in the context of a situation where what one does, perhaps in a specific role, is already largely established. As Clark puts it, 'what is doing the work in such cases is not so much the individual's cogitations as the larger social and institutional structures in which the individual is embedded' (1997, p. 182). Indeed, he claims that, in extreme cases, where a situation and associated role are highly constrained, the role of internal states in regulating a participant's behaviour is so minimal that a 'zero-intelligence trader, a pigeon, a rat, a human trader, or, in the worst cases, a coin-flipping device' could do the job (1997, p. 184).

This indicates that, in many instances, we can understand behaviour by appreciating its wider context and paying little attention to internal psychology.

Letting situations do the work is very different from relying on an internalised belief-desire psychology and there is a simple reason why it is much easier and more effective. Bermúdez (2003) and Morton (1996), among others, note the considerable cognitive work involved in predicting several interacting people by considering their mental states. The actions of each person will affect the mental states of others, thus affecting their actions, which affect others' mental states and so forth. By the time you have worked out what one person is thinking, you will need to reassess what they are going to do in the light of what another person has said and done. With even a few people interacting in an open-ended, unconstrained situation, the task of prediction starts to look decidedly intractable. Given that time and cognitive resources are limited, a different strategy is required. This is where equipment and associated norms come in. Even when we are not dealing directly with other people, it is easy to see how equipment can lessen the burden on internal cognitive resources. Haugeland (1998, p. 234) offers the example of knowing the way to San Jose:

> . . . the internal guidance systems and the road itself must be closely coupled. [. . .] . . . much as an internal map or program, learned and stored in memory, would [. . .] have to be deemed *part of* an intelligent system that used it to get to San Jose, so I suggest the *road* should be considered *integral* to my ability.[15]

Relying on the road, rather than internal guidance systems, also allows one to interpret the behaviour of others. If everyone were to use internal and perhaps quite different guidance systems to regulate their behaviour in all manner of situations, the task of predicting them could be a very difficult one. However, if the guidance systems are embodied in the road itself, in the form of its direction and boundaries, in conjunction with the signs that appear along it, the same guidance system is now accessible to all. You need not worry about what is hidden in people's heads because the guidance system they are following is out there in the world for all to see.

One might retort that there is still the issue of whether a given individual will or will not follow the signs. However, the signs are not just there; they are there for all to follow. In other words, it is generally pretty clear that signs are signs. The task of predicting individuals is replaced by shared predictability, achieved via environmental structures that are available to everyone concerned.

It is also important to note that we not only *predict* people by assuming that they share the same situational understanding. We also manipulate each other's behaviour through instruction, criticism and debate. If someone does not follow a norm, they have not just rendered themselves unpredictable; they have often done something that is regarded as wrong, something that is perhaps to be criticised, challenged or corrected. So we make each other predictable by putting norms in the world for all to follow and also by interacting with each other in such a way as to influence behaviour so that it conforms to a greater degree with norms. In those cases where a situation is unfamiliar, the best bet is often not to attempt to predict someone's behaviour but to assume that the other person is a competent participant, ask them what is going on or what one is expected to do and then modify one's own behaviour accordingly. The emphasis, as Kusch (1999) and Morton (2003) have both stressed, is not simply on trying to predict unpredictable people but on making them and ourselves more predictable.

Social situations and belief-desire psychology

I have suggested in this chapter that social understanding is inseparable from interaction with a shared social environment. This emphasis on interaction is to be contrasted with the assumption of a perspective of *detached contemplation* that characterises many descriptions of FP. Gordon (1996, p. 11) distinguishes between 'hot' and 'cold' methodologies for interpreting others. A cold methodology is observational and detached, whereas a hot methodology involves engagement of one's own emotional and motivational capacities. Theory theories are cold but some formulations of simulation involve a less detached understanding of others. However, even simulation theories like Gordon's fail to clearly distinguish between engagement of emotional resources in spectatorial contexts and those cases where understanding proceeds through bodily interactions with shared situations. Hence I suggest that FP fails to accommodate an important aspect of the structure of social understanding, a largely practical familiarity with situations that is presupposed by FP and often operates without FP. Indeed, many of the cases where social understanding and interaction break down seem to be explicable in terms of a lack of practical familiarity, rather than a failure to assign the right propositional attitudes. Consider the bewilderment that often accompanies the commencement of a new job or attending an unfamiliar committee for the first time, which is gradually alleviated by increasing familiarity with context-specific norms, roles and the way equipment is used. As one learns to inhabit this context and respond appropriately to shared cues, one becomes better able to interpret and co-ordinate with others. FP is at best an incomplete description of 'commonsense psychology', given that it neglects a situational understanding that is more widespread than FP and does not depend upon FP. Central to the failure of FP to accommodate situational understanding is its emphasis on the internal cognitive capacities of individuals. It is both phenomenologically and cognitively implausible to suggest that our negotiation of the social world depends on factors that are wholly internalised.

The question arises as to how situational and psychological understanding relate to each other. At one extreme is the view that they are distinct kinds of social cognition. Cummins (2001) goes some way towards formulating such a position but focuses on social norms, rather than offering a more general conception of situational understanding. Citing experimental data, she suggests that FP abilities and an understanding of social norms have discrete developmental paths. The latter is evident first, in the guise of an ability to detect social rule violations, whereas the former emerges more gradually and has several distinct developmental stages (pp. 90–96).

At the other extreme is the view that there is nothing more to FP than an ability to participate in social situations. Baker (1999) leans towards this, in her claim that intentional psychology is inseparable from a more general 'commonsense conception' (p. 13), the latter being similar to what I have described as situational understanding.

I doubt that either extreme is tenable. It seems implausible to suggest that situational understanding has a wholly separate developmental trajectory to psychological understanding, given that an appreciation of situations plays a considerable role in constraining and thus facilitating psychological interpretation. The ability to constrain interpretation is surely an important part of the ability to apply intentional psychology, rather than something wholly distinct. However, it is also clear that understanding someone in psychological terms involves more than interpreting her as a bearer of roles or as an anonymous participant in a context of equipment and associated norms. Hence an account of social situations fails to accommodate the fact that we do not just experience others as bearers of roles, users of tools and followers of norms but as loci of experience and agency. An additional account is required of how we understand that people are distinctive in this way. One way to go would be to argue that FP, construed as the attribution of internal propositional attitude states, facilitates psychological understanding but has a more limited role than is often claimed. However, in Chapter 5, I will argue that an understanding of the meaning of actions, gestures and expressions can be obtained perceptually, without the need for inference, and that this perceptual grasp is foundational to our sense of others as 'people', as subjects of experience and instigators of action. Perception of action, gesture and expression is, I will argue, a process that engages one's own bodily responsiveness. It is not a detached, dis-embodied, theoretical affair and is quite unlike FP.

5
Perceiving Actions

In Chapter 4, I argued that the interpretation and explanation of action owes much to situational factors. Given that situational understanding is normative, it can account not only for why an action was performed but also for why it ought to have been performed. Furthermore, it can do so without involving propositional attitudes. Not all situational understanding relates to particular actions. For example, interpretations of what commuters do every morning and evening address routine and lengthy patterns of activity. But there are plenty of other cases where situational factors enable us to understand or explain why a specific action was performed, perhaps by showing that a seemingly anomalous action was, after all, warranted given a situation. For example, 'why did he just get up and leave?' can be met with 'because he's 17 years old and people under 18 aren't allowed in this bar after 6.00 pm'. However, the question 'why did A do p?' already assumes that an action of some description has been performed by A, even though the reason for its performance is unknown. It might be argued that taking something to be an action requires a grasp of FP. As indicated by the developmental evidence discussed in Chapter 4, it is unlikely that an ability to attribute internal propositional attitudes is required in order to recognise a behaviour as an action. However, it might be argued that understanding p to be an action still requires the attribution of internal mental states of some sort to A, a proto-FP, if you like. My aim in this chapter is to show that this is not so. I will suggest that the kind of understanding involved in grasping both that others are agents and that specific behaviours are actions differs from FP in two important respects:

(a) Actions, gestures and expressions are usually perceived, rather than inferred on the basis of perceived behaviour.

121

(b) Perception of others' actions, gestures and expressions involves one's own bodily responsiveness, in a way that even simulation theories of FP fail to accommodate.

The claim that we perceive actions is ambiguous. It could be taken to mean merely that we can perceive that p is an action. However, the stronger claim could be made that it is possible to perceive that p is directed at a particular object or even why p is directed at that object. I will argue that it is generally possible to perceive a behaviour as an action and to perceive something of its goal structure. Towards the end of the chapter, I will also suggest that we can sometimes perceive the reason why an action was performed, at least in those cases where the reason takes the form of a shared situation. My argument will apply to expressions and gestures, as well as object-directed actions. In cases where a why question is better answered through an appeal to psychological factors, I leave open, for now, the possibility of there being a role for an FP-style understanding, involving the positing of unperceivable internal states.

In order to assess the extent to which the argument of this chapter is critical of FP, it is worth reflecting on the question of how encompassing FP's role is claimed to be. Does anyone maintain that it is required in order to recognise a set of movements as an action? As will be clear from Chapter 1, almost all accounts of FP assume that it is employed to understand or explain *why* an action was performed or is likely to be performed. But when it comes to appreciating that something is an action, directed at a particular object in a particular way, the matter is less clear. Many discussions do indicate that the attribution of internal mental states is what allows us to distinguish actions from mechanical behaviours. For example, Meltzoff (1995, p. 838) remarks:

> Failure to attribute mental states to people confronts one with a bewildering series of movements, a jumble of behaviour that is difficult to predict and even harder to explain. At a rough approximation, this may be something like the state of children with autism.

Meltzoff contrasts behaviour-reading with the kind of mentalistic understanding that even 3-year-olds have. He construes the latter not as an ability to perceive the meaning of behaviour but to 'read below surface behaviour', adding that a fully developed adult FP involves a more sophisticated representational understanding of internal mental states, including beliefs (p. 838). Hence, on some accounts at least, it looks as though an understanding of action requires an ability to infer the presence of hidden mental states as causes. However, this need not imply that the appreciation of action is non-perceptual. Churchland (1991, pp. 57–58) acknowledges that behaviour is already packaged in the form of actions, rather than 'kinematically described', before we even begin to theorise as to its causes. He accounts for this by maintaining that perception is theory-laden and that the theory in question is FP.

My task in this chapter is to show that our understanding of others is largely, and often wholly, perceptual and also that this perceptual appreciation does not rely upon FP. (This is not to suggest that perception is non-conceptual; perception can involve concepts without involving FP. The relationship between conceptual understanding and perceptual experience will be briefly addressed in Chapter 6.) Perception of others' agency engages one's own motor and affective resources in a way that neither theory nor simulation theories accommodate. That so much depends upon perception does not make us mere readers of mechanical behaviour, as opposed to mind-readers. A clear division between observable behaviour and unobservable mental states is, I will suggest, an artificial and misleading imposition on our understanding of action, gesture and expression.

Experiencing others

Although I suggested in Chapter 2 that we should be wary of appealing to commonsense concepts and everyday intuitions, it does seem intuitive to suggest that we *experience* others as agents, *see* their emotions in their expressions and *perceive* the meaningfulness of their gestures. Indeed, it is difficult to imagine what it would be like to perceive the behaviour of another human being as purely mechanical and only afterwards to assign underlying mental states as its causes. Of course, proponents of FP can acknowledge that mentalistic interpretations of others' behaviour come naturally and effortlessly to us, so much so that it seems to us that we do just see their emotions, intentions and so forth. At the same time, they can claim that processes of theorising, simulating or both go on tacitly and serve to provide the mentalistic gloss that we take for granted when understanding behaviour. However, a considerable and diverse body of work suggests that this is not the case. For example, everyday intuitions are supported by numerous phenomenological descriptions, which not only indicate that our grasp of others is largely perceptual but also emphasise that this perceptual grasp is quite primitive, a more basic constituent of interpersonal experience than theorising or simulating. Phenomenology alone cannot repudiate the claim that what looks like an experiential rather than inferential grasp of other people actually depends upon 'sub-personal' inference processes. However, as Petit (1999), Gallagher (2001a,b), Thompson (2001) and others have noted, phenomenological descriptions are complemented by recent findings in neuroscience, which indicate that we can perceive action, expression and gesture, without the need for modelling or inference. I will begin by briefly outlining three phenomenological descriptions of our most fundamental intersubjective achievements, offered by Husserl, Scheler and Merleau-Ponty, before reviewing and critically discussing the relevant neurobiological evidence.

Phenomenological approaches attempt, in various ways, to make explicit and clarify the structure of intersubjective experience. In so doing, phenomenologists have argued that theoretical cognition, inference and analogy do not provide the basic awareness of others upon which interpersonal understanding and interaction rest. The agency of others is somehow experienced *in* their behaviour rather than inferred from it. The emphasis is placed upon perceptual and affective awareness of others as animate organisms, an awareness that is not detached or theoretical but inextricable from bodily responsiveness of self to other. Agency is not perceived in the standoffish way that one can encounter a stone; behavioural responsiveness to others is constitutive of the ability to perceive their behaviour as meaningful.

Perhaps the most intricate (and difficult) phenomenological discussion of intersubjectivity is that offered by Husserl in his *Fifth Cartesian Meditation*. Husserl rejects the view that an awareness of others is achieved through inference or analogy. Such views assume that another person is first encountered as a kind of object, distinct from oneself, with which one then comes to identify in a certain way. However, he claims that any experience of an *objective* world already has an appreciation of other experiential subjects sewn into its structure. An objective world just is a world that is 'there for everyone, accessible in respect of its Objects to everyone' (p. 91). Husserl's argument for this claim appeals to the manner in which we experience entities as objective, as independent of a particular perspective upon them. He notes that we do not simply experience an object, such as a chair, as an actuality. Instead, the chair, as it is presented to us, reflects various salient possibilities for perception and action. One could walk round it to reveal its hidden profiles, sit on it, look upon it from the other side of the room and so forth. Perception of the chair is not just a matter of what is given to a particular perspective; it also incorporates a 'horizon' of possibilities. We perceive not just an appearance but an appearance of something and we do so because every appearance offers up the possibility of various other appearances. Actualities and possibilities are thus co-constitutive of our experiences of things (pp. 44–45).[1] Husserl claims that a sense of the objective is constituted by the inclusion of possibilities that involve other people into experience. An appreciation of something as objective, as more than just a reflection of one's own concerns, is constituted by the possibility of its being experienced and manipulated by others. Hence an acknowledgement of others as loci of experience and activity is presupposed by the possibility of experiencing and thinking about an objective world. Any grasp of them as objects within an objective world consequently presupposes a more basic appreciation of them as experiential subjects.

To articulate the nature of this appreciation, Husserl attempts to formulate a transcendental theory of 'empathy' (p. 92), a description of the foundational apprehension of others as like me and yet distinct from me that underlies all interpersonal understanding. His phenomenological method involves what he calls a reduction to the 'sphere of ownness', a discarding of all experiential structures that incorporate or presuppose a sense of other people. What is left is a peculiar experiential world, an 'abstraction' (p. 93) devoid of any sense of another person, or, as Husserl puts it, a world from which *'all constitutional effects of intentionality relating immediately or mediately to other subjectivity'* have been extracted (p. 93). It is unclear whether this procedure is proposed as a sort of thought experiment or whether it is an experiential state that one is actually invited to achieve. However, setting aside such methodological issues, it is instructive to consider what Husserl claims to discover through the procedure. He aims to make explicit the structure of our most basic awareness of others by contrasting the sphere of ownness or 'primordial sphere' with fully enriched intersubjectivity and describing the order of stages via which the gulf between them is crossed. So he starts with a state in which a sense of others is completely absent from experience and asks what the first stage of intersubjectivity must look like. This stage will involve our most foundational sense of other people. Husserl envisages the project as an exercise in 'static' phenomenology, an account of the layers that are present in fully developed, adult intersubjective experience. However, his descriptions may also apply to developmental accounts, given that the more foundational levels will, presumably, arise first. As Smith (2003, p. 235) puts it, 'what is foundationally first is also genetically first'.

Although a sense of others has been removed from the primordial sphere, Husserl claims that some kind of pre-objective realm of experience still remains, sustained by perception and kinaesthesia (p. 97). He takes this as the starting point from which to address the question of how an appreciation of other experiential subjects can be built up or, in Husserl's terms, of:

> . . . how we are to understand the fact that the ego has, and can always go on forming, in himself such intentionalities of a different kind, intentionalities with an existence-sense whereby *he wholly transcends his own being.*

(p. 105)

Husserl suggests that the first step out of solipsistic experience must be an awareness of the other's body as an animate organism like oneself. He proposes that a pre-reflective, non-inferential 'analogizing apperception' is involved, which somehow links perception of the other organism directly to one's awareness of oneself as a locus of experience (p. 111). This 'analogising' is not a process that associates distinct objects of experience. The bond between self and other is part of experience, rather than something that is inferred. This bond, Husserl claims, is achieved through a passive 'pairing' of certain aspects of self and other: '*ego* and *alter ego* are always and necessarily *given in an original "pairing"*' (p. 112). Just as a knife and fork are grouped together in an experiential gestalt, so too one's own body and that of the other are somehow associated, allowing the other's body to 'appropriate from mine the sense: animate organism' (p. 113). There must be a basic, immediate connection between self and other, which allows one to experience the other as an animate agent. Once this foundational bond between self and other is established, Husserl suggests that building up the higher strata of intersubjectivity and culture, which involve various differentiations between self and other, is relatively easy (p. 129). So the hard part is to explain how the other can be experienced as an animate organism at all, without falling back on inference or analogy.

Although I will agree with Husserl's emphasis on the primitive, experiential nature of the self-other relation, I think his account may be misleading in at least two respects. First of all, he states that the other's body 'appropriates from mine' its sense as an animate organism. However, it is arguable that self and other appropriate that sense from each other and that neither is given as what it is before the other. Second, although Husserl emphasises experience of others, rather than inference, his descriptions could apply equally to spectatorial perception of another person and to reciprocal interaction between people. However, it is arguable that the nature of the pairing will be better understood if we take embodied interaction between people as a starting point, rather than experience of one body by another.

Both of these themes are apparent in the writings of Scheler and Merleau-Ponty. Scheler (1954) focuses specifically on perception of emotion in expression and claims that we have a pre-theoretical, perceptual sense of others as animate organisms. He considers cases of having fellow-feelings or pitying someone and argues that empathetic and sympathetic experiences of this nature presuppose a more basic appreciation of others as experiential subjects. One does not understand someone as a person *by* pitying her; that she is a possible object of one's pity is already understood. It is this presupposed sense of others that Scheler attempts to make explicit:

> One may look at the face of a yelling child as a merely physical object, or one may look at it (i.e. in the normal way) as an expression of pain, hunger, etc., though without therefore pitying the child; the two things are utterly different. Thus experiences of pity and fellow-feeling are always additional to an experience in the other which is already grasped and understood.
>
> (1954, p. 8)

Before any transference of feeling between self and other, any attribution of states to the other, any theorising, analogy, or inference, she is already given as *one like me* (p. 9). She is not an internal consciousness that inhabits a perceivable body. Rather, she is perceived *as* a locus of experience. Her expressions are not external clues to inner states; emotional experience presents itself in her visible expressions and is grasped with a kind of immediacy. The body as a mere *object* is an abstraction from the perceived meaningfulness of expressive phenomena:

> . . . that 'experiences' occur there is given for us *in* expressive phenomena – again, not by inference, but directly, as a sort of primary 'perception'. It is *in* the blush that we perceive shame, *in* the laughter joy.
>
> (p. 10)

This 'primary givenness' of others, Scheler claims, is the basis of other interpersonal abilities, such as imitation. Imitation rests upon an understanding of the meaningfulness of gestures, an understanding which is not achieved by inferring underlying mental states from behaviour but through perception; 'the impulse to imitate only arises when we have already apprehended the gesture *as* an expression of fear or joy' (p. 10).

Scheler's view, like that of Husserl, appeals to some kind of basic asso-ciation between one's own experiences and the activities others. This allows perceived phenomena to be perceived *as* expressions; 'the rela-tionships between expression and experience have a fundamental basis of connection' (p. 11). The connection, Scheler claims, comprises the 'primitive givenness of "the other"' (p. 31), the basis of interpersonal and social understanding. It is seldom recognised or articulated and so the problem of intersubjectivity is misconstrued as that of connecting two entities that begin life experientially cut off from each other.[2] In contrast, Scheler claims that the appreciation of others as animate forms always involves 'some degree of undifferentiated identification' (p. 31). One does not fully distinguish oneself from others and experience them as wholly distinct entities, detached from one's own experiencing.

Merleau-Ponty similarly claims that others are encountered perceptu-ally. Like Scheler, he rejects the idea of a gulf between internalised subjects, to be bridged by inference from behaviour to agency. The meaning of behaviour, he suggests, is perceptually apparent in a man-ner that is prior to any intellectualised divide between distinct subjects that philosophers might impose (1964a, pp. 17–18). My own body is a sense-giving orientation through which all experience is structured, as opposed to a mere object with which I am uniquely familiar. And the bodies of others are not encountered as objects either:

> Just as my body, as the system of all my holds on the world, founds the unity of the objects which I perceive, in the same way the body of the other – as the bearer of symbolic behaviors and of the behavior of true reality – tears itself away from being one of my phenomena, offers me the task of a true communication . . .
>
> (1964a, p. 18)

Another person is not first encountered as an object, as 'one of my phe-nomena'. Rather, others are experienced as those to whom one can stand in communicative relations. Hence Merleau-Ponty emphasises communicative gestures, in addition to expressions and bodily behav-iours more generally. But how is it that a body is apprehended as a locus of experience and as a potential communicative interactant, rather than as an object in motion? In his essay 'The Child's Relations with Others', he offers a developmental account of the structure of intersubjectivity. This account rejects the commonplace assumption that 'since I cannot have direct access to the psyche of another [. . .] I must grant that I seize the other's psyche only indirectly, mediated by its bodily appearances'

(1964a, p. 114) and proposes that young infants' responsiveness to facial expressions and their ability to imitate them cannot be based upon inference or analogy. The infant could not have a sufficiently developed perceptual appreciation of its own body to facilitate the complicated task of mapping others' actions onto its own. Hence the ability to imitate must have its source in some kind of direct mapping between perception and proprioception.[3] Merleau-Ponty asks 'have we the means of systematically comparing the body of the other as seen by me with my body as sensed by me?' He claims that this is indeed so and that the other's agency is directly apprehended in his behaviour; 'it is in his conduct, in the manner in which the other deals with the world, that I will be able to discover his consciousness' (pp. 116–117). This understanding requires, he claims, a link between the perception of others and the goal-oriented potentialities of one's own body:

> If I am a consciousness turned toward things, I can meet in things the actions of another and find in them a meaning, because they are themes of possible activity of my own body.
>
> (p. 117)

Like Scheler, Merleau-Ponty indicates that intersubjectivity is founded on an undifferentiated awareness of agency, through which self and other gradually emerge as distinct beings but are never wholly separate from each other.

Similar claims concerning the embodied, practical, perceptual nature of our appreciation of other people and the relatedness of self to other can be drawn from several other phenomenologists. For example, Sartre, whose account of self and other I will discuss in Chapter 6, suggests that 'the original bond with the Other first arises in connection with the relation between my body and the Other's body' (1989, p. 361). My aim here is not to arbitrate between these various accounts or debate over the often quite subtle differences between them. Instead, I want to stress the consensus that intersubjectivity is a matter of bodily, perceptual, affective relatedness between people. This applies both to our understanding of specific actions, gestures and expressions and to our sense of others as animate agents and loci of experience, as *people*.

Evidence from neuroscience

One response to these phenomenological claims is to state that it is simply not possible to perceive agency and experience in others.

Phenomenological, and perhaps everyday, intuition might suggest that we do so but scientifically informed intuition suggests otherwise. Actions, it might be asserted, are movements that are initiated in certain ways by internal cognitive processes. So the only way of finding out whether a movement is an action is to find out whether it was caused by the right kind of cognitive process. As we cannot see the relevant processes, we postulate actions by means of inference or analogy.

However, the claim that we can perceive actions, intentions, goals, emotions, meanings and even thoughts is quite compatible with empirical science. Indeed, it is a view that is increasingly supported by recent scientific findings. Although Meltzoff, as quoted earlier in this chapter, seems to think that mental states are underlying causes of behaviour, he and his collaborators have done much to illuminate the close connection between action and perception of action. For example, Meltzoff and Moore (1977) demonstrate that young infants and even neonates are able to imitate the facial expressions and gestures of adults. As they would have had insufficient perceptual exposure to their own gestures to acquire such mappings through learning, it would seem that there is an innate connection between proprioception and perception. One senses one's own expressions and gestures proprioceptively but somehow maps this proprioceptive awareness onto a perceptual awareness of others.[4]

Recent findings in neuroscience concerning so-called 'mirror neurons' further support the claim that there is an innate link between proprioception and perception. They also suggest that this link facilitates a perceptual appreciation of action, gesture and expression. Mirror neurons were first discovered in area F5 of the ventral premotor cortex of monkeys by means of electrophysiological studies (Gallese, Fadiga, Fogassi and Rizzolatti, 1996; Rizzolatti, Fadiga, Fogassi and Gallese, 1996) and have since been found in other cortical areas (Rizzolatti, Craighero and Fadiga, 2002, p. 37). There is also strong evidence for the existence of a mirror system in humans. Although direct recording of individual neurons is not ordinarily an option with human subjects, due to ethical and legal constraints, studies have been conducted using magnetoencephalography (MEG), transcranial magnetic simulation (TMS) and positron emission tomography (PET).[5]

The discovery of mirror neurons was preceded by that of 'canonical neurons', the other class of neuron in area F5. Canonical neurons have both visual and motor properties; they discharge when one performs a particular action and also when an object congruent with that same kind of action is perceived visually (Fogassi and Gallese 2002, p. 15).

Likewise, mirror neurons have perceptual and motor properties. However, rather than matching actions with perceived objects, they match actions performed with actions perceived. In monkeys, mirror neurons discharge when another monkey is seen performing a hand action. They do not discharge when the target object is observed while the action is not. And response is also significantly diminished or absent when a tool, rather than the hand, is employed to manipulate an object. Responses are variably specific to 'kinds' of action. Some cells are tuned to general categories of action, such as 'grasping manipulating, tearing, holding objects', whereas others are also receptive to the *manner* in which an object is grasped or held (Fogassi and Gallese, 2002, p. 16). In addition to these perceptual properties, they discharge during performance of certain kinds of action and match observed actions with actions performed. For example, a cell that responds during perception of another monkey reaching for food may respond in the same way when the observer reaches for food. This matching between action and perception of action is variably refined. Strictly congruent neurons match quite specific similarities between perception and performance, such as 'firmly grasping an object'. Broadly congruent neurons are sensitive to less specific similarities, such as just 'grasping'. There are also broadly congruent neurons that match sequential actions. For example, in monkeys, some cells will discharge when an experimenter places food in front of the monkey and then when the monkey reaches for it (Fogassi and Gallese, 2002, pp. 15–19).

Interestingly, mirror neurons do not appear to be tuned to *movements*, characterised as physical changes in posture, but to the structure of action. Observation of an action being mimicked in the absence of a target object results in a substantially weakened or absent response, suggesting that it is goal structure, rather than physical behaviour, that is important. That mirror neurons are selective to the teleological structure of action, rather than to the physical structure of behaviour, is also illustrated by the difference between strictly and broadly congruent cells. The latter pick up on the goal structure of an action, such as grasping an object, whereas the former are also receptive to the 'style' of the action, the way in which that goal is achieved, such as its being a precision grip, for example (Rizzolatti, Craighero and Fadiga, 2002, p. 37).

It is claimed that the mirror system in humans is more elaborate and has additional properties. For example, we routinely use our bodies to make communicative gestures, which do not have target objects, and there is evidence that the human mirror system is receptive to these

(Rizzolatti, Craighero and Fadiga, 2002, p. 41). We also employ an elaborate range of facial expressions when communicating, and it has been suggested that there is a specialised mirror system for matching the facial expressions of others with one's own (Studdert-Kennedy, 2002). Of further interest is the observation that monkey F5 is homologous to Broca's area in humans, which is associated with linguistic ability. So the possibility arises that our mirror system plays some role in facilitating verbal communication or that it is at least very closely associated with verbal communication (Rizzolatti, Craighero and Fadiga, 2002, pp. 42–43). Humans also differ from monkeys in their ability to imitate, which may play a considerable role in the development of communication. And it has been suggested that the mirror system could well support this ability. For example, Wohlschläger and Bekkering (2002) claim that the human mirror system is a necessary but not sufficient condition for imitation.

Much of the current philosophical and scientific interest in mirror neurons is focused around their implications for our understanding of intersubjectivity and, more specifically, their implications for the theory-simulation debate. Gallese and Goldman propose that mirror neurons are a precursor to mature intersubjective abilities and that their presence supports simulation theories over theory theories:

> The activity of mirror neurons, and the fact that observers undergo motor facilitation in the same muscular groups as those utilized by target agents, are findings that accord well with simulation theory but would not be predicted by theory theory.
>
> (1998, p. 493)

Theory theory suggests that intersubjective understanding does not require *sharing* the mental states of others. As Stone and Davies (1996, pp. 126–127) put it, 'according to [theory theory], other people are objects in our environment, and the task of understanding them is no different, in principle, from the task of understanding the behaviour of other, more inert, objects'. Given the theory theory, one would not expect to find a system matching action observation with action performance. But simulation points to just such a mapping. Gallese and Goldman suggest that the mirror system 'seems to be nature's way of getting the observer into the same "mental shoes" as the target – exactly what the conjectured simulation heuristic aims to do' (1998, pp. 497–498). They argue that it is part of the simulation mechanism and may also be an evolutionary precursor to full-blown simulation. Simulation could have originated in a sensitivity to the goals of action and later developed into a more complicated modelling of full-fledged belief-desire psychology.

However, it is doubtful that mirror neurons complement simulation theories in this way. As Gallagher (2001a, 2007) points out, the term 'simulation' suggests that another person is first perceived and then simulated. But evidence from mirror neurons does not point to a two-step process: 'perception of action is already an understanding of the action; there is no extra step involved that could count as a simulation routine' (2001a, p. 102). Gallagher (2007) appeals to phenomenology in order to challenge the view that we use *explicit* simulation to appreciate others as agents with rich mental lives. The argument is pretty simple: this view does not cohere with experience. We frequently experience others as agents without having any awareness of adopting their points of view, putting ourselves in their shoes or pretending to have their mental states. One does not see a person and then use one's mind as a model with which to interpret her as an agent. One just *sees her as an agent*. However, this still leaves open the possibility that an implicit or 'subpersonal' routine is responsible for what seems, phenomenologically, to be a perceptual appreciation of others. Gallagher also challenges this view. He notes that mirror neurons fire only 30 to 100 milliseconds after visual stimulation. Hence their response is very swift. Given this, he suggests that, if we think of vision as a temporally extended process, it is quite conceivable that mirror neuron responses are integral to perception at the functional as well as phenomenological level. In any case, there is simply no place for a discrete modelling process that acts upon perceptual outputs. Mirror neuron response is directly elicited by perceptual stimuli, just like other elements of the visual process. This view, he notes, is made all the more plausible if one admits that vision is an enactive process, meaning one that incorporates motor responsiveness.

Various philosophers and psychologists accept that all vision is 'enactive' in some sense. Objects do not appear to us in a manner that is detached from our preoccupations and capacities. Terrain is encountered not simply as there but as navigable; cups do not just appear as detached entities but as graspable; chairs are sittable on and so forth. The view that our bodily potentialities contribute to perception has a distinguished history in both phenomenology and psychology. As Gibson (1979) famously puts it, objects are perceived as 'affording' various behaviours. And Merleau-Ponty (1962) offers a detailed phenomenological description of how our bodily capacities shape our perception of things, which complements Gibson's view in several respects. Such views have been developed in various ways by more recent authors. For example, Noë (2004) draws on both Gibson's work and on phenomenological reflection to argue that all perception involves sensorimotor skills. It is a matter of active, skilful, bodily engagement with the world, rather than the passive uptake of environmental information.

If the view that vision, more generally, involves motor processes is accepted, a parity argument can be offered for the conclusion that mirror neurons are integral to perception of action. Canonical neurons associate perceived objects with compatible actions. Given the view that perception of objects involves motor capacities and also that canonical neurons are found at an early stage of visual processing, it seems highly likely that these cells play a role in perception. Mirror neurons are found in the same areas of the brain and participate in the same stages of processing. So, if we take cells that pair actions with perceived objects as part of the perceptual system, there is no good reason to exclude cells that pair actions with perceived actions.

However, it might still be argued, on behalf of simulation theory, that all perception involves simulated action. Could it be that both mirror neurons and canonical neurons are part of a subpersonal simulation routine that participates in the process of perception? As Gallagher (2007) notes, that a type of cell contributes to both perception and action does not imply that the former function amounts to a modelling of the latter. The sole fact that perception and action use some of the same processes does not warrant the claim that one of these uses is a simulation of the other, even though it does suggest that perception and action are interconnected and functionally similar in certain respects. The hypothesised function of mirror neurons does indicate that perception of action is achieved in virtue of similarities between one's own bodily capacities and those of others. However, this kind of isomorphism does not imply modelling. So, although we can admit that perception relies on what Heal calls co-cognition, meaning that it is a process that utilises similarities between A and B, it is not a simulation process that utilises those similarities by employing A as a model or partial model of B.

The view that mirror neurons facilitate *perception*, rather than modelling, is endorsed by many of the neuroscientists most closely associated with their discovery and subsequent study. For example, Fogassi and Gallese take it that 'perception, far from being just the final outcome of sensory integration, is the result of sensorimotor coupling' (2002, p. 27). They go on to suggest that, thanks to the mirror system, it is possible to perceive the meaningfulness of behaviour, thus circumventing the need to rely wholly or even mostly on an ability to infer internal mental states as underlying behavioural causes:

> What we would like to emphasize is that when 'reading the mind' of conspecifics whose actions we are observing, we rely *also*, if not mostly, on a series of explicit behavioral signals, that we can detect from their observed behavior. These signals are intrinsically meaningful to the extent that they enable the activation of equivalent inner representations on the observer/mind-attributer's side.
>
> (2002, p. 30)

Neither simulation nor theory theories account for how we are initially aware of another person as a locus of experience and agency or for how we grasp that actions, gestures and expressions are meaningful behaviours, rather than mechanical movements. Mirror neurons, assuming they facilitate an inter-modal bridge between perception and action, show how this understanding of others can rest upon a shared, practical, bodily, affective relatedness, rather than an inference made on the basis of some theory or a modelling process.[6]

Of course, mirror neurons alone do not add up to a comprehensive explanation of our sense of others. In fact, they do not even account for the differentiation between self and other; that x discharges when I perform an action and also when you perform a similar action does not explain how I experience one action as mine and the other as yours. But they do at least show how a *perceptual*, albeit undifferentiated, grasp of agency is possible. Hence the problem of understanding others is perhaps not that of bridging a gap between two distinct and hidden mental lives but of distinguishing between them, given the starting point of an awareness of agency that is, to some degree, undifferentiated.

How do mirror neurons manage to differentiate between the agencies of self and other? The simple answer is that perhaps they do not. However, all we need in order to allow for the possibility of distinguishing between the two is something less that a complete resonance of self to other, a complete replication of the perceptual and motor state of A by B. So I do not think there is a problem here. Mirror neurons facilitate a perceptual connection but the assumption that other processes involved in perception and action do differentiate between the two (by responding to one and not the other or by responding to both but differently) allows for the formation of a distinction. What we need in order to experience someone as 'another person', rather than as a 'thing' or as 'oneself' is a form of experiencing that involves neither total identification nor total detachment (Zahavi, 2007). It is also worth recalling that Fogassi and Gallese (2002) refer to a class of mirror neurons that match sequential actions, such as when a monkey perceives someone placing food on the table and also when that monkey grabs the food. This suggests a motor responsiveness that complements, rather than duplicates, the actions of others.

It would seem then that phenomenological descriptions and work in neuroscience can complement each other, in suggesting that our primary access to others is neither a matter of theorising nor simulating but of a perceptual, bodily receptivity. Thus there is the possibility of mutual illumination between these two very different fields. Husserlian phenomenology and research on mirror neurons can interact and complement each other in several ways. Husserl's account rests on an intersubjective achievement whose nature is unclear. What could a pre-objective bodily analogising actually be, aside from the judgement that another body is relevantly like one's own, which is precisely the kind of inferential move that Husserl rejects? Work on mirror neurons can lend some support to Husserl, by showing what such a relation might consist of and how it is possible. As Gallagher (2001b, pp. 95–96) notes, the problem concerns just which aspect of the other's body Husserl thinks we pair with our own and how. Mirror neurons, he argues, are part of the solution; they show how an inter-modal link between proprioception and perception of *action* might be possible. Hence neurobiological findings can provide support for Husserl and can also feed into the interpretation of phenomenological descriptions, by clarifying the kind of relation described and showing how it need not be something irrevocably vague or mysterious. Likewise, Husserl's claims can complement recent work on mirror neurons, by peeling back the layers of intersubjectivity to reveal a basic sense of others, the existence and nature of which is largely ignored by the recent FP literature. He thus provides a phenomenological framework through which the role of mirror neurons might be contextualised, interpreted and explained.

Such a marriage may require some reinterpretation of Husserl. For example, Smith (2003, p. 239) suggests that Husserl's *Fifth Meditation* is 'over-intellectualized', in emphasising relations between stationary bodies rather than mobile, interacting agents. He goes on to discuss Husserl's unpublished work, which places a more explicit emphasis on the role of instincts, drives and behaviours in the constitution of intersubjectivity.[7] It is movement, rather than bodily appearance, which is paired and links perception with kinaesthesis. However, it is doubtful that Husserl, even in *Cartesian Meditations*, envisages a pairing between *bodies*. For example, he claims that 'the experienced animate organism of another continues to prove itself as actually an animate organism, solely in its changing but incessantly *harmonious "behaviour"*' (p. 114). It is through perception of movement that the analogising between self and other occurs, perhaps via an extended sequence of perceived movements being harmoniously matched with a coherent sequence of motor patterns.

The neuroscience also complements aspects of the descriptions offered by Scheler and Merleau-Ponty. Both phenomenologists suggest that an understanding of others begins with an undifferentiated experience of agency, gesture and emotion, rather than with a subject of experience who somehow manages to assign a mental life to a complicated object in his perceptual field. An innate inter-modal link between action, expression and gesture and their perception supports such claims. Merleau-Ponty postulates just such a link but is unable to defend the view that it is innate in nature. Mirror neurons provide a resource with which to do so (Gallagher and Meltzoff, 1996).

Another project that might benefit from cooperation between phenomenology and neuroscience is the progressive refinement of psychological categories. (By 'cooperation', I mean an ongoing critical dialogue between the two, rather than the reshaping of one field of study so as to conform to the metaphysical and epistemological presuppositions of the other, as I will make clear in Chapter 8.) Husserl, Scheler and Merleau-Ponty emphasise slightly different aspects of our experience of others. Husserl emphasises the perception of animate agency. Scheler focuses more specifically on expression and Merleau-Ponty highlights the importance of communicative gesture. Hence I have, up to this point, distinguished between actions, gestures and expressions. This distinction is not arbitrary. Scientific work also suggests that there are genuine psychological distinctions to be drawn between these kinds of bodily activity. For example, Gallagher (2005a, Chapter 5) discusses the case of Ian Waterman, who lost all proprioception below the neck, as a result of 'de-afferentation'. As a result, Waterman cannot determine the position of any of his limbs or co-ordinate his actions unless he is able to perceive them visually. However, his conversational gesturing (but not ostensive gesturing) is normal in the absence of visual guidance, suggesting that certain kinds of gesture are quite different from object-directed actions. Indeed, Gallagher suggests that gestures are more closely associated with language than they are with intentional action.[8] There is also evidence of a decoupling between the perception of action and expression. For example, Hobson (2002, p. 56) discusses results showing that, in certain experimental conditions, autistic children seem to be insensitive to the emotional attitudes of people, while still remarking on their actions.

Hence our experience of others' behaviour is not homogeneous but involves perceptual receptivity to different kinds of experience and activity. The ongoing task of differentiating these is, I suggest, something that phenomenology and science can both contribute to. For current purposes, I will stick to a tripartite distinction between gesture, expression and action. However, it is worth stressing that all three categories can be sub-divided. For example, Goldwin-Meadow (1999, p. 422) notes that, even if we restrict ourselves to conversational gestures, it is possible to distinguish several subcategories. The category 'action' is also very broad. What I want to emphasise here, in referring to 'action perception', is that we can perceive (a) that a behaviour is goal-directed, (b) what it is directed towards, (c) the manner or style of the behaviour, and (d) that sub-units of a goal-directed behaviour participate in that behaviour, rather than being mere mechanical movements. I have referred to the combination of these as a perception of action. However, various kinds of action can be distinguished. An action can be goal-directed without being premeditated or preceded by intentions of which a person is aware. For example you can take a sip from a drink while talking with a friend, without intending to do so beforehand. So actions that are preceded by explicit intentions are only a subclass of the goal-directed actions to which mirror neurons are receptive. There is a further contrast to be drawn between, for example, reaching for a glass of water and putting one step in front of the other. The former involves a discrete unit of behaviour that is individuated by its goal. However, putting one foot forward while walking is not usually itself a goal-directed behaviour but, rather, part of a larger pattern of goal-directed activity. It would seem likely that mirror neurons apply to both, given that they are claimed to be responsive to the 'styles' of conduct involved in goal-directed performances.

There is also considerable philosophical debate over what actions actually are (see, for example, Davidson, 1980) and it might be argued that goal-directed behaviour alone does not add up to action. However, I am not concerned with which behaviours we choose to call 'actions' so much as with what it is that we are able to perceive (consisting of (a) to (d), above) and of the contribution that this makes to interpersonal interpretation, interaction and coordination. Hence, if one wants to claim that actions are states that are caused by specific beliefs and desires or by reasons that take the form of psychological states, then many of the behaviours that I call actions will have to be re-labelled as goal-directed or purposive behaviours. However, as will be argued later in this chapter and in Chapter 7, in most cases where we seek and offer reasons for action, these reasons do not take the form of posited internal psychological states. Hence to restrict the category of action by emphasising FP-type causes will be to restrict it too far.

The mirror system: applications and limitations

The kind of perceptual appreciation and bodily responsiveness that mirror neurons are hypothesised to facilitate has very broad application. In all those cases where we are able to visually perceive another person's behaviour, a perceptual grasp of action, expression and gesture will make a considerable contribution to interpretation. There are, of course, many other cases where we interpret behaviour in the absence of perceptual access, such as when we respond to email, read about behaviour or hear about it from others. Hence these perceptual abilities will not be applied in all cases. However, if our *sense* of people as loci of agency and experience is acquired through a perceptual-motor coupling, as suggested by Husserl, Scheler and Merleau-Ponty, then we would not be able to interpret any behaviour as action, in the absence of such a coupling. By analogy, we can understand something of the way in which a particular painter uses colours by relying on what we have been told and without seeing any of the relevant paintings. However, this understanding still presupposes the ability to see.

Although a perceptual-motor coupling may play a role in many or all of our perceptual encounters with others and even lie at the source of our sense that there are others, it is perhaps most evident in cases of intricate bodily coordination between people. FP, as noted, tends to adopt a voyeuristic account of intersubjectivity, which is a far cry from pastimes such as dancing or sport. When two people dance together (good dancers, that is), it is unlikely that the elaborate and complementary interplay of movements and gestures between them is modulated by assignment of inter-related propositional attitudes and resultant behaviour predictions, such as 'A believes p and desires q. So, all things being equal, A will move her right hand up while moving her left hand sideways, at the same time as putting her left foot forward and then swiftly moving it back', followed by 'I desire to complement A and A will be complemented by movements p, q and r, which I will therefore initiate'. This would make substantial demands on our cognitive resources and is at odds with the phenomenology of being attuned to another's body, of being responsive to her in a way that blends together perception and action in the form of seamless mutual coordination. Furthermore, the finely co-ordinated movements we see in dance require very swift reaction times (Rotondo and Boker, 2002, p. 160), surely too swift to allow for a complicated inference as to the internal states of another person, followed by action performance. So it is difficult to see how appreciation of a succession of internal mental states could enable this kind of coordination.

There are many other familiar scenarios where perception of behaviour is closely tied to behavioural response. A crowd at a football match will react in a variety of ways to action on the pitch. The link between perception of an event on the pitch and bodily response to it has a kind of phenomenological immediacy, as though the response is directly solicited by the perception or even indissociable from perception of what is happening. For example, we might talk about watching a 'tense moment', as we quite literally tense the muscles in our arms. This sense of immediacy sits well with work on mirror neurons, which suggests that motor mimicry of others, though normally suppressed at the spinal level, is often manifest to varying degrees (Rizzolatti and Arbib, 1998, p. 190). Rotondo and Boker (2002, p. 151) note various contexts in which mirroring and complementary gestures are apparent. For example:

> In an informal group, people may cross their legs at similar angles, hold their arms in similar positions, even simultaneously perform head or hand motions. To a point, such mirrored or matched positions can be of benefit to the continuity of the conversation; however, if people see such displays as deliberate attempts to mimic, it can bring about feelings of discomfort and a desire to break the established symmetry.

Boker and Rotondo suggest that 'the interplay between symmetry formation and symmetry breaking in posture and gaze' is 'integral to the process of communication' and not a product of some already established psychological understanding (2002, p. 165). Interpersonal interaction is partly composed of a mutual, practical attunement that pervades communication and is especially evident in activities such as dancing (p. 160). Rizzolatti and Arbib (1998) go so far as to hypothesise that bodily interactions between self and other, facilitated by an intermodal mapping between perception and action, amount to a kind of primitive dialogue, which was an evolutionary precursor to linguistic communication. Action p of A is directly apprehended by B as being action p. Sometimes B's motor facilitation, integral to this perception, is not wholly inhibited. Thus B's response with a similar or complementary gesture allows A to see that B has recognised the meaning of her action and so forth, as a shared context of mutual bodily attunement develops. The ability to regulate inhibition of motor response facilitates voluntary signalling and a form of dialogical interaction is made possible.

Hence both phenomenological descriptions and work in neuroscience emphasise the way in which grasping others as people and taking their behaviour to be meaningful is a matter of relatedness. In other words, contrary to FP, one does not ordinarily understand someone from a detached perspective and then, perhaps, relate to them. Instead, our sense that another is an agent and that an action is occurring is partly constituted by our bodily relatedness to them. Sometimes, this relatedness can, in a context of interaction, do most or all of the work required to coordinate with others. In other contexts, it may only be part of the story. Even so, it seems that work on mirror neurons, complemented by phenomenology, has the potential both to cast considerable light on the structure of intersubjectivity and to call into question the presupposition of detachment that pervades the FP literature.

There is a great deal of optimism regarding the contribution that mirror neurons can make to an understanding of intersubjectivity. For example, Ramachandran (2000, p. 4) speculates that 'mirror neurons will do for psychology what DNA did for biology: they will provide a unifying framework and help explain a host of mental abilities that have hitherto remained mysterious and inaccessible to experiments'. However, it is important to note that others are more cautious. For example, Stamenov (2002) observes that both humans and monkeys have mirror systems but only humans have language, inferring from this that mirror neurons are not the primary facilitator of human linguistic ability. Addressing the more general significance of mirror neurons, he notes that their activity is encapsulated, automatic and so quite different from interpersonal understanding. And, in monkeys, the cross-modal mapping facilitated by mirror neurons is 'numb and dumb, unconscious, selfless and agentless' (p. 269). For similar reasons, Knoblich and Jordan (2002) argue that the mirror system is far from sufficient for sophisticated action co-ordination, even though it may play a part. As they note, macaques possess a mirror system but they do not imitate and are rather poor at social coordination. They suggest that, in the macaque, motor receptivity to the effects of conspecifics' actions has the somewhat less interesting function of ensuring that the monkey manages to grab some food before others eat it all (pp. 116–117).

However, even if such concerns are well founded, the existence of a cross-modal mapping between perception and action, regardless of its precise nature, could still be of considerable significance. Indeed, that mirror neurons are part of a low level, automatic process tallies well with the claim that we perceive agency, rather than infer it. Hence they can make an important contribution to intersubjective ability, even though they are only part of the puzzle.

It is also arguable that a perceptual-motor coupling only plays a role in some cases of perception and may be a dispensable source of information regarding gesture, expression and action. Returning to phenomenology, Smith (2003) points out that Husserl's conditions for empathetic pairing need to be fairly abstract, given that an appreciation of other people can still be acquired in cases of sensory impairment. If the link between perception and motor readiness is restricted to the visual modality, it clearly cannot be foundational to intersubjectivity, given that congenitally blind people manage to lead rich interpersonal lives.[9] The same point applies to mirror neurons. If they are exclusively associated with the visual modality, then they cannot be an indispensable ingredient of intersubjectivity. However, although much of the research on mirror neurons has been concerned with visual-motor couplings, recent studies have also reported mirror neurons that are receptive to sound. For example, some respond during motor performance of an action and also to the perceived sound of the same action being performed by someone else (Rizzolatti and Craighero, 2004, p. 173). So it seems that the mirror system may well have more general applicability. Indeed, why stop with vision and hearing? There is surely much to be said about the intimate connections between touching and being touched.[10]

Another question to be addressed is whether human motor responsiveness is specific to other humans. Suppose that the mirror system is just as active when we perceive a cat as it is when we perceive another person. This would suggest that its capacity to illuminate inter*personal* understanding is limited to say the least, given that cat interpretation is a far cry from fully enriched interpersonal interpretation. Rizzolatti and Craighero (2004, p. 179) report that mirror systems in different areas of the human brain do indeed respond to various activities of non-human animals, such as biting, regardless of whether it is performed by a monkey, dog or human. However, they do not respond to actions that are far removed from the observer's own behavioural repertoire. For example, the human mirror system does not respond to perception of a barking dog. This suggests that response is much more robust and wide-ranging when it comes to other humans. So we need not be too worried about putting interpersonal experience on a par with person-dog experience. Mirror neurons only suggest a limited degree of continuity between how we perceive the activities of humans and how we perceive those of non-human animals.

However, even if the role of the mirror system is fairly pervasive in our interpretations of others and perhaps even a prerequisite for an appreciation that others are agents, it is arguable that we are able to assign agency to a perceived movement in the absence of a mirror system response. For example, Heider and Simmel famously asked subjects to watch a film involving two geometrical shapes and to describe the interactions between them. They found that, in certain cases of structured interaction, subjects would interpret what they saw in terms of 'motives' and 'sentiments' (Heider, 1958, pp. 31–32). Movements were also described in terms of goal-directedness, intent, trying and so forth even though they were performed by simple, inanimate shapes and bore little relation to the structure of human action. It is debatable as to whether such interpretations are, like an appreciation of human action, perceptual in nature or whether they involve a process of inference. Nevertheless, under the assumption that the mirror system is not responsive in any way to such patterns of movement, they at least suggest that there are cases where actions are ascribed on the basis of perceptual information without the aid of a perceptual-motor coupling. This does not contradict the view that mirror neurons play an important role in action perception. What it does suggest is that there may be other routes too.

Hence there is some uncertainty concerning the scope of mirror system activity and how central it is to interpersonal understanding. Indeed, we should remain open to the possibility that many claims concerning the interpersonal function of the mirror system will end up being repudiated. However, even if this were to happen, work on mirror neurons can still teach an important lesson, which is that perception of agency and experience is not something that is a priori impossible but something that we can take seriously as an empirical possibility. These studies have also served to draw attention to an important aspect of interpersonal experience; the extent to which it involves bodily responsiveness.

Emotion in expression and meaning in gesture

Resistance to the view that we can perceive emotions, intentions and communicated meanings is founded largely on the assumption, integral to FP, that mental states are internal and *cause* observable behaviour. For example, Wellman claims that, according to commonsense psychology, 'mental states, such as beliefs and desires, are private, internal, and not observable in others' (1990, p. 107). The same, I assume, is also alleged to be the case for some if not all of the features of our mental lives that I have claimed to be perceivable. I argued in Chapter 2 that we should be wary about any appeal to a 'commonsense' psychology. But, as it happens, I do think the view that we perceive much of other people's mental lives is most likely a 'commonsensical' view. As Trevarthan (1993, p. 122) puts it, 'it is simply untrue that human mental states are unobservable, to humans. We can detect the mind states of other people instantly from their expressions, with no training'. A problem with claims like this is that a speedy response to a stimulus need not add up to perceptual recognition. Furthermore, it is not clear from such claims just what it is that we perceive. What is it to perceive a 'mind state'? Stern makes a helpful distinction. Focusing on perception of feeling, he distinguishes 'vitality affects' from 'relational affects'. The former refer to the subtle qualities of an expression. For example, a smile is not simply happy. It can also '"explode" or "dawn" or "fade"' and these aspects blend with the more general quality of happiness (1993, p. 206). The latter are not as manifest in expression and include feelings of being secure, attached, alone, loved, separated and so forth.[11] Stern suggests that relational affects are not directly perceivable but that vitality affects are. One can perceive the subtle qualities of happiness in 'temporal contours of intensity' that are observable on the face (p. 210). However, one could still argue that what is perceived is not a feeling but just what he says: changing contours of intensity. So how do we defend the view that what is actually perceived is the feeling, the meaning or the intention?

The way to go is to reject the view that there is a firm distinction between internal mental states and their external, bodily manifestations. Consider the experience of interpreting another person. How often does it seem to be a matter of reaching behind what is perceptually available, of figuring out what hides behind the shield? I think it is fair to say that such experiences are unusual. One ordinarily experiences a thinking, feeling person, who is fully present in the experience, rather than a mechanism behind which lurks a mind that cannot be experienced. A way of thinking about mental states and behaviours, which accommodates such intuitions, can be developed from Husserl's account of horizons. Recall that, according to Husserl, one does not perceive an *appearance*; one perceives an *appearance of an object* and one does so in virtue of salient possibilities that are integrated into the experience. The possibilities that surround an experienced object are referred to by Husserl as the object's 'horizon'. These possibilities are *there* in the experience, but as possibilities rather than actualities. What actually appears and the possibilities that surround it together constitute a sense of the object.

I suggest that we can apply much the same view to mental states and behaviour. What one sees is not an outer indicator of an internal hidden thing but the presence of an experience, emotion, intention or meaning. It does not appear in its entirety but then neither does a perceived object. Our sense of both is composed not just of what is actually there but of the associated horizon of experiential and practical possibilities. Of course, there is a disanalogy here. Integral to the horizon that constitutes the experience of a chair is the sense that one can walk around it and see the other side. This clearly does not apply in the case of mental states, which are not displayed on the backs of people's heads. However, that the horizons are different in structure is to be expected, given that people and inanimate objects are indeed experienced as quite different from each other. But what is the nature of this difference? Among the possibilities that are offered by others' expressions, gestures and actions are possibilities for communication and, as I will argue in Chapter 6, thoughts, feelings and meanings that are glimpsed in an expression or gesture can be progressively revealed through interaction. People can become more or less open to each other and the possibilities implied in a perceived gesture can be actualised in the context of sustained communication.

Husserl is clear that the space of salient possibilities that comprises an object's horizon is also a space of bodily potentialities. Horizons do not incorporate the entire space of conceivability but are 'predelineated' and central to this predelineation is an 'I can and do, but I can also do otherwise than I am doing' (1960, p. 45). This complements the claim that motor responsiveness structures perception. The possibilities that surround a chair and participate in my experience of what it is are shaped by bodily capacities and dispositions. The same may be said of other people, although the possibilities that they afford are quite different, given that the agent-object and agent-agent bond are different in character.

Gallagher (2001a, p. 190) suggests that intersubjectivity involves, for the most part, body-reading rather than mind-reading. This might suggest a clear distinction between the two (although it is not Gallagher's intention to do so). What I want to suggest is that what one perceives is quite literally an emotion, an intention or even a thought. One perceives only an aspect of it but then again no act of perception engulfs a thing in its entirety and concurrently seizes hold of all the possibilities that it has to offer. It might seem strange to proponents of FP that a mental state is partly present in behaviour. However, my phenomenological case is complemented by a variety of findings in psychology. Consider the relationship between emotion and expression. Ekman (2003) discusses the finding that making an expression can lead one to feel an emotion and remarks that

> Generating emotional experience, changing your physiology by deliberately assuming the appearance of an emotion, is probably not the most common way people express emotion. But it may occur more often than we initially think.
>
> (p. 37)

He proceeds to list several ways in which emotions can be created and manipulated by bodily activities. Given the inter-relationship between feeling and expressing, it seems that the feeling cannot be cleanly dissociated from its expression. Merleau-Ponty puts the point more strongly:

> We must reject the prejudice which makes 'inner realities' out of love, hate or anger, leaving them accessible to one single witness: the person who feels them. Anger, shame, hate, and love are not psychic facts hidden at the bottom of another's consciousness: they are types of behaviour or styles of conduct which are visible from the outside. They exist *on* their face or *in* those gestures, not hidden behind them.
>
> (1964b, pp. 52–53)

Campbell (1997) makes the complementary point that feelings are often individuated through their expression (pp. 48–49). She uses the term 'feeling' in a broad sense, to accommodate standard inventories of emotions, in addition to a host of subtly different feelings that are referred to in literature and throughout everyday life. She also argues that the individuation of feeling can be a collaborative endeavour and that expression not only plays an individuating role but can also determine the intentional object of the feeling (p. 76). Hence certain feelings are what they are and are about what they are about in virtue of the way in which they are expressed.

An objection to this is that people frequently conceal their feelings, indicating that one can have a feeling without displaying it in any way.

This being the case, it is a short step to the claim that feelings are internal states that are contingently manifested in expressions. However, as Campbell (p. 183) notes, it is unlikely that one could experience and yet wholly conceal a feeling on every occasion that it arises without that feeling, each time it recurs, being diminished or altered in some way. Hence that we sometimes conceal, at least in part, a feeling is not sufficient to repudiate the claim that expression participates in feeling. Indeed, the very term 'concealment' suggests that feelings are usually there for all to see but are sometimes hidden, rather than that people sometimes inhibit the outer effects of a distinct inner state. One disguises, conceals or hides one's feelings, rather than their contingent effects.

It is also arguable that the meaning of certain object-directed actions is neither something that one has in mind before the action, in the form of a prior intention, nor something that one has in mind during the action. Rather, the unfolding action itself and its eventual outcome, both available for all to see, together determine its meaning and whether it even has a meaning. Merleau-Ponty (1964b, p. 19) illustrates this through a discussion of the relationship between thought and action in Cézanné's art:

> What he expresses cannot [. . .] be the translation of a clearly defined thought, since such clear thoughts are those which have already been uttered by ourselves or by others. 'Conception' cannot precede 'execution'. There is nothing but a vague fever before the act of artistic expression, and only the work itself, completed and understood, is proof that there was *something* rather than *nothing* to be said.

An analogous point can be made with regard to certain actions in sport and other practical contexts, which I discussed in Chapter 4. Such actions are often solicited and regulated by situations, rather than by prior intentions. Perhaps, in some cases, the meaning of an action or whether it has a clear meaning will depend upon its actual outcome.

Turning to gesture, there is plenty of evidence to suggest that gestures do not merely communicate thought and that thought processes are also partly embodied in gesture. One can literally see thought in the making, at least to a degree. Goldwin-Meadow (1999) discusses the variety of gestures employed in conjunction with speech and reviews evidence suggesting that they have a communicative function. The meaning of a gesture is reliably interpreted by most people in the same way. It also seems that gestures can communicate aspects of thought that are not conveyed in speech. As Goldwin-Meadow puts it:

> Because gesture rests on different representational devices from speech, and is not dictated by standards of form as in speech, it has the potential to offer a different view into the mind of the speaker.
>
> (p. 422)

She offers the example of talking about a coastline while using gesture to outline its structure and notes that the representational medium of gesture is better suited to communicating some details than speech, given that the latter would require one to formulate a cumbersome and most likely unclear account of its idiosyncratic undulations. Goldwin-Meadow remarks that people also tend to gesture in private and that blind people gesture normally, even when addressing other blind people, indicating that gesture may have an intrapersonal as well as an interpersonal role. Otherwise, why gesture if nobody is receptive to it? She cites evidence indicating that gesture has a number of intra-personal functions. For example, it can facilitate memory retrieval. It can also reduce cognitive burden; gesturing while performing certain tasks improves performance, perhaps by encoding information spatially and thus relying on spatial, rather than verbal memory. She also proposes that gesture plays a role in the formation of new thoughts. Some thoughts are expressed in the medium of gesture before they become fully articulate and their embodiment in gesture is perhaps itself part of the process via which they are clarified and developed to a stage where they become articulable. Such a system makes good sense, given that gesture and speech are very different forms of representation. Thus it seems likely that certain kinds of ideas will be better formed and expressed through one than the other (p. 427). Goldwin-Meadow adds that gesture may provide a good nurturing environment in which to culture ideas, as, unlike speech, it is immune from potentially disruptive criticisms that might be offered both by oneself and by others in response to what one says.[12]

Given the likely intra-personal roles of gesture and the inter-personal perceptual sensitivity that we have to it, it would seem that it is possible to perceive something of the structure of thought. Gestures, expressions and actions are not just external expressions of internal thought processes; they are part of those processes. Hence we really can perceive, to some extent, the mental lives of others.[13]

It is worth drawing attention to a further implication of the view that thoughts are partly constituted by gesture and feelings by expression.

Given that dispositions towards certain gestures and expressions, and sometimes actual gestures and expressions, can be directly elicited by perception of somebody else's behaviour, it follows that people directly influence each other's mental lives through interaction. We do so not in a systematic or blunt way, amounting to thought programming or anything sinister like that but in a much more delicate, fragile way. I will suggest in Chapter 6 that this permeability and mutual influence is especially apparent in interpersonal interactions such as good conversations, which rely not so much on an ability to assign mental states as an ability to participate in shared experience.

Explaining action without FP

If we combine perception of action, gesture and expression with the situational understanding discussed in Chapters 4 and 5, we get a sophisticated understanding of action without any input required from FP. Situations are generally presupposed as contexts for interpretation. Thus, when we perceive that A is reaching for x, the broader meaning of the action is usually given in the form of the shared situation. Hence in many cases it is possible to perceive that an action is occurring, what it is directed at and also *why* it is occurring. Most of the time there is no question as to *why*, given that everything we need in order to make sense of the perceived action is part of the situation into which it fits. So, as Schutz (1967) and Gallagher (2001a) both note, when we turn to everyday social encounters, we find that experience alone is usually enough and that there is no need to embark on a search for reasons.

A considerable amount of work can be done with situational understanding and action perception, sometimes supported by knowledge of idiosyncratic traits. This applies not just to interpretation, interaction and coordination but also to explanation. Explanations of perceived actions often take the form of a reference to relevant features of a situation that the party requiring the explanation did not have access to or failed to notice. Reasons can be situational norms, rather than mental states or reasoning processes. Other explanations appeal to idiosyncratic traits and dispositions. Unlike situational norms, these are not reasons in the normative sense of 'reason'. That is, they do not specify why someone ought to have acted in a certain way. However, they do explain why an action occurred or is likely to occur. So, when we perceive an action, we can explain its occurrence in terms of roles, norms, artefact functions, individual circumstances, character traits, projects, idiosyncratic commitments with associated norms and a host of other factors, none of which is FP or implies FP. In Chapter 4, I offered a number of rather brief situational explanations, along the lines of:

'Why did he reach down?' 'Because there was a £20 note on the pavement.'
'What is she doing?' 'She's the ticket inspector.'
'Why aren't we moving?' 'The light's still on red.'

However, situational interpretations of perceived actions can be much more elaborate than this. Actions are interpreted by progressively adding layers of surrounding situational context and moving 'outward', rather than by moving 'inward' and postulating internal states as causes. Consider the following passage from Schutz:

If I observe, or even hear about, a man tightening a nut, my first interpretive scheme will picture him as joining together two parts of an apparatus with a wrench. The further information that the event is taking place in an automobile factory permits me to place the operation within the total context of 'automobile' manufacturing. If I know in addition that the man is an auto worker, then I can assume a great deal about him, for instance, that he comes to work every morning and goes home every night, that he picks up his check every payday, and so on. I can then bring him into a wider context of meaning by applying to him the ideal type 'urban worker' or, more, specifically, 'Berlin worker of the year 1931'. And once I have established the fact that the man is a German and a Berliner, then all the corresponding interpretive schemes become applicable to him.
(1967, pp. 192–193)

The interpretive process that Schutz describes involves the integration of action perception and situational understanding. It is seldom a process that we need to go through explicitly, as situations are, for the most part, already given. However, in cases where the reason for an action is unknown, the ability to understand it frequently involves coming to appreciate the context in which it is embedded. This process of contextualisation is ignored by the FP literature, which tends to place an exclusive emphasis on internal states as reasons for actions. Take this passage from Wellman (1990, p. 8):

John's going to the store to buy groceries, for example, is explained by John's desire to eat and his belief that he can buy food at the grocery store. Similarly, I may decide to go to the grocery store rather than to the drugstore because I desire to get food, not pharmaceuticals, and I believe that food is found at the grocery store.

When compared to the passage from Schutz, this explanation seems curiously empty. Stating that the action is an outcome of internal states goes no way to explaining why it occurred. Consider the following explanations of why John went to the grocery store:

It was shopping day.
John was just passing by on his way back from work and thought he might as well pop in.
They had a special offer on tomatoes.
John had some spare change and he fancied an apple and a can of soda.
John is cooking for friends tomorrow and the shop won't be open then.
John is a health inspector and it's his job to check the quality of all food sold in the area; he's just bought a selection of foodstuffs to take back to the laboratory.
John was doing some shopping for the old lady down the road.
John wanted to keep a conversation going with Sandra. So he followed her into the grocery store and did some shopping himself, so as not to make it too obvious.
John is a chef and he went in to buy some food for his restaurant.

Some of these do refer to psychological states, which may or may not be hidden causes of behaviour. However, all of them also appeal to situational factors that serve to contextualise the action and, in so doing, facilitate its interpretation. Hence, even if something like FP does participate in some explanations of why an action occurred, it does so in conjunction with an outward moving, contextualising, situational understanding. Furthermore, most or all those interpersonal encounters that do not provoke why questions proceed quite happily without FP. Perception of action, gesture and expression in shared situations does all the work. So FP plays, at most, a rather limited role in explanation and prediction. In Chapter 7, I will address the question of what role, if any, the attribution of internal propositional attitudes to predict and explain behaviour does actually play. Before turning to that, I want to further explore the contribution made by bodily responsiveness, interaction and relatedness to interpersonal understanding. Although these factors have been neglected by the FP literature, I will argue in Chapter 6 that most interpersonal understanding is inextricable from frameworks of interaction.

6
The Second Person

A central theme of Chapter 5 was that perception of agency is not a detached affair; bodily responsiveness to people is integral to perception of them. I will further pursue this theme here by emphasising the extent to which interpersonal understanding is embedded in structures of interaction that are facilitated by mutual bodily responsiveness. Throughout the chapter, I will focus on two closely related distinctions:

i. The distinction between second-person and third-person understanding. That is, the difference between understanding someone as a 'you' and understanding someone as a 'he' or 'she'.
ii. The distinction between understanding someone from a detached, inactive standpoint and understanding her through one's interactions with her.

Participants in the FP debate tend to assume that interpersonal understanding can be adequately characterised by focusing exclusively on the first- to third-person relation. There is no mention of any difference between addressing a 'you' and scrutinising a 'he' or 'she'. Neither is there any acknowledgement that observational and interactive understanding might have quite different structures.

A small number of recent critics have suggested that the orthodox emphasis on third-person observational understanding is misleading. For example, Gallagher (2001a) emphasises both interaction and the first- to second-person relation, proposing that interpersonal understanding is ordinarily a matter of 'second-person interaction', rather than 'third-person observation', and that neither theory nor simulation have a role to play in most cases of second-person interaction. Thus he not only criticises the view that we ordinarily rely upon a 'theory' to interpret people but also the assumption that we do so by adopting a 'theoretical' attitude towards them. It is important to keep the two criticisms distinct, as one can make use of a theory without adopting a theoretical stance. For example, doctors employ medical theories in contexts of practice (Churchland, 1998b). Hobson (1993a, 2002) offers a similar view to Gallagher. Focusing on intersubjective development, he stresses the extent to which the understanding that parent and child have of each other emerges through contexts of relatedness. Like Gallagher, he indicates that it is more a matter of I-you interaction than theorising about a 'he' or 'she'. Hobson makes the further claim that our sense of people as *people*, rather than complicated objects, is constituted by our relatedness to them. An affective, bodily receptivity comprises a kind of stance or way of experiencing things and it is only through this stance that entities can be revealed as people.

I am sympathetic to such views and will argue in this chapter that (a) an I-you relation is a better starting point for an exploration of inter-subjectivity than an I-he/she relation or an I-it relation, (b) affective, bodily receptivity to others is constitutive of our sense of them as people and (c) interactive understanding is quite different in character from detached theorising. First of all, I will discuss the difference between an I-you relation and an I-she/he/it relation, exploring the relationship between 'second-person understanding' and 'interaction' in the process. Following this, I will offer a phenomenological illustration of how a bodily, affective responsiveness underlies a sense of people as *people*. Then I will turn to interaction. Gallagher suggests that second-person interaction is the norm and that theoretical stances towards others are rare. I will argue that understanding through interaction is even more widespread than he indicates. Even in cases where interaction might seem to be absent, thoughts about people are accompanied by a variety of bodily responses, which can amount to a kind of 'simulated interaction'. Hence I acknowledge a role for simulation, not as 'A modelling B' but as 'A modelling interaction between two parties, one of which is often A'. Although the role of interaction is more conspicuous in second-person cases, it extends to seemingly detached third-person cases too, in the form of simulated interaction. Interactive understanding is quite different in structure from observational understanding. In order to make the difference clear, I will return to the theme of embodied, embedded cognition. Other people, I will suggest, are not complicated moving objects to be interpreted via the exercise of one's internal cognitive mechanisms. The ability to interpret is not possessed by one, the other or both parties in the form of wholly internalised cognitive abilities. Rather, it is embedded in the interaction between people and is to be understood as a matter of relatedness between them.

Wherefore art Thou?

What is distinctive about experiencing and understanding someone in the second-person? Hobson (1993a, p. 105) states that his use of the distinction between second- and third-person relations follows that of Buber (1958). Buber's *I and Thou* is a somewhat poetic, mystical work. However, it is still possible to extract some interesting claims from it. Buber suggests that the relationship between I and Thou is not a matter of two previously discrete beings coming into contact with each other. Instead, the relation is primary and its two parts are inextricable. He refers to 'I-Thou' as a 'primary word' but does not mean this in a linguistic sense. Instead, he wants to emphasise the primitive nature of the I-Thou relation, which he thinks is more fundamental to our phenomenology than self and other construed as unrelated beings.

According to Buber, the term 'Thou' does not refer to a kind of entity that we first recognise and then address as Thou. Rather, the I-Thou relation is a stance or way of experiencing and it is only through this stance that a being can be encountered as 'Thou' rather than 'it'. And to be able to encounter a being as Thou just is to be able to encounter her as a person, rather than an object. So the I-Thou relation is a kind of openness to the possibility of people. Buber contrasts this with the I-it relation, through which things are encountered as impersonal objects. He restricts the term 'experience' to the latter; one experiences objects but one does not experience people in the same sense. Instead, I-Thou opens up 'the world of relation' (p. 6). People are not experienced in the detached way that a rock might be, as a sense of what people are consists of a distinctive kind of relatedness to them. I do not simply look upon another person but 'take my stand in relation to him' (p. 9). He is experienced as what he is through that 'stand'.

Of course, we do not always address other people in the mode of Thou and a person that one encounters as Thou can also be encountered as he or she or, as Buber puts it, as 'it'. However, when we experience people, rather than stones and the like, through an I-it relation, we do not just take them to be objects. A sense of them as people has its source in I-Thou but, even when they are not addressed through this stance, we continue to grasp them as people in so far as we appreciate their *potentiality* to take up the position of Thou (p. 33). This claim is perhaps complemented by various everyday remarks, such as 'what will he do when I tell him that?'; 'she's really interesting to talk to'; 'what's the best way to approach her about this issue?'; 'I can't wait to meet him'; 'she's great fun to be with' and so forth. A potential Thou is not simply a temporary It but a Thou in waiting. So third-person experience remains *personal*. However, given the primacy of I-Thou, our appreciation of the personal cannot be adequately grasped by any investigation that focuses exclusively on the 'it'. Indeed, Buber remarks that nobody who lived life exclusively through an I-it stance would be a complete person, as to be a person is to be able to enter into relations with other people (p. 34).

If Buber is right, FP amounts to an inadvertent denial of the personal, rather than a characterisation of interpersonal understanding. But can his claims be developed into an argument? One problem is that he simply asserts the primordial nature of I-Thou and says little more about its character. Schutz, as discussed in Chapter 3, offers a slightly clearer account of what the relation consists of. Whereas Buber claims that I-Thou is not affectively structured and that feeling merely accompanies it (p. 81), Schutz emphasises a kind of bodily relatedness, which comprises an openness and permeability to the experiences of another. In Chapter 5, I argued that we do indeed have a perceptual appreciation of agency and experience, which involves a multi-faceted, bodily, affective responsiveness that is quite different in character from our responsiveness to inanimate objects. However, Schutz's account indicates that there is more to a Thou orientation than just having this kind of response. An I-Thou relation involves mutual receptivity to and synchronisation of experience and activity. The relevant bodily responsiveness is incorporated into intricate patterns of ongoing interaction between people and it is through these interactions that an appreciation of what is distinctive about people is most manifest.

Thus, if we follow Schutz, it would seem that the term 'second-person interaction' does refer to a distinctive way of encountering people. Second-person experience cannot be decoupled from interaction, given that a Thou-orientation consists of patterns of relatedness that are embedded in interaction. In this chapter, I will defend just such a view. However, before I do so, some further clarification of the terms 'second-person' and 'interaction' is required.

The term 'second-person experience' cannot refer to a distinctive kind of experience that is reliably correlated with linguistic use of the second-person pronoun or with addressing someone verbally. Looking into someone's eyes and sincerely saying 'I love you' is a far cry from saying 'can you give me another bag please' to a shop assistant. While the former is a deeply personal experience, the latter could accommodate a variety of stances towards the other person, including, in the extreme case, a failure to even register her as anything more than a means of getting a shopping bag. Perhaps, as indicated by Gallagher, the relevant distinction between second- and third-person maps onto that between interaction and observation. However, interaction between people is not restricted to instances where they are addressed in the second-person. There are many cases of interaction where we regard the other person as a 'he' or 'she', such as competitive interaction, where we sometimes ask 'what is he going to do next?'. And routine exchanges like asking for the shopping bag, where the word 'you' is employed but the other person is encountered as little, if anything, more than the embodiment of a role, are still interactions with people rather than observations of them. So an account is needed of the relevant kind of interaction and of the sense in which it can be said to take a 'second-person' form.

To add to the problem, there are various other relations, in addition to 'I-you' and the 'I-he/she/it', which can be further differentiated into those that involve observation and those that involve some kind of interaction. Consider 'us looking at you' or 'us interacting with you' (where 'you' can be singular or plural), 'you and me interacting with each other while theorising about her', 'us watching you interacting with her/them' and so forth. All of these could potentially serve as linguistic clues that point to distinctive forms of experiencing or understanding. So it is important not to impose an overly restrictive linguistic distinction between second- and third-person pronouns onto the structure of social life.

Third-person experience is not a homogeneous category either. Buber's description of experience does not distinguish between I-it and I-he/she. However, even when we encounter people in the third-person, we do not experience and understand them as complex objects, despite what the language of certain proponents of FP might suggest. People are encountered as objects only in those contexts where interpersonal understanding is wholly absent. Although trampling over screaming bodies in order to reach the fire exit of a burning theatre may amount to regarding them as objects, one is not, in that context, seeing them as people at all. A third-person stance is not an objective stance (Goldie, 2000, pp. 181–182). This does not bode well for theory theory, which fails to make any such distinction.

The third-person encompasses several different ways of relating to people. A third-person stance might be adopted towards somebody out of dislike, as a refusal to engage with her as 'you', or because communication is physically impossible. Actively ignoring somebody is very different from observing him with interest from afar or spying on him. Many other distinctions can be drawn. A distance might be retained out of respect, fear or shyness. One could regard another person with the aim of manipulating her. Or one might sympathise with her, feel pity towards her or adopt a stance of curiosity towards her activities. So the label 'third-person' fails to do justice to the numerous different stances or attitudes that we adopt towards each other. Some of these involve quite different ways of experiencing people. The experience of ignoring a person or pretending not to see him is different from that of watching his movements with indifference. Third-person encounters also make various different interpretive demands. While watching someone on the other side of the street, one may be content to simply observe her, relying wholly on the kind of experiential appreciation I described in Chapter 5 and refraining from further interpretive efforts. In sympathising with someone, there is emotional engagement and a sense of relatedness. Thoughts about her will reflect this relatedness, perhaps taking the form 'what shall I do?' or 'what can I do?', rather than just 'what is she thinking or feeling?' Other interpretive efforts will be more preoccupied with the relevance of an activity to one's own concerns; 'did he leave in a hurry because he's annoyed with me?; 'does what she just said suggest that I'll lose my job?' In other cases, we might just be curious as to the meaning of a passing stranger's seemingly incongruous activities. And the list goes on. In none of these scenarios is the other simply experienced as a kind of object. There are many ways of relating to and distancing oneself from people but the neutral, detached stance through which one might examine a quartz crystal captures none of them. It would amount to an indifference to personhood, an absence of intersubjectivity.

Which of our diverse interpersonal relations should the term 'second-person interaction' accommodate? Hobson and Gallagher both emphasise patterns of dialogical interaction, of the kind that characterise, for example, a good conversation. And the relevant contrast between second- and third-person experience tracks, to some extent at least, differences in how second- and third-person pronouns operate in the context of conversation. Stawarska (2007) notes that the third-person can operate as a substitute for a noun phrase, such as 'the person next door'. Hence it can be employed to refer, in a stable fashion, to a particular entity that is being discussed. However, 'I' and 'you' do not require pre-established referents in the same way. Furthermore, while the referent of 'she' or 'he' stays constant, 'I' and 'you' are indexicals that are reversed in an ongoing fashion as the narrative proceeds, with each party being addressed as 'you' and responding as 'I'. The movement of 'you' and 'I' reflects the pattern of interaction between participants. The stability of 'he' or 'she' is indicative of that party's non-participant status. Stawarska appeals to the work of Benveniste, who emphasises the contrast between first- and second-person pronouns on the one hand, and the third-person pronoun on the other, remarking that Arab grammarians define 'I' as 'the speaker', 'you' as 'the addressee' and 'she' or 'he' as 'the one who is absent'. The way in which we relate to others as people, she argues, is better understood by emphasising typical I-you relations than I-she/he relations, given that the latter often involve an absence of interpersonal relatedness. This is exemplified by the frequent irritation that people express when referred to as 'he' or 'she' while they are present. Understanding someone in the third-person is not the essence of intersubjectivity but a withdrawal from it and, in some cases, a refusal of it.

Thus, in discussing second-person interaction, what I have in mind is an experience of interpersonal relatedness that is embedded in patterned, dialogical interactions between people.[1] Aside from those cases where we rely wholly on shared norms and roles, almost all interpersonal relations involve reciprocity of gesture, word or expression, rather than being a matter of the detached scrutiny of one party by another. This reciprocity can involve brief mutual greetings, smiles, nods, waves and so forth or it may take the form of a lengthy pattern of verbal and non-verbal interaction. What I want to look at here is the extent to which our appreciation of what people are and what they do is embedded in patterns of communicative, bodily interaction. I will start by offering a phenomenological illustration of how a distinctive kind of bodily sensitivity can be, at the same time, a sense of another as a person. Then I will discuss pre-linguistic dialogical relations between infants and caregivers, before turning to the role played by patterns of bodily relatedness in adult conversation.

Sartre on intersubjectivity

In Chapter 5, I appealed to both phenomenological descriptions and findings in neurobiology to argue that appreciating someone as a locus of experience and agency involves a distinctive kind of bodily responsiveness comprised, at least in part, of patterns of motor-readiness and an affective sensitivity to gestures and expressions. The contribution made by this responsiveness is not always apparent to casual reflection, given that the relevant responses are incorporated into perception of other people and need not take the form of conspicuous feelings of one's own body. However, on some occasions when we encounter another person, there are quite pronounced changes in how our bodies feel and, with a bit of phenomenological reflection, it can be seen that these changes structure the way in which that person is experienced. Certain such experiences serve as the basis for Sartre's account of inter-subjectivity in *Being and Nothingness* and it is to his discussion that I now turn in order to further illustrate the inextricability of the sense 'another person' from affective, bodily response. I do not wish to endorse every aspect of Sartre's view. My aim is to use his discussion to illustrate *that* intersubjectivity is a matter of bodily relatedness, rather than to illustrate the form that this relatedness usually takes.

Sartre claims that our experience of others is direct; it does not orig-inate in an inference from observable behaviour to hidden mental states. He appeals to the feeling of 'shame' to illustrate how others are encountered as *others*, rather than inanimate entities. One can be peep-ing through a keyhole, spying on someone else's private pastimes and, when engrossed in such activities, one is not explicitly aware of one's own body as an object. However, things suddenly change when a creak is heard on the stair behind and one becomes aware of being looked upon by another. According to Sartre, this awareness does not take the form of an inference but of a self-altering feeling, through which one's body becomes conspicuous. He describes it as follows:

> I have just made an awkward or vulgar gesture. This gesture clings to me; I neither judge it nor blame it. I simply live it. [. . .] But now suddenly I raise my head. Somebody was there and has seen me. Suddenly I realize the vulgarity of my gesture, and I am ashamed.
>
> (p. 221)

It is clear that what he calls 'shame' is a kind of affective, bodily response. It is 'an immediate shudder which runs through me from head to foot without any discursive preparation' (p. 222). Registering the presence of another involves a change in one's own orientation towards the world, a *feeling* of being scrutinised that breaks up the coherence of one's prior concerns. The project of spying, in which one was previously absorbed, disintegrates. One is no longer a locus of prac-tical projects but an entity that stands before somebody else, an object for them. This affective re-orientation, Sartre suggests, does not just accompany the experience of another person. It *is* itself a sense of 'the Other'. Shame is not merely a feeling of one's own body, given that a modification of how one's body feels is at the same time the sense that someone is present. As he puts it, 'I am ashamed of myself as I *appear* to the Other' (p. 222).

It might be objected that one's relationship to another person must be recognised *before* one can feel ashamed. Shame is either an evaluative judgement that is made regarding one's conduct in a given social situation or, alternatively, a feeling that one has, having appraised a situation in a certain way. But, whichever the case, the relevant interpersonal context is already understood. The simplest response to this is to note that, although 'shame' could be understood in such ways, Sartre means something different by it. For Sartre, shame is not an attitude that is adopted towards a pre-established self-other relation but is constitutive of that relation. It is thus analogous to Scheler's 'primitive givenness' of the other. Just as the latter constitutes a sense of the other and is presupposed by feelings like sympathy and empathy, Sartrean shame is presupposed by the kind of 'shame' that one might feel after one's relationship to another has been established.

Sartre does not take affective transformation of self before the other to be a one-off event but a dynamic process of interaction, whereby self and other engage in a play of mutual objectification. He paints a rather bleak picture of intersubjectivity, which, he claims, often takes the form of a doomed attempt by both parties to relate to each other as people and, at the same time, to objectify them. For example, he construes love as the attempt to possess another person as an object. This will always fail, as the moment you possess someone in this way, you lose the sense of her as a person and it was precisely the person that you sought to possess (p. 376). He stresses a tension in interpersonal experience, an unstable dynamic between freedom and objectification. Before the other, one loses one's status as a locus of projects and purposes, instead becoming thing-like. One escapes this predicament by objectifying the other, thus freeing oneself from her own objectifying gaze. So we have an ongoing dynamic between people, where interaction is characterised in terms of strategies to objectify others and to constrain their potential to turn things around, to keep them contained. This direct, perceptual, affective interaction is, Sartre says, more primitive than any theoretical or detached understanding that one might employ. The other is experienced with immediacy and no inference, theorising or modelling is required; she 'is present to me without any intermediary as a transcendence which is not mine' (p. 270).

Sartre claims that the feeling of shame reveals what he calls 'the look' of the other. By 'the look', he means something more abstract than a pair of eyes gazing at one:

> Of course, what *most often* manifests a look is the convergence of two ocular globes in my direction. But the look will be given just as well on occasion where there is a rustling in the branches, or the sound of a footstep followed by silence, or the slight opening of a shutter, or a light movement of a curtain.
>
> (p. 257)

So the look is not something in the world with a physically identifiable structure. But surely, if a rustling in the branches can do it, some kind of cognitive process is required in order to infer the presence of another from changes in inanimate objects? Sartre acknowledges that the look does not guarantee another person's presence on any particular occasion. One can sense the look, only to find that the shadowy figure at the side of the path is, after all, a shrub. However, he is not making a point about whether and how we know for sure that another person is present. Instead, he is describing the structure of our sense of the personal. His claim is that shame involves a kind of responsiveness that is itself our openness to the possibility of others. It embodies the relation that he calls 'being-seen-by-another' and Sartre suggests that our sense of someone being a person consists of the 'permanent possibility of *being-seen-by-him*' (p. 257). One can objectify the other to some extent so as to keep her contained but, Sartre claims, the other is never experienced as wholly object-like. Something cannot be experienced as both a person and a *mere* thing. The sense that she is a person is preserved by her potentiality to manifest the look; 'the Other is in no way given to us as an object. The objectivation of the Other would be the collapse of his being-as-a-look' (p. 268).

Hence an openness to the possibility of others and our sense that they are quite different from objects is, according to Sartre, composed of an affective, bodily responsiveness. An appreciation of people is relational. It involves permeability to them in the guise of a certain feeling, a disposition to be affected by them in a particular way. Sartre's account, like Buber's, implies that any study of intersubjectivity that focuses exclusively on how people are encountered via detached theorising will fail to articulate our appreciation of what is distinctive about them. People will not be revealed as people to a disinterested cogniser who is not open to them.

Although Sartre recognises that the look can be instantiated in different scenarios, such as a creaking stair, the opening of a door or the sound of laughter, he recognises the primacy of embodied interaction, claiming that 'the Other is originally given to me as a *body in situation*' (p. 344). However, this is not to suggest that a physical body is apprehended and that mental states are then postulated as the causes of bodily movements. For Sartre, a sense of the Other as an experiencing agent or 'for-itself', rather than an object or 'in-itself', is tied up with the way in which her body is experienced. The other's body is perceived *as* a locus of experiences and projects. This perception is at the same time an affective transformation of one's own body, which one becomes aware of as an object situated within the context of the other's projects. As Sartre puts it, 'the original bond with the Other', upon which the objectifying interplay between self and other is based, 'first arises in connection with the relation between my body and the Other's body' (p. 361).

Sartre's description of Being-for-others emphasises an irresolvable tension in interpersonal relations. One might protest that it is, at best, a description of certain pathological relationships and fails to capture the mutual openness that characterises many forms of interpersonal experience and interaction. Indeed, Merleau-Ponty suggests that Sartrean objectification before the gaze of another is something that only happens in certain cases where interaction fails to proceed smoothly. On some occasions,

> . . . each of us feels his actions to be not taken up and understood, but observed as if they were an insect's. This is what happens, for instance, when I fall under the gaze of a stranger.
>
> (1962, p. 361)

It is phenomenologically implausible to maintain, as Sartre does, that the reciprocity embodied in a conversation between friends is a dance of mutual objectification or that the smile of a lover is 'the death of my possibilities' (p. 271). Furthermore, Sartre has a very individualistic understanding of practical possibilities. He does not take account of joint projects, in which two or more parties work together to open up and nurture a shared space of possibilities. Of course, he could maintain that the conflictual relations he discusses are more fundamental to our appreciation of others than experiences that involve sharing and mutual openness. However, his discussion includes no argument for such a claim. So I can see no reason not to adopt a more accommodating account of intersubjectivity, according to which Sartrean conflict only applies in certain, perhaps pathological, cases.

However, we can accept all these criticisms and still draw an important lesson from Sartre. Although he focuses on certain interpersonal relations, which are perhaps untypical, his descriptions do draw attention to features of interpersonal experience that are more generally applicable. In emphasising the 'danger' and 'uneasiness' that we sometimes sense in experiencing others (p. 275), he makes salient the extent to which senses of self and of other are locked together in experience. Ways in which we experience other people are also ways in which we experience ourselves. Invasion of one's own possibilities is an extreme instance of something that is more generally the case, the permeability of self to the experiences and activities of others. Furthermore, his claim that a kind of felt bodily response is, at the same time, our sense of others indicates that interpersonal relatedness is a matter of mutual bodily receptivity. Sartre's discussion also emphasises structured interpersonal interaction. He does not make a distinction between I-Thou and I-he/she/it. And examples such as 'the sound of a footstep' suggest a sense of the presence of a 'he' or 'she', rather than an orientation towards a 'you'. However, he does stress the way in which sustained face-to-face interactions involve a to-ing and fro-ing between participants. He construes such patterns of interaction in terms of each party attempting to contain or objectify the other. However, if such negative connotations are left aside, what we are left with is a dialogical structure, a back and forth movement between a 'you' and an 'I', rather than a static relation between a detached observer and an observed third-person. Hence we can draw from Sartre the view that intersubjectivity is best construed as a matter of bodily reciprocity embedded in ongoing interaction.

A proponent of FP might argue that FP underlies the kind of bodily, affective receptivity that Sartre describes. For example, A is ashamed before B because A believes that B believes that spying is wrong; A also believes that spying is wrong; A believes that B has seen A and so forth. So what looks like a bodily responsiveness that contributes to perception is actually supported by largely tacit abilities to attribute various internal mental states. But the question arises as to why we *should* reinterpret the experience in these terms, even though we can, if we want, impose an FP framework upon it. One reason to resist such a move is that complicated patterns of gestural and expressive interaction between people, incorporating a distinctive kind of mutual perceptual-affective receptivity, are evident in exchanges between parents and very young children long before the latter are claimed to develop FP abilities. As I will discuss in the next section, various accounts of early parent-child interaction complement some of the claims I have drawn from Sartre but without emphasising conflict. I will also argue that adult interpersonal understanding, although supplemented by spoken language, continues to depend upon such perceptual-affective relations in a way that FP fails to recognise.

Interaction

It is odd that FP does not pick up on the importance of interaction and relatedness between people. As I noted in Chapter 2, undergraduate students, in responding to a questionnaire that addressed their intuitive view of interpersonal understanding, seldom offered anything resembling FP. However, the most consistent theme that emerged, which was remarked upon in 60% of my 2005 questionnaires, was the connection between understanding and relatedness, with an emphasis on conversation. Here are two such responses, both quoted verbatim:

> Understanding others for me comes through the interaction of that person with myself. What makes it different than with that of a rock is that you engage with the person and feed your understanding of them from the responses and reactions they give.
>
> I guess the main difference between interacting with a rock and a person is the level of response – essentially it's a two way system. When I'm talking to a person I can converse and receive or at least observe a reaction, even if this may be silence. That's to say that understanding is not necessarily verbal.

I think these responses are pretty much right. The key point can be couched in terms of embodied, embedded cognition. The ability to interpret other people is not wholly internalised but is partly composed of structured patterns of interaction with relevant features of the environment (that is, with people). So it is a mistake to think of interpersonal understanding in terms of an internal cognitive ability that can be deployed in contexts of both observation and interaction, given that the ability cannot be dissociated from the interaction. Furthermore, people are not just objects of cognition or objects that are manipulated so as to facilitate cognition. What they do is integral to the cognitive achievement. It is the relations between people that constitute their ability to interpret each other.

There are many varieties of social interaction, which require and facilitate different kinds and levels of social understanding. The example of navigating a subway system, discussed in Chapter 4, is a case where much of the burden of interaction and coordination is placed upon the shared world. It is a case of embodied, embedded cognition but one that relies on norms, roles and functions more so than on an understanding generated by one-to-one interactions between people. The contribution made by others' expressions, gestures and actions to the interpretive process is negligible in many such cases. It is a different matter when we turn to conversation. Conversations come in several varieties. A verbal exchange between a mortgage broker and a house purchaser or between a salesperson and a client may be quite rigidly constrained by the relevant norms and roles. A casual conversation with a stranger on a train may, as it progresses, become far less constrained. Conversation can serve several different purposes too. We might converse so as to give/receive/exchange information, to solicit and share opinions, seek reassurance, provoke, placate or console someone, facilitate mutual cooperation or maybe because we are expected to make conversation in a given situation. And it is very often the case that we just engage in conversation for conversation's sake. Face-to-face conversation consists of intricate, ongoing patterns of interaction between parties, involving words, tones, expressions, gestures and actions. As noted by one of the students quoted above, even silence can convey meaning.

Structured interaction is evident from a very early age, before spoken language develops. It is well established that very young infants respond to emotional expressions and gestures with attention, gaze, expression and sometimes imitation. Hobson (1993a,b, 2002) appeals to numerous studies of autistic and typical children of various ages to make the stronger claim that infant-parent exchanges take the form of a proto-dialogue, which is enabled by mutual perception of affect in expression, during structured interaction. He suggests that, although young infants are unable to conceptualise intentional states, they display 'capacities to *perceive* a range of overt, bodily-expressed attitudes in other people' (1993a, p. 103). Interactions do not generally take the form of simple, brief perception-response exchanges. They are often lengthy and complicated, involving distinguishable stages such as initiation, mutual orientation, greeting, play dialogue and, finally, affective disengagement (2002, p. 35). He claims that early interaction involves neither 'behaviour-reading' nor 'mind-reading' on the part of the infant. As I argued in Chapter 5, one need not *infer* meaning from behaviour; one perceives it *in* the behaviour. As Hobson puts it, infants have 'direct perception of and natural engagement with person-related meanings that are apprehended *in* the expressions and behaviour of other persons' (1993a, p. 117).

Hobson argues that early interpersonal abilities do not depend on an infant's internal capacities, operating without the aid of interaction; 'it is not the case that to begin with, behaviour is perceived in a cool, detached way' (1993b, p. 214). They instead involve a mutual receptivity that is partly constituted by and grows through affective, bodily interaction. Parent and child together configure a framework for their exchanges, through patterned reciprocity of gesture, expression and affect. Hence structured interaction with others is inextricable from an infant's developing ability to understand and relate to them. This kind of mutual responsiveness, Hobson suggests, is integral to our sense of others as people. The sense of being with another person involves a characteristic bodily relatedness, which does not ordinarily accompany our experiences of inanimate objects.

Others have made similar claims on the basis of a range of ecological studies that emphasise interactions between infants and caregivers in familiar environments, rather than the exercise of cognitive skills in response to unfamiliar, observed situations. For example, Neisser (1993) proposes that 'face-to-face interaction between individuals establishes a sense of an inter-personal self that is very different from anything the inanimate environment can offer' (p. 3). One does not merely perceive behaviour but also perceives its 'reciprocity with one's own', through the bodily relatedness that characterises interaction. Almost every encounter we have with others is not observational but, rather, 'mutually regulated' (p. 10). Neisser reports that young infants have what he calls 'protoconversations' from the age of six to eight weeks, composed of ongoing, structured patterns of mutual bodily response. Various experimental findings indicate that infants' responses to the expressions and gestures of parents are communicative in nature, rather than being mere reactions. For example, one well-known experiment involved two scenarios. In the first, infant and mother interacted with each other via closed-circuit television. In the second, the infant was shown a videotape of the mother behaving as she normally would during interaction. Infants reacted normally in the closed-circuit television scenario but became quickly distressed when watching a videotape, where none of their responses were reciprocated (Neisser, 1993, p. 17). Hence infants do not just *respond* to the expressions and gestures of a caregiver; behaviour regulation goes both ways. Early intersubjectivity is not a matter of detached, disembodied perception and inference.

It involves a mutual bodily attunement, regulated and enhanced through patterned interactions. Trevarthan (1993, p. 137) puts it nicely:

> The two subjects become entrained on one beat, so the pattern of engagement draws them along in a duet of synchronized or alternating parts [. . .] to the regulation of which both contribute.

As with a musical duet, what is important is not just the responses elicited but a sense of relatedness, cooperation and sharing. As Stern (1993, p. 205) remarks, 'the crucial event is not only the feeling experienced but also the experience of interpersonal evocation or regulation or sharing'. This is quite different in character from an understanding that depends wholly upon the internal cognitive capacities of individuals. It is not a matter of deploying internal abilities so as to interpret an observed situation and act accordingly but of interacting with people in such a way as to create the conditions that facilitate mutual understanding and coordination.[2]

Gallagher (2001a) argues that this kind of interaction is sufficient to facilitate most adult social achievements too. As noted in Chapter 4, proponents of FP tend to regard early perceptual and affective abilities as steps en route to a fully fledged FP. Consider the three mechanisms postulated by Baron-Cohen (1995, Chapter 4), which are claimed to come into operation before the ability to attribute propositional attitudes:

a. A perceptual 'intentionality detector'.
b. An 'eye direction detector' which, amongst other things, triggers arousal and affective response when somebody else is looking at you.
c. A 'shared attention mechanism' that enables an appreciation that one is looking at the same object as somebody else.

Baron-Cohen regards these as developmental precursors to a theory of mind mechanism and suggests that they continue to support the function of that mechanism in adults. However, according to Gallagher, such early abilities remain the *primary* source of interpersonal understanding even in adults. He lists a range of practical and perceptual abilities, including 'imitation, intentionality detection, eye-tracking, the perception of intentional and goal-related movements, and the perception of meaning and emotion in movement and posture' (2001a, p. 90). Taken together, these, he suggests, can usually do all the work without any need to resort to FP. Propositional attitude attribution is a specialised, marginal skill that is not required in order to negotiate most social situations.[3]

Gallagher distinguishes between strong and weak pragmatic claims that might be made on behalf of FP, the former being that it is widespread or even ubiquitous and the latter being that it is something we resort to only sometimes, in the guise of theory, simulation or a combination of the two. He poses the following question:

In the situation of talking with someone else about a third person, it seems possible to describe our attitude toward the person under discussion as theoretical or as involving a simulation of the other person's mental states. But does the same description capture the dynamics of our interaction with our interlocutor?

(2001a, p. 93)

The answer, he says, is no. Theory and simulation both involve a third-person, observational stance towards others, which is quite different from understanding through interaction and something we resort to only infrequently. Hence only the weak pragmatic claim should be accepted.

However, I will suggest that not even this much should be conceded. Any form of understanding deserving of the label 'inter*personal*' will involve, to some extent, the kind of bodily, affective receptivity and interaction described above. The presence of interaction is much more salient in some cases but is, I will argue, far more widespread than it might appear to be. Even supposedly detached, voyeuristic contemplation is often in fact a kind of interactive understanding. First of all, I will emphasise the contribution made by perceptual-affective interaction to adults' social understanding. Then I will address the question of how far the scope of interactive understanding extends.

That affective, perceptual interaction plays a central role in adult as well as infant interpersonal relations can be illustrated by looking at cases where it is disrupted. Cole (1998, 2001a,b) addresses the contribution made by facial expression and its perception to interpersonal interaction, by exploring cases where the ability to express oneself facially or to perceive facial expressions is impaired or absent. He notes the biological uniqueness of the human face and its capacity for expressiveness, also observing that interactions between people usually involve an intricate interplay of perception of expression and expressive response. Breakdown of this interaction occurs in those with certain facial problems, such as Möbius syndrome, a form of facial paralysis. As a consequence, the ability to interpret and relate to others is substantially impaired. As Cole observes, 'those with facial differences describe a loss of social relatedness leading to profound social isolation and to an impoverished sense of self' (2001b, p. 478). He describes the predicament of one subject with facial paralysis as follows:

> . . . without the feedback and reinforcement between people that facial gestures provide, there was little relatedness and engagement. Her loss of facial responsiveness made her feel somehow invalidated at her very core.
>
> (1998, p. 10)

The social difficulties that some people with facial problems face also make salient the extent to which interaction involves mutual regulation, with each party playing an active role in structuring exchanges. As Cole (2001a, p. 61) observes, 'people with facial disfigurement often become passive, only ever reacting to others and never daring to control conversations and interactions themselves'. Similarly, Hull (1990) describes how becoming blind deprived him of an expressive relatedness that people ordinarily take for granted. This deprivation, he says, 'tends to make you passive in getting to know people' (p. 97), leading to mutual awkwardness and problems with initiating and withdrawing from conversations.[4]

Such cases illustrate how dialogical interaction of expression and feeling contributes to interpersonal understanding. Perception of another's expression involves an affective response, which is often manifested in one's own expression. The other person responds to this and so forth. Expressions and gestures are not usually interpreted from a detached, observational standpoint but in the context of their being solicited and modified in response to one's own expressions and gestures. This interplay constitutes an openness or receptivity between people; a dynamic framework within which the task of mutual understanding is played out. We do not have to appeal to clinical cases in order to appreciate this. Most of us have had the experience of a conversation where we feel detached from the other participant, as though we have somehow failed to make contact. On occasions, the dance of expression, gesture and eye contact fails to flow, the conversation breaks down and we feel a failure to 'connect'. Breakdowns of mutual understanding need not take the form of an inability to infer the relevant intentional states. They more often involve a *feeling* of distance, an absence of the to-and-fro of expression and gesture that ordinarily operates as a harmonious backdrop for mutual understanding. What is interesting about these situations is not only the extent to which the capacity to interpret the other person is affected by that person's lack of response but also the accompanying experience of one's own social abilities being somehow diminished. It is not just that the other person fails to give out certain cues and is therefore difficult to interpret. The absence of such cues affects one's own responsiveness. The spontaneous tendency to gesture, smile and more generally express oneself diminishes. In conjunction with this, one can feel hollow, empty, awkward, distant, removed from it all or a host of other ways that reflect an unusual and uncomfortable lack of relatedness.[5]

What we see in such cases is not just the social failure of one person but a loss of relatedness that affects the ability of each to interpret the other. People are permeable to each other and our abilities to relate and interpret depend, to a considerable extent, on how others respond to us. But how can a lack of expression on the part of another person diminish one's own feelings and interpretive abilities? There is evidence that lack of expression on the part of one party is met by lack of expression by the other (Buck, 1993, p. 230). And, as discussed in Chapter 5, evidence from mirror neurons and other sources suggests that reciprocity of expression is not a matter of making considered decisions as to how to respond but, more often, of a response being directly solicited by another person's behaviour. In so far as gesture and expression are constitutive of thought processes, an unresponsive person can indeed have a direct effect upon one's interpretive abilities by influencing one's gestures and expressions.

Throughout this section, I have referred to the role of 'affect' in regulating interpersonal understanding. It is important to be clear about what is meant by this term. The task of defining 'affect' or 'feeling' is not an easy one. As Hobson remarks, there is 'no precise meaning to the term "affect"' (1993b, p. 212). However, the relevant contrast between affective interaction and FP can be drawn without the need to formulate a strict definition of 'affect' or a comprehensive taxonomy of affects. By 'affects', I mean a variety of bodily responses to stimuli. These responses are 'felt'. However, the way in which they are felt need not take the form of a perception of one's own bodily state, as affects can contribute to experiences of things other than the body (Ratcliffe, 2004b, 2005c,d). Elsewhere, I have argued this point by drawing an analogy between tactile feelings and feelings more generally (2005c, forthcoming). When we touch something, we experience a *relation* between ourselves and the object, rather than simply a feeling of our own body *or* a feeling of the object. However, which side of the relation takes up the experiential foreground varies from case to case. It can be the part of one's body that is doing the touching or the object that is being touched. In other words, the object of the feeling can be oneself or something other than oneself. The same, I suggest, applies to the 'feelings' or 'affects' involved in interpersonal interaction. A particular feeling may be most salient as a sense of how things are with one's own body or, alternatively, as a way in which another person is experienced.

I also want to stress the inextricability of feeling and its manifestation in expression and gesture. As discussed in Chapter 5, feelings are perceived in others' expressions and gestures. And the perception of feeling itself involves feelings, which are themselves bound up with expressions and gestures. Hence two important differences between affective interaction and FP-style attribution of mental states are:

(a) We interact with people by *responding* to feelings with feelings, partly constituted by expression and gesture, rather than by *conceptualising* feelings or *attributing* them.
(b) Patterns of affective response are inextricable from interaction, rather than being the product of internalised abilities that are deployed during interaction.

Affective interaction, as I have described it here, would seem to be non-conceptual. Hence it might be objected that it has no bearing on the sophisticated conceptual understanding that adults often employ when interacting with each other. However, it would be wrong to maintain that the ability to appreciate people conceptually can be cleanly dissociated from expressive and gestural interaction. I have argued that a bodily receptivity to others is integral to our perceptual experience of them. We perceive actions through activation of our own motor systems. And our sense that we are in the presence of a person is, I have suggested, also comprised of a kind of bodily receptivity that structures experience. Hence the issue of what is and is not conceptual hinges, in part, on what we take the relevant 'experience' to consist of. Should experiences of people and of actions, expressions and gestures be regarded as conceptual in nature? There are various possibilities. For example:

i. Conceptual understanding is embedded in the structure of the experience and not neatly dissociable from it.
ii. Concepts such as 'person' and 'action' originate in certain kinds of experience but are not part of those experiences. They are instead part of our talk and thought about certain experiential objects.

iii. Concepts that we learn shape the ways in which we experience.
iv. Concepts are applied during experience but concept application is dissociable from experiencing.

Many more options can be listed, not all of which will be mutually exclusive. The problem in deciding between them is that there are many different concepts of 'concept' and which position we opt for will depend on what we take concepts to be. I certainly do not want to deny that perceptual experience has conceptual structure, at least in some sense of 'conceptual'. As I argued in Chapters 3 and 4, we experience the world as a realm of norms, roles and functions. This surely involves a kind of conceptual appreciation, although one with a rather different structure to FP. I am sympathetic to the view expressed by Noë (2004, Chapter 3) that concepts originate in skilled perception and that the line between perceptual experience and conceptual thought is not an easy one to draw (pp. 117–118). Consider gesture, for example. As discussed in Chapter 5, conversational gestures have inter- and intrapersonal roles, both of which can serve to reveal something of what a participant is thinking. Interpersonal gesturing is not a form of action comparable to intentional action, but a kind of embodied communication, more closely allied to speech in both its phenomenology and its neurobiology. In our interactions with others, appreciation of gesture is sometimes inextricable from appreciation of a conversational narrative. As Gallagher puts it:

> Gesture is not a form of instrumental action that takes place within a virtual or narrative space. Rather, gesture is an action that helps to *create* the narrative space that is shared in the communicative situation.
> (2005a, p. 117)

If gestures do indeed embody communicative meanings in a quasi-linguistic way, the distinction between a linguistic, conceptual understanding and a receptiveness to non-conceptual bodily activities may be far from clear. However, for current purposes, and to avoid a lengthy detour concerning the nature of concepts, I want to settle for the weaker claim that our *ability* to understand each other conceptually is embedded in our practical, affective, bodily relations. This need not imply that some or all of the relevant concepts are themselves constituted by patterns of bodily responsiveness, only that the ability to successfully apply them is. Affective interaction is not wholly distinct from conceptual understanding but is, rather, an indispensable ingredient of that understanding.

We do not simply possess an internal ability to interpret people conceptually, which is applied in the same way during observation and interaction. This, I will now suggest, is apparent from everyday conversations, which clearly incorporate conceptual content given that they involve language. (And it is worth noting that linguistic ability is generally not claimed to depend upon FP ability. Thus the introduction of conversation need not amount to the introduction of FP.)

Conversational interaction

According to Hobson (2002, p. 42), early affective interaction serves as scaffolding for the development of language, meaning that the development of linguistic communication is embedded in and nurtured by affective, bodily dialogue. Adult conversation continues to be regulated and supported by patterns of non-linguistic interaction, as is evident from face-to-face conversational interactions that involve the cooperative construction of shared narratives. Hobson notes that his account of affective interaction is complemented by the work of Bruner and others on the role of narrative interaction in interpersonal interpretation. For example, Bruner and Feldman (1993) argue that the primary deficit involved in autism is not, as is often maintained, an impaired capacity to attribute internal mental states. They suggest that it is better characterised as a failure to fully participate in the narratives that are typically generated through interpersonal interaction. In linguistic interactions, autistic subjects fail to extend a previous speaker's comment or grasp 'where it is "going"' and their ability to tell coherent stories is impaired (p. 274). They lack the ability or inclination to tell a story or to elaborate upon the narratives of others in spontaneous and relevant ways. Even high functioning autistic people seldom develop someone else's comment in such a way as to move to a new and pertinent topic. Bruner and Feldman argue that these 'patterns of narration', which are near absent in autism, facilitate the kinds of achievement that typical theory of mind tasks detect. Hence prevalent accounts of FP are misleading, given that an ability to interpret people is embedded in patterns of narrative interaction, rather than in observational, individualistic cognition. Children's developing understanding of the psychological states of others is inextricable from their ability to participate in shared narratives:

> I am proposing, then, that knowledge of intentional states is encoded in the story-making of normal children from about two or three

years of age, or even earlier in the (narratively) formatted 'play' that is so prominent among normal children and their caregivers.

(1993, p. 274)

In support of such claims, it is worth noting that most versions of the false belief task do not simply test children's ability to attribute mental states but require them to interpret a narrative that is acted out between two 'people'.[6] Bruner and Feldman's view is compatible with Hobson's, as narrative abilities are claimed to develop out of and remain embedded in the kind of bodily proto-conversation that Hobson and others attribute to younger children. Hence impaired affective interaction will be followed by impaired narrative abilities. Bruner and Feldman acknowledge that feeling ordinarily plays a central role in narrative interaction. As they tellingly note of conversational interactions between an interviewer and autistic children:

> Although all but one of the subjects manifestly enjoyed having the conversations, the interviewer felt she had failed. In spite of the appearance of so much talk, she nevertheless felt that she had been unable to make contact.
>
> (p. 277)

As noted earlier, a breakdown of interpersonal understanding often takes the form of a failure to connect affectively, as opposed to a failure to assign appropriate intentional states. People are permeable to each other and a consistent lack of response on the part of one can lead to a feeling of disconnectedness on the part of the other. As Trevarthan puts it, in healthy interactions between people, 'expressions of the self "invade" the mind of the other, making the moving body of the self resonant with impulses that can move the other's body too' (1993, p. 151), rather like the interaction described by Sartre but with an emphasis on communion rather than conflict.

This emphasis on permeability is complemented by the observation that conversation serves not only to communicate thoughts and information but also seems to generate thoughts. For example, as noted by Morton, a phenomenon common to philosophical discussion is that 'as you argue you find yourself defending beliefs you did not know you had' (2003, p. 163). Perhaps you did not have them beforehand, at least not in the form of a clear, articulate viewpoint. Indeed, it is arguable that many thoughts, interpretations and viewpoints that emerge through conversation owe their creation to several people. They belong to nobody in particular and are shared products of interaction. Here's how Donald (1991, p. 257) describes the modern dinner party:

> Talk flows freely, almost entirely in the narrative mode. Stories are told and disputed; and a collective version of recent events is gradually hammered out as the meal progresses.

Such conversations are regulated by the interplay of expression, gesture and action. Expressions and gestures are partly constitutive of feelings and thoughts. Thus reciprocity of gesture and expression can also involve, to some extent, mutual regulation of thoughts and feelings. Patterns of interaction between people can involve considerable synchrony, as their thoughts and activities are regulated by their interaction. As discussed in Chapter 5, this can be conveyed in terms of Husserl's concept of a 'horizon'. To experience something as a particular kind of object is not just to register an actuality. Salient possibilities that are integral to the experience, such as seeing the object from another angle, walking around it or sitting upon it, contribute to a sense of what the object is. I suggested that much the same applies to experiences of people but that the relevant possibilities are communicative, rather than observational or manipulative. The communicative possibilities that constitute the horizons of perceived gestures and expressions are seized upon by complementary responses, which incorporate further possibilities. It is not a matter of inferring internal mental states but of reciprocating in such a way as to actualise potentialities that are *there* in a person's gestures, expressions, tones and so forth. Mutual understanding is a collaborative exercise, which can involve each participant becoming increasingly open to the communicative possibilities that the other affords. Consider the following description offered by Merleau-Ponty:

> In the experience of dialogue, there is constituted between the other person and myself a common ground; my thought and his are interwoven into a single fabric, my words and those of my interlocutor are called forth by the state of the discussion, and they are inserted into a shared operation of which neither of us is the creator. We have here a dual being, where the other is for me no longer a mere bit of behaviour in my transcendental field, nor I in his; we are collaborators for each other in consummate reciprocity. Our perspectives merge into each other, and we co-exist through a common world.
>
> (1962, p. 354)

To understand others as people is to participate in or to be open to the possibility of participation in the communion that they afford, rather than to interpret them as objects. That would be to withdraw from the personal altogether. Of course, lying, deception, insincerity and concealment of thoughts are commonplace. Hence other people do have 'hidden' mental states in some sense of the term. However, a situation in which one hid everything or misled the other party in every respect would amount to a total breakdown of communication. Specific instances of concealment and insincerity presuppose a more general background of communion, even if interaction is sometimes manipulated in certain ways so as to forward concealed agendas. The assumption that understanding sincere conversation and understanding deceit have the same psychological structure, consisting of inferring a hidden mental state on the basis of observed behaviour, is questionable to say the least. To suggest that lies and sincere pronouncements are both articulate symptoms of hidden states is to use the term 'hidden' in a quite different way, given that everyday language contrasts hidden states with those that are not hidden, rather than taking all states to be hidden. As suggested in Chapter 5, the language of 'concealment' and related notions indicates an asymmetry between cases where one is open to people and other cases where one attempts to hide mental states.

Even if the strong claim that thoughts are co-constructed through interaction or even shared and distributed between participants is rejected, it is still clear that patterned interaction, during the course of conversation, is integral to interpretive ability. Face-to-face conversations are sculpted by a subtle, harmonious interplay of feeling, gesture, expression and action. As Trevarthan puts it, conversation is 'full of an immediate interpersonal vitality that goes beyond, or beneath, the words' (1993, p. 159). Inarticulate 'accompaniments' to verbal exchanges play a significant role in the interpretation and development of remarks. For example, if a comment is met by a smile, one may develop that comment further. One understands, through her smile, that another has understood and sympathised. The construction of conversational narratives is not simply a matter of having the capacity to assign mental states and respond accordingly. In conversational interaction between an 'I' and a 'you', both parties are interpreted within a mutually created context. Understanding is progressively shaped and focused by an evolving narrative, the development of which is supported by interaction of gesture, movement, expression and tone. One does not need to predict what another will say, think or do from a neutral, detached perspective or assign internal states by observing behaviour. A shared context is co-constructed through interaction and it is within this developing context that one interprets. Interpretations are supported, revised or rejected through interaction, through a frown, a laugh or a grimace. In order to understand another, one does not 'read' from afar; one acts, gestures, smiles, speaks and responds. Understanding through conversation is a multi-faceted process, in which others' activities partly constitute the ability to understand them. It is not a matter of detached observation of behaviour or deployment of a pre-given internal capacity. Each party actively investigates with word, gesture and expression, soliciting behaviour from the other in such a way as to make them increasingly intelligible and perhaps predictable.

Face-to-face communicative interaction is a cooperative endeavour, which dispenses with the need to employ complicated internal mechanisms to work out what others are thinking, given that they are usually quite happy to assist in interpretation and thus take the place of such mechanisms. As Morton (2003) argues, much of social life is characterised by the mutual attempts of people to make themselves intelligible to each other; 'by acting in particular ways we can create the conditions under which people are predictable' (p. 27).[7] By making yourself predictable, you facilitate others' abilities to interact with you in predictable ways and thus make them predictable too.

It is also worth noting that conversation is not just a matter of two parties coming together to construct a shared framework for interaction. Much of that framework is brought with them into the exchange, in the form of shared norms and roles that regulate interaction. Many of the relevant norms are specific to face-to-face conversation. As Goffman puts it:

> . . . conversation has a little life of its own and makes demands on its own behalf. It is a little social system with its own boundary-maintaining tendencies; it is a little patch of commitment and loyalty with its own heroes and its own villains.
>
> (1982, pp. 113–114)

He describes the ways in which conversations are regulated by shared standards of deference and demeanour, rules of etiquette, and procedures for moving from transgressions to the restoration of order. Much of this order is, as he puts it, 'ceremonial' (p. 115). In addition, Goffman notes the fragility of the conversational enterprise; conversations often involve complex patterns of mutual performance that are susceptible to interference from a wide range of factors. For example, as discussed earlier, the unease of one participant can permeate interaction so as to precipitate its breakdown (Goffman, 1982, p. 126).

Various others have suggested shared norms that facilitate speaker interpretation during conversation. For example, Grice (1989, p. 26) proposes that conversation is ordinarily regulated by a general 'Cooperative Principle':

> Make your conversational contribution such as is required, at the stage at which it occurs, by the accepted purpose or direction of the talk exchange in which you are engaged.

According to Grice, conversation is characterised by the largely tacit acceptance that one ought to abide by this principle if one cares about communicating successfully. He also discusses several more specific conversational maxims.[8]

However, could it be that all this is facilitated by FP? Although the surface structure of what is going on looks quite different from FP, could it still be supported by an implicit, subpersonal FP, involving a theory of mind and/or simulation routines? I think we can dispense with such suggestions. Theory and simulation are both offered as explanations of how we accomplish something quite specific, the attribution of internal propositional attitude states in the service of predicting and explaining behaviour. However, what we do in conversation is quite different in structure; the ability is constituted by the interaction. If we do not do x at all, then there is no place for capacities that are postulated in order to account for how it is that we manage to do x.

The question remains as to whether FP has a role in certain other contexts. After all, not every instance of interpersonal understanding involves face-to-face interaction. In conjunction with new technologies, there is an increasing tendency to communicate with people at a distance, rather than through face-to-face conversations. In addition to the more traditional medium of letters, we have telephone calls, emails, text messages, chat rooms and so on. So might FP have some role to play in some or all of those scenarios where the other person is not perceived and where we might thus have to theorise as to her mental states?

In most instances of interpretation, I suggest that shared situations, combined with second-person interaction, render an additional ability to infer internal mental states on the basis of behaviour redundant. The more one withdraws from face-to-face conversations, the more one tends to rely on pre-established norms to do the interpretive work. Some communicative scenarios, especially those that involve routine financial matters and the like, involve nothing more than an exchange of information. There is therefore no need to understand anything of what a person is actually thinking, just what is said. Many such interactions also tend to rely heavily on pre-established norms and, in cases such as telephone sales, pre-scripted performances. Cases where intricate shared narratives are constructed by telephone tend to involve conversations between friends or those who share a situation. In such cases, the 'rules of engagement' are largely pre-established, so that both parties are already predictable to each other. The same goes for prolonged e-mail exchanges. The lengthy and elaborate first- to second-person exchanges between strangers, which (I am told) take place in Internet chat rooms, are also constrained by norms (some of which will be explicitly imposed and specific to chat rooms), in addition to shared interests. Furthermore, whether a chat room facilitates fully enriched interpersonal understanding is debatable. Perhaps part of the appeal of such things is the mystery and unpredictability of a curiously impersonal, distant respondent.

Given that situational understanding and second-person interaction both make important contributions to social life, the question arises as to how they relate to each other. Which comes first? Gurwitsch takes community and situation to play the primary role in regulating social interaction and interpretation. Sartre, in contrast, claims that embodied, conflictual relations have primacy over Heideggerian Being-with-others and, by implication, Gurwitschian situational understanding (1989, p. 429). Schutz, although offering a very different account to that of Sartre, also prioritises the personal over the situational.

I suggest a diplomatic solution, applicable to both phenomenological and developmental perspectives: situational understanding and second-person interaction are co-constitutive of interpersonal understanding and neither is more fundamental than the other. A bodily receptiveness comprises our core sense of the distinctiveness of people. However, as Gurwitsch observes, a mere sense of the personal does not add up to a fully enriched interpretation of a person's activities, or to structured interaction and coordination. Most, if not all, of our interactions and interpretations are structured by shared situations; a situational appreciation is generally taken for granted when we interpret people. However, interactions can also serve to create shared situations that can then serve as a basis for mutual interpretation, as indicated by Hobson's account of parent and child together configuring a framework for increasingly complex exchanges. As Hobson (2002, Chapter 2) notes, adult-child interactions often involve structured play or games, which become more intricate as norms of interaction become established and operate as scaffolding for further interaction. However, it is clear that not all such shared patterns are *created* through the interaction of parent and child. The parent already inhabits an intricate framework of normatively configured situations, passed on from previous generations. So pre-established norms will play some role in shaping the way in which interpersonal interactions and relations develop. This not only applies to the enculturation of infants. Adults can also be explicitly or implicitly guided through interaction, so as to become competent participants in situations that they were previously unfamiliar with, thus rendering them more easily interpretable and better able to interpret others.[9]

Pre-established situations are not set in stone; they can be reshaped through interaction's between people. We inherit situations but, through our interactions, we modify them. Hence there is a complex relationship between established norms and interpersonal interactions, involving two-way feedback between them. Clark (1997, pp. 186–187), although he emphasises the extent to which behaviour is regulated by external structures, still acknowledges that individuals can re-structure the wholes in which they participate. And Kusch (2007) argues that entrenched social institutions regulate our conduct and that we also modify each other's behaviour through explicit criticism and discussion, sometimes challenging and re-shaping established parameters of activity in the process.[10]

Simulation or Simulated interaction?

Earlier in this chapter, I said that I would argue that the role of interaction and bodily relatedness even extends to cases of third-person observation. It is to this task that I now turn. I acknowledge that we do attribute psychological states to people, of which I shall say more in Chapter 7. But what I do not want to concede is that any form of understanding that warrants the label 'interpersonal' can fail to involve the kind of practical, bodily receptivity to others outlined here and in Chapter 5. Our understanding of others never involves treating them as objects in the manner suggested by theory theories. Bodily receptivity is constitutive of our sense of people as *people* and so any understanding that fails to incorporate it is impersonal. What about simulation? This, at least, seems to acknowledge the emotional dimensions of interpersonal understanding, thus preserving the claim that we understand others as people, while still characterising certain instances of interpersonal understanding in terms of the attribution of internal mental states on the basis of behavioural observations. As Gordon puts it, simulation is a 'hot' methodology, which engages our own emotional, motivational and practical reasoning resources, as opposed to a 'cold' methodology that allows us to remain detached from the object of study (1996, p. 11). I argued in Chapter 5 that implicit simulation is actually a case of perception. So the only option left is the view that we employ explicit simulation. However, I suggest that accounts of explicit simulation fail to accommodate the extent to which our experiences and interpretations of others are facilitated by our interactions with them, misconstruing the relationship 'A with B' as 'A modelling B'.

The difference between theory and simulation is made vivid by Ravenscoft's description of observing a distressed climber. One watches the increasingly exhausted climber reach in desperation for something to hold on to, knowing full well that a fatal fall is imminent. Each time his hand slips, he tries again, knowing that his predicament is growing increasingly dire. Ravenscroft points out that, as one looks on, one's phenomenology is unlike that of the theorist:

> When we empathise with the distressed climber we do not merely hold a series of propositions about his mental life. We personally experience states very much like his. [. . .] We experience what it is like to be the distressed climber.
>
> (1998, p. 172)

Hence Ravenscroft suggests that, when it comes to such cases, simulation is a more phenomenologically acceptable account than theory; detached propositional attitude attribution alone does not explain our experiential engagement with the climber. However, this kind of emotional engagement cannot simply be characterised as *feeling what it is like to be someone else*. Goldie (1999, 2000, Chapter 7) points out that there are a number of different ways in which we identify with others. We can 'put ourselves in their shoes' and imagine how we would feel in their situation. Alternatively, we might empathise with them and try to imagine what it is actually like *for them*, rather than how it would feel *if you were them*. Both of these are different from sympathy, which involves feeling *for* them, rather than *like* them. We might also have a more general understanding of the situation, taking the form of a narrative constructed around the person's predicament. And we may experience some emotional contagion, which, Goldie suggests, is not really a way of relating *to* somebody. So what might we experience when we watch the climber? The experience would, I think, involve all these responses, in addition to a presupposed receptivity to her as a *person*, which is not itself a product of simulation. One might experience an overwhelming desire to somehow assist, a feeling of intense fear in one's own chest, a recollection of the overwhelming panic one experienced in a similar situation. One might also 'catch' a pervading emotion, as gasps from the surrounding crowd 'seep in'. And, if one is a climber oneself, one might have a grasp of the climber's normatively configured situation, a shared context of procedures, norms and functions, involving various items of equipment.

There is a lot more going on than identification and such experiences are not adequately characterised in terms of modelling or replication. One has a complex of different relations with the distressed climber. And, I suggest, these relations are essentially practical, bodily and self-involving. One does not simply 'look upon' the climber and imaginatively identify with him or model him. One perceives his movements, makes slight movements in response, clenches one's fists, grimaces and engages in an intricate, albeit one-sided, bodily dialogue with him. It is partly through this bodily dialogue that one is *open* to the climber's predicament. Even when we observe someone in the third-person, our bodies are responsive to them in a variety of complementary ways. Hence I suggest that first- to third-person experience also often incorporates interaction. One does not replicate the person's predicament; one responds to it.

Consider an alternative scenario where one is not even in perceptual contact with another person but, instead, anticipating what he will do when next encountered. The experience is seldom, if ever, a matter of 'hopping into his head' or 'putting oneself in his position' but of imagining a kind of interaction. 'Simulating' what another will do often involves playing the part of oneself and imagining various interactions. One's own words and actions are simulated as much as theirs. Patterns of interaction and interpersonal narratives are imagined; these can serve as preparation for anticipated interactions. On other occasions, we might, to some degree, adopt another person's perspective. However, what is simulated is still often interaction between her and other people. Hence the phenomenological structure of solitary 'simulating' is not usually 'A as B' but several permutations of 'A with B' (although I will concede, in Chapter 7, that there is also a place for certain other imaginative exercises that could be described as 'modelling' people). Take the example of simulating one's own future possibilities: 'If I pretend *realistically* that there is an intruder in the house I *might* find myself surprisingly brave – or cowardly' (Gordon, 1995a, p. 63). Even though this is proposed as an example of self-simulation, it is actually an example of simulated interaction. What is imagined is a series of interactions between oneself and the intruder. Imaginative understanding of people is generally interactive and dialogical, as opposed to being a modelling of one person by another. Simulated interaction has a perceptual, bodily and affective quality, which is sometimes quite subtle. Often, when 'simulating', one becomes aware of changing one's facial expressions, moving one's tongue, lips and jaw as one imagines speaking, clenching one's fists, moving one's body in a communicative fashion, smiling, nodding or even laughing.

Anticipating interactions with people often involves various other factors, in addition to and sometimes instead of simulated interaction. For example, when we imagine what A will do when she finds out what B has done, we might invoke character traits, recollect memories of previous interactions between A and B in similar circumstances, consider what ought to be done in such a situation or discuss what is at stake for A, given her situation, projects, commitments, motivations and so forth. So it would seem that the ability to anticipate interaction is multifaceted and heterogeneous. It is also worth noting that, when we interpret a third-party, we often do so in the context of discussion with someone else. Interpretation of the third-party, C, is often not achieved by A or B but through interaction between A and B.

I suggest that interaction with others is our primary mode of interpersonal understanding. When reflecting on others from a solitary perspective, we do not ordinarily adopt a theoretical stance and neither do we employ all our bodily reactions in the service of a modelling process. Rather, we 'internalise' interaction in order to generate thought, often engaging in actual movements and expressions, of the kind that we might make during actual interaction, as part of the interpretive process. When observing others or thinking about them, we often generate a kind of dialogical understanding by imagining and, to some degree, enacting interpersonal engagement. Clark makes an analogous point with respect to mathematical abilities, arguing that we do not use external props to aid internalised mathematical abilities. The manipulation of external structures, whether by using one's fingers or manipulating figures on paper, comes first and is then, to some degree, internalised:

> . . . we can mentally simulate the external arena and hence, at times, internalize cognitive competencies that are nonetheless rooted in manipulations of the external world.
>
> (1997, p. 61)

Likewise, I suggest that identifying with others is not simply a matter of using internal resources to model their predicaments but something that Vygotsky claimed to apply more generally, 'the internal reconstruction of an external operation' (1978, p. 56).[11] Not all observation of people will involve simulated interaction. However, as argued in Chapter 5, even when we observe others in a rather detached way, perception of them engages our own motor systems. This perception does not amount to 'simulated interaction' but it is still an active appreciation of others as people, a receptivity to the possibility of interaction, which is presupposed by simulation and quite different in structure from the detached appreciation of complex objects that characterises theory theory.

Denying people

The theme of this chapter has been that FP's emphasis on detached, spectatorial comprehension is highly misleading. It emphasises individualistic deployment of cognitive abilities, whereas interpersonal abilities are actually constituted by the relatedness between people and are most evident in contexts of sustained interaction, such as conversations. Perhaps more troubling is the fact that FP fails to accommodate a bodily responsiveness which, I have suggested, is constitutive of the personal. FP, in so far as it construes interpersonal understanding as a species of objective, mechanistic understanding, amounts to a denial of the personal, a far cry from the structure of any 'commonsense', 'folk' or 'everyday' appreciation of people. This latter criticism applies to all theory theories of FP but not to those versions of simulation, such as Gordon's, that emphasise an affective, experiential appreciation of people. That said, even Gordon neglects the extent to which understanding relies on interaction in shared situations, rather than on a process of imaginative projection.

Mechanistic thinking (by which I mean understanding entities solely in terms of physical, casual processes that are often quite complicated) is of course a legitimate and often productive mode of theorising in many contexts. It is not a mistake to employ (at least sometimes) this kind of thinking when theorising about human beings and their various traits. The mistake is to assume that people ordinarily do something along such lines. In order to describe the structure of interpersonal understanding, one should respect what is distinctive about it, rather than imposing upon it, from the outset, the structure of an alien theoretical enterprise.

However, despite everything I have said so far, it can still be maintained that people employ a 'belief-desire psychology' in everyday life. If we emphasise people, situations, interaction and the ability to perceive much of mental life, we get a kind of understanding that is quite different in character to FP. However, even if FP is a misleading account of the *manner* in which we interpret others, it can be argued that it at least identifies the right *concepts*. Propositional attitudes, principally beliefs and desires, may not be ubiquitous features of interpersonal understanding. However, they are surely central to cases where we explicitly understand or explain someone's behaviour in psychological terms. And, although I have argued that many mental states are partly constituted by behaviour, I have not stated that this is so with 'belief' and 'desire'. So can we still preserve the claim that people sometimes, perhaps only as part of a marginal practice, attribute internal propositional attitude states so as to predict and explain what other people do? This will be the topic of Chapter 7.

7
Beliefs and Desires

So far, I have argued that much of social life can proceed quite happily without belief-desire psychology. Perception of people's activities, embedded in shared situations, is often all we need to facilitate the level of understanding required for successful interaction and coordination. Even when we explain actions in terms of reasons, we often do so by referring to aspects of situations, rather than to psychological states. In addition to this, I have argued that FP is a misleading description of any truly *personal* understanding, in so far as it characterises a participant appreciation of people as a detached appreciation of complex mechanisms.

I do not want to deny that we frequently employ psychological terms when describing ourselves and each other. However, I have suggested that many so-called 'internal' mental states are partly constituted by expression and gesture. They are not 'hidden' in the way that most proponents of FP claim they are and the distinction between internal mental states and their external bodily expressions is sometimes misleading. Nevertheless, it could be that certain other kinds of mental states are understood by the 'folk' to be wholly internal and that an appeal to such states plays a key role in some interpretations of behaviour. Thus it is arguable that FP, in emphasising 'belief' and 'desire', has at least identified some of the right concepts, even if it overextends their scope and fails to appreciate the extent to which an ability to deploy them is embedded in shared situations and interpersonal interactions. These concepts will be the focus of the current chapter. Given that much of social understanding can proceed without explicitly or implicitly invoking them, I will restrict my attention to (a) those cases where 'belief', 'desire' and related terms feature explicitly in everyday talk and (b) examples of belief-desire explanation that are offered by proponents of FP.

Philosophical uses of the terms 'belief' and 'desire' do not map neatly onto everyday uses. This in itself need not be a problem; a technical term could be used to pick out a conceptual unity in our thinking that is not as clearly reflected by everyday talk. However, I will argue that these terms, as employed throughout the FP literature, do not succeed. The problem is not that they fail to pick up on *any* of our concepts but that they accommodate far too many of them. 'Belief' and 'desire' are abstract placeholders for a wide range of states that we manage to distinguish in our everyday discourse about people.[1] We do not have a set of 'core uses' with a few anomalies surrounding it. Rather, where FP imposes order, everyday interpretation accommodates diversity.

The standard approach in the FP literature is to construe both beliefs and desires as propositional attitudes.[2] In other words, they are attitudes that can be conveyed in the form 'A believes that p' or 'B desires that q', where p and q are propositions, such as 'the cat is hungry', 'today is Monday', 'Durham is in England' and so forth. For example, Wellman describes the character of belief as follows:

> Believing is the mental attitude of conviction, the thought that something is true. It is the attitude that takes a description ('the car is green') as corresponding (to some degree) to a state of affairs in the world.
>
> (1990, p. 61)

A range of examples are offered by the FP folk in order to illustrate the effectiveness of belief-desire understanding, conceived of in this way. Many involve simple and banal scenarios, whereas others involve complicated interpersonal narratives, often taken from classic literary texts. For example, Fodor (1987) appeals to Shakespeare's A *Midsummer Night's Dream* and to Conan Doyle's *The Speckled Band*. In what follows, I will argue that, even in the simple cases, belief-desire explanations that are asserted to be intuitive are actually quite inadequate, as they fail to differentiate a range of subtly different psychological states that everyday narratives distinguish with ease. They also fail to acknowledge the role of situational understanding, which operates in conjunction with psychological understanding and, in some cases, instead of the psychological understanding that is allegedly doing the work.

Everyday 'Belief' and 'Desire'

Needham (1972) observes that talk of belief is rife in academic disciplines such as anthropology but that the meaning of the term is seldom made clear. He goes on to argue that it has no core meaning in such contexts but is a placeholder for a diverse range of states. Anthropological use departs from everyday use in various respects but, as Needham notes, the heterogeneity of 'belief' is even more conspicuous in everyday discourse. I suggest that the same applies with regard to the relationship between philosophical and everyday uses. The former is more restrictive than the latter but still refers to a mixed bag of psychological and situational predicaments. Proponents of FP might claim to operate with a clear, specific understanding of belief. However, as I will show, the illustrations of belief-desire psychology that they actually offer suggest otherwise.

First of all, how do everyday and philosophical uses part company? Turning to the former, Needham suggests that 'belief' has many meanings within our culture and that there is considerable inter-cultural variety too. I will focus on intra-cultural variety here. Needham offers the example of A asking B whether B will accept something, such as biscuit or another cup of tea, and B replying 'I believe I won't' (1972, p. 40). The meaning of this utterance is not adequately conveyed by 'B believes that not p', where p is the proposition 'B will accept a biscuit'. The utterance could have different meanings in different contexts. However, it is never simply a matter of denying a proposition. It might be a way of politely declining an offer or, if uttered in a different way, an indignant response to an unreasonable request, intended to emphasise the extent of one's objection to the demand.

Other uses of 'belief' abound. For example, depending on how it is uttered, 'I don't believe it', can convey astonishment, disappointment or incredulity, where only the latter has the form 'A believes that not p'. Similarly, 'I can't believe you did that!' can express anger, disgust, embarrassment, disappointment, admiration and so forth.

'Belief' is also often used to express a state of uncertainty, whereas FP belief is employed more generally, also accommodating states that we would ordinarily refer to as 'knowing'.[3] For example, 'there's a lion in the room' is different from 'careful, I believe there may be a lion in the room'. One is a statement of fact whereas the other indicates only the suspicion of a lion being present. FP 'belief' can respect such differences by distinguishing 'A believes there is a lion in the room' from 'A believes there may well be a lion in the room'. However, this is still a departure from everyday use. Employing the term 'belief', as FP does, to refer to all instances of 'taking something to be the case' also involves extending its use to instances that we would not remark upon at all. If a person walks into a room and sits on a chair, we would not ordinarily describe her psychology in terms of believing or knowing there is a chair and wanting to sit down. As argued in Chapter 4, in so far as the relevant details are presupposed in the form of a shared situation, talk and thought about what a particular individual 'knows' or 'believes' is redundant.

Everyday assertions like 'I don't believe that' might seem to better complement the FP use of the term. However, such assertions can involve a variety of different objects, including moral positions, religious commitments, events that are alleged to have occurred and so on. It is arguable that 'not believing' is not the same attitude in every case; different objects of belief might implicate quite different attitudes. For example, one could dispassionately disagree with an empirical claim on the basis of evidence or, in contrast, *feel* strongly that a moral claim or perhaps an accusation is wrong.

The assertion 'I don't believe you' sometimes involve a very general attitude towards a person, rather than towards a specific proposition that has been expressed. For example, when, in the last days of a decaying relationship, A turns to B and says, 'I just don't believe you; I've heard it all before', it is not a matter of A believing that B has asserted the truth of a proposition, p, which B believes or knows to be false. Rather, it is a more general expression of A's lack of trust in B. 'I don't believe you', directed at B, can even be uttered in conjunction with the acknowledgement that B's utterance is offered sincerely, in the sense that B does not take it to be false. The 'belief' expresses a more general appraisal of B's character and capacity for commitment; the likelihood that B will lapse back into old ways, fail to keep promises and so forth. In other cases, 'believe' is used to communicate an ideological commitment to someone or something, rather than trust or confidence. People often talk of believing *in* a cause, a way of life, a person or a course of action.

Of course, our proponent of FP could translate such talk into FP terms. In the above example, 'I don't believe you' might become 'A believes that not p', where p is the proposition that 'B is committed to a relationship between A and B'. Thus the superficial divergence between everyday and FP use of 'belief' is not itself an objection to FP; it does not preclude the possibility of FP being able to accommodate the content of such remarks. Nevertheless, the differences between FP and everyday uses do serve to show that the concept of belief that FP takes to be central to social life cannot simply be read off everyday discourse.

Much the same applies to 'desire'. The closely related term 'want' is more commonly used than 'desire' in everyday Anglophone discourse.

Both terms are used to refer to many different psychological predicaments, which we distinguish by appreciating something of the broader context in which they are employed. 'Wanting/desiring an ice cream' might be a matter of seeing an ice cream van on a hot day and then feeling a visceral urge. The kind of 'feeling' that motivates the eventual decision to have an ice cream is quite different in character from A's desire to have sex with B. This in turn is different from 'desiring friendship', which may take the form of a desperate feeling of loneliness or a sense of estrangement that pervades one's life as a whole. And the term 'desire' accommodates a host of other motivational structures that may be very different in character from each other. Consider an expressed desire for world peace. This might be uttered with little conviction and with no impact on the speaker's more general behaviour. Or it could be a deeply entrenched commitment that shapes a person's more general outlook on life and fuels a multitude of activities. Furthermore, the term 'desire' is closely associated but not synonymous with various other terms, such as 'yearn', hope', 'wish' and 'seek'. All of this suggests a multitude of different psychological states, rather than a unitary kind of motivation. Hence, as Dancy (2000, p. 11) notes, 'desire', as employed in philosophical discussions of motivation, is 'a term of art'.

'Belief' and 'Desire' in FP

Do the FP terms 'belief' and 'desire' succeed in identifying two distinctive kinds of attitude that underlie everyday talk and thought about people's activities? Proponents of FP tend either to use these terms without any further qualification or to state that 'belief' and 'desire' are propositional attitudes with distinct roles, belief being informational and desire motivational. But what is meant by a 'propositional attitude'? It is important to distinguish propositional attitudes from what we might call 'sentential attitudes'. A sentential attitude is an attitude towards a sentence, such as B believing that the sentence 'Arthur is the current Queen of England' is true. Other sentential attitudes will similarly take the form of judgements as to the truth or falsehood of sentences. Any account that restricted itself to sentential attitudes would fail to accommodate most of our judgements concerning psychological states, which take the form 'B believes that p is the case', rather than 'B believes that sentence p is true'. In other words, propositional attitudes are usually attitudes towards states of affairs that can be expressed as propositions, rather than towards sentences that describe those states of affairs.

It could be maintained that thought is embodied in a representational medium that is linguistic in nature and that all thought is therefore linguistic. However, debates as to the nature of mental representation need not have any implications for the distinction between propositional and sentential attitudes. Even if all thought is somehow language-like in structure, a clear distinction between assenting to the truth of a sentence and taking a state of affairs to be the case is still integrated into it.[4] There is a difference between thinking about something and thinking about a sentence about something. Given that people do, of course, think of each other as having attitudes to things other than sentences, the objects of belief and desire need to be understood more broadly. What about the attitudes themselves? Are 'believing' and 'desiring' distinctive kinds of attitude, which can have linguistic or non-linguistic objects? The examples typically offered by proponents of FP suggest that they are using 'belief' and 'desire' in a very broad way, so broad that the terms fail to pick out homogeneous psychological categories. Consider the following example:

> When a normal person is looking at a traffic light which changes from red to green, she usually comes to believe that it has changed from red to green.
>
> (Stich and Ravenscroft, 1996, p. 126)

What is being claimed here? It would seem from this description that we interpret A as looking at x occurring and then coming to believe that x has occurred. But does this track everyday interpretations and explanations of why people respond to traffic lights as they do? First of all, it is unlikely that we assign any mental states in most such scenarios. That people share the same situations and have the same access to events is a commonplace presupposition of interpretation. When sitting in a room with A, we do not, ordinarily at least, assign hundreds of beliefs to A concerning what is going on in the room, such as 'A believes that there is a chair to her left', 'A believes there is a bowl of fruit in the corner', 'A believes I am sitting in the chair', 'A can hear me saying hello' and so forth. The same goes for traffic lights. They are taken for granted as part of a shared situation within which *we* interpret each other.

However, our proponent of FP might respond that, although we do not actually assign beliefs in most such cases, we still appreciate that people have them, which is why examples like the one offered above are so intuitive. But are they intuitive? What form is the 'belief' that the light has changed from red to green claimed to take? Let us assume that the relevant believer is a driver taking the same early morning trip to work that she has taken five days a week for the last twenty years. She stops at a familiar set of lights and waits for them to change to green, just as she has done on so many other occasions. Does she see the lights change, then believe that they have changed and finally act on the basis of that belief by moving the car forward? Alternatively, it could be that, as the lights change, her body responds with seeming immediacy to the perceived object by manipulating the controls of the car in a habitual fashion. Is there a distinct state of believing here or are perception and action so closely tied together that there is no place in between for an additional 'belief'? By analogy, consider a description of a tennis player 'believing' that the ball is approaching at 120 miles per hour and 'desiring' to hit it. As indicated in Chapter 4, such descriptions misleadingly chop up seamless purposive activity into distinct informational and motivational components.

The traffic lights example also fails to distinguish between someone who has never seen a traffic light or driven a car before and the routine situation that I have just described. Would both people have the same mental state of 'believing that the light has changed from red to green'? This is unlikely. In one case, the person's experience of the event is shaped by a framework of norms associated with driving, which serve to specify a pattern of activity. In the other, it has no such context. One response to this is to maintain that the description offered by Stich and Ravenscroft is only intended to apply to belief attribution in typical cases. So it is unfair to start referring to people from other cultures seeing traffics lights for the first time. But, if this is so, the example is misleading. If we assume that the person is an accomplished driver, she most likely does not come to form a belief about an object, which can be cleanly dissociated from norms of activity. The light changing to green means 'drive now' and perception is closely tied to behavioural response. In the case of a novice driver, the changing lights might be explicitly entertained. And, unlike the expert, she may have to pause and think about what to do next. However, perception of the lights is again inseparable from a sense of their practical significance. They are still perceived as meaning 'drive now', even though there is a gap between perception and subsequent performance. So, either the example wrongly characterises various quite different kinds of experience in terms of the same propositional attitude or, alternatively, a propositional attitude is not itself a distinctive kind of psychological state but a rather abstract way of talking about various psychological predicaments.

However, it might be objected that I have just described what is *actually* going on, rather than what the 'folk' *think* is going on. So perhaps I am being unfair to FP. Regardless of whether the person really does have a belief about the lights, the fact remains that everyday 'folk' take him to have such a belief and FP is an account of what they think. However, simple, everyday descriptions make a range of more subtle discriminations between psychological and situational predicaments. Hence the problem lies with Stich and Ravenscroft's example, rather than with an everyday understanding of people. Consider the following:

1. John pulled up at the lights. As they changed and he started to move, his thoughts were wholly elsewhere, with Jane.
2. John was surprised to see the brand new traffic lights at the end of the street. Indeed, his attention was only drawn to them when they changed from green to red, at which point he brought the car to an abrupt stop.
3. John was not especially concerned by the lights for the first minute or so. But, as time dragged on, he became increasingly preoccupied with them, willing them to change. When he finally saw them change, he had to look at them again before he actually believed it.

It is possible to concoct dozens of narratives along such lines, all picking out subtly different psychological and situational predicaments. These cannot simply be classified into normal cases, exemplified by the applicability of FP belief, plus a range of exceptional cases. There is no normal case, just a diversity of cases. Everyday discourse and understanding do not, of course, incorporate an explicit and comprehensive inventory of mental state categories. Nevertheless, it is at least apparent from the differences between the three situations described above that we make all sorts of subtle distinctions, which are not included in FP explanations, and that these can be communicated fairly easily in the form of brief narratives.

Such problems are rife throughout the FP literature, which markets vague and unhelpful statements about beliefs and desires as platitudes that anyone with any sense would assent to. For example:

> . . . it is trivially easy to explain why John will carry his umbrella with him: it is because he *believes* it will rain and he *wants* to stay dry.
>
> (Frith and Happé, 1999, p. 2)

Is it trivially easy to explain why John will carry his umbrella? Consider the following accounts of his behaviour:

1. As always, John switched off his alarm clock and got out of bed at 7:30. He dressed, ate breakfast, picked up his briefcase and umbrella and set off to work at the usual time of 8:30.
2. John opened the door and saw the unusually dark sky. He went back into the house and picked up his umbrella.

These suggest quite different explanations of why John carries his umbrella. In the first case, his behaviour is habitual and his picking up the umbrella is part of a larger pattern of routine activity. At no point does he entertain the thought that it will rain. In the second, he looks up at the sky, explicitly considers the likelihood of rain and interrupts his schedule to retrieve an umbrella. Imposition of the terms 'believes' and 'wants' does not succeed in distinguishing these scenarios, even though most everyday descriptions, even rather crude ones, would manage to convey the difference. There are many other possible explanations of John's carrying an umbrella, some of which do not even refer to characteristics of John. Suppose it is pouring with rain and everyone is carrying an umbrella. If someone asks why John is carrying an umbrella, 'it's raining' should suffice as an answer, given the assumption that one's respondent appreciates something of the norms associated with umbrella use. In cases where this does not suffice, the respondent has not appreciated the relevant norms. Reference to John's beliefs and desires will not help her to do so.

Where psychological factors do crop up, they can take the form of generalisations along the lines of 'people don't like getting wet' or even 'it's not nice being wet', rather than posited ingredients of John's psychology. Such generalisations do not seem to be the product of a core FP. Instead, they are most likely a disparate set of learned, content-specific generalisations concerning the relationships between various scenarios and associated psychological states. But what if John's behaviour does not conform to situational norms and familiar generalisations? Suppose that everyone else is holding an umbrella while an umbrella-less John is leaping around in the rain, singing happily and getting drenched. Would 'John believes it is raining and he desires to get wet' suffice as an explanation here? Again, it would not. It does not add anything more to our understanding than 'he is leaping around in the rain, grinning and getting increasingly wet'. Consider the old joke 'why did the chicken cross the road?' The alleged humour lies in the answer 'to get to the other side' being completely uninformative. Now consider:

Why did the chicken cross the road?
Because it believed there was another side and it desired to get there.[5]

This is no more informative than the usual punch line. Yet the translation from the old joke to the new one proceeds in just the same way as FP translations of statements about goal-directed behaviour into psychological 'explanations'. Suppose John's dancing in the rain or a person crossing the road are both unexpected behaviours that require explanation. What is often needed is an account of relevant norms, projects, pastimes and commitments. Alternatively, there may be special circumstances that explain the suspension of certain more usually applicable norms, such as 'he did it for a bet'.

When we do appeal to psychological states, explanations need not take the form of 'reason' explanations, in the narrow sense of 'reason', meaning why John *ought* to have done p given certain information or, more permissively, why it was *reasonable* for John to have done p. For example, 'I forgot', 'I wasn't paying attention', 'I was in a really bad mood', 'I wasn't with it at the time', 'I was just feeling really happy; I don't know why', 'he wasn't thinking straight', 'he's irrational', 'she's mad', 'it's all in her head' and so forth. Explanations only stop at specific psychological episodes or dispositions when we have given up trying to rationalise behaviour in terms of shared norms. Hence psychological factors tend to feature as reasons in a broad sense; they make an action understandable but do not do so by showing why it was the/a reasonable thing to do. The norms that feature in explanations of behaviour do, of course, include norms of good *reasoning*, in addition to situational norms. However, there is a difference between reasoning and having a reason. And, as I will argue later in this chapter, norms of reasoning are not generally understood as characteristics of internal mental processes, any more than situational norms are.

Although having a headache, being tired or being in a bad mood can all make an action understandable in certain cases, it is a different matter when we turn to various psychological predicaments that go by the names 'belief' and 'desire'. Beliefs and desires alone do not serve as 'reasons' in either sense of the term. If I ask why Fred crossed the road, only to be told that he believed the Loch Ness Monster was chasing him but that it would not cross the road because traffic lights irritated its skin, this would not amount to any kind of reason, given that the mental state contents are far more baffling than the behaviour. A mental state only contributes to a reason for an action if the action is more understandable in the light of that state than it would have been without it. And an acceptable reason involves an implicit or explicit reference to circumstances in which such a state is appropriately acquired or at least understandable. The 'belief that p' only contributes to a reason explanation if it is accompanied by situational and other considerations that make clear why one might take things to be that way. 'I didn't come out because I believed it was raining' is not a reason unless the belief that it was raining is also shown to be understandable, through an appeal to factors such as the person's receiving accurate or misleading information. If someone explains the belief by saying 'I don't know why; I just did', this would amount to absence of a reason.[6] Thus explanations that cite beliefs and desires are not explanations at all, unless they explicitly include an account of relevant situational factors or implicitly implicate an appropriate kind of situation.[7]

In the case of actions arising from mistaken beliefs, an explanation will often involve an account of how the situation was taken to be, plus a further account of why it was taken to be that way. The action is explained by showing that (a) it would have been reasonable had the situation been the way it was taken to be and (b) the actual situation was such as to make the mistake understandable. For example, 'Tom asked the traffic warden to arrest the two thugs because Tom believed she was a police officer' explains the action by (a) describing how Tom took the situation to be, in such a way as to show that Tom's behaviour would have been appropriate had the situation been that way and (b) assuming that the recipient will recognise the similarity between traffic wardens' uniforms and those of police officers. Although a psychological state does feature in the explanation, the reason consists of the situation, both as it actually was and as it was taken to be. In fact, it is arguable that, although the explanation makes Tom's behaviour understandable, it does not show that there *was* a reason for his behaviour but that there *would have been* a reason had the situation been as he took it to be. However, the distinction is not so clear-cut. It is not that the situation Tom took to apply did not apply at all. If the two thugs really were up to no good, then there would indeed be a reason for 'getting them arrested', even if not for 'getting them arrested by a traffic warden'.

It is also worth noting that 'taking things to be' a certain way is not a unitary attitude, a point I will further stress in the remainder of this chapter. Hence the FP term 'belief' fails to identify a distinctive psychological category that features in reason-explanations, even allowing that beliefs are not themselves reasons. Furthermore, as argued in Chapter 4, many reason explanations do not involve psychological states at all. Where a situation was as A took it to be but B was not party to all aspects of it, A's behaviour can be explained to B by drawing attention to the relevant features of the situation. And, in cases where a situation is shared by both parties, an explanation is not usually required.

A distinction is sometimes made between 'normative' and 'motivating' reasons (see, for example, Dancy, 2000, p. 20). One can state that an action p was reasonable given situation x, thus supplying a normative reason in the form of the situation. However, one can also state that 'Tom did p because of situation x'. In this case, the situation did not just make the action understandable; it also motivated it. Situations, as I have described them, can play both roles. In many cases, motivating and normative reasons will turn out to be the same. However, it might be argued that my view runs into problems in those cases where they come apart. When there are several normative reasons that make an action reasonable, the question arises as to which of them actually motivated it. Perhaps FP comes in here? I suggest that, where normative reasons do not serve to specify motivating reasons, we can rely upon various other sources, such as perception of expression and gesture, verbal communications and knowledge of idiosyncratic traits. In cases where such information fails to differentiate or is unavailable, we are left with a situation where we just do not know what motivated the action, rather than one in which we bring an additional FP ability to bear on things.

Experience and belief

Examples offered on behalf of FP are misleading in other ways too. For instance, there is a pervasive failing throughout the literature to distinguish experiences of things from inferences that might be made on the basis of those experiences. The latter may involve sentences that express propositions. However, experiencing something is rather different from entertaining a linguistic description of it. Consider the following:

> If you see a person running to catch up with a just-departing train, for example, you interpret the person as an intentional agent, who *believes* that there is a just-departing train, and who *wants* to get on it.
>
> (Scholl and Leslie, 1999, p. 131)

Although the terms 'believe' and 'want' are used in what looks like the same way as the umbrella example, very different situational and psychological predicaments could be involved, even if we take umbrella case 2, where 'it will rain' and 'I do not want to get wet' are explicitly entertained. Compare 'Jane believes that the Eiffel Tower is in Paris' to 'Jane believes that her train is about to leave'. In the former, the 'belief' may well amount to no more than her explicitly assenting to the truth of a particular sentence or having a disposition to do so, with no associated experiences and no connection with any of her actions, save her explicit utterances (assuming she is not planning to visit the Eiffel Tower). But now let us suppose that Jane is trying to get to her best friend's wedding and will not make it in time unless she boards the train. Jane's belief that the train is about to leave looks like a state in which experience and action are very closely tied together. The way that the train 'appears to Jane' is infused with emotion. Her experience of it is at the same time a reflection of her own predicament. Her running, the sight of the train, the sound of the whistle, the shutting of the doors, a sense of urgency and a background of concerns and projects all blend together seamlessly. Just about any everyday description of the two cases would succeed in communicating the significant differences between them but stating that utterances and actions are caused by 'beliefs' and 'wants' or 'desires' does not. The two 'beliefs' seem to be very different states, connected in very different ways to experience and action. Adding desires does not help either. Jane's desire to get on the train may be quite different in nature to her desire to visit the Eiffel Tower.

This point applies to emotionally structured experiences more generally. Most recent philosophical accounts of emotion acknowledge that emotions are often, if not always, intentional states. However, this is not to say that emotions are combinations of propositional attitudes, which can be neatly divided into informational and motivational components, or of propositional attitudes and non-propositional feelings. The term 'intentional state' is more encompassing than 'propositional attitude'. Almost all theorists of emotion acknowledge that the intentionality of emotions and the ways in which they influence behaviour will not be captured by treating them as propositional attitudes. An emotion is, among other things, a way in which an entity or situation is experienced. Objects appear to us as 'frightening', situations are experienced as 'urgent' and so forth.[8] In emotional experience, bodily dispositions, idiosyncratic concerns and aspects of an experienced situation all blend together.[9]

Emotional experience is not a matter of having certain informational and/or motivational propositional attitudes. And everyday narratives do not indicate otherwise. So we can either take propositional attitudes to be a way of talking about such predicaments, employed by certain philosophers, or we can take them to be posited ingredients of human psychology that the 'folk' are actually committed to. If we opt for the former, propositional attitudes look like artificial impositions upon a diverse range of psychological and situational predicaments that are picked up on by everyday experience and talk. And, if we opt for the latter, it would seem that FP is false; everyday interpretations of people are not structured by unitary categories of 'belief' and 'desire' or by the broader category 'propositional attitude'.

Another way to go would be to restrict the role of FP to the interpretation of sentential attitudes that do involve assenting to a linguistically expressed proposition. However, although sentential attitudes have a role to play in interpersonal understanding, they are ineffective on their own. Some explanations may single out a person's attitude to certain sentences that she has read, heard or formulated. However, any account that omits emotional experiences, experiences more generally, perception of agency, gesture and intention, normatively configured situations, character, motivation, habitual tendencies and so forth will be so partial that it will be an extremely impoverished account of the 'folk' appreciation of people. Furthermore, sentential attitudes do not motivate people. Desiring that sentence p is true is just a matter of desiring (in some sense of 'desire') the state of affairs expressed by p. The sentence itself is not what matters.

Hence, if the propositional attitudes of 'believing' and 'desiring' are taken to be central to social life, they must be more broadly construed. This being the case, they will encompass a variety of phenomena that people recognise to be distinct. Thus I suggest that they are abstract placeholders rather than ingredients of a 'folk' way of thinking.[10] As I will now argue, this becomes all the more apparent once we recognise that the motivational/informational distinction at the heart of FP is not respected by much of our thought and talk about people.

Beliefs, desires and commitments

Stich and Ravenscroft offer the following as an illustration of how the folk understanding of desire operates:

> If a person sitting at a bar wants to order a beer, and if she has no stronger desire to do something that is incompatible with ordering a beer, then typically she will order a beer.

> (1996, p. 126)

But suppose that the person in question is an alcoholic, who desires a beer more than anything else in the world but, after much procrastination and sweating, leaves the bar to go home and does so due to her resolution to abstain. It could be maintained that there is no tension between this case and the one above, given that the alcoholic has a stronger desire to go home. However, the 'desires' in question are different in character. One is clearly 'stronger', in the sense of being an intense bodily urge for a beer, but the other has a different form rather than being simply 'weaker'; it is a more general commitment to reshape a life, to act contrary to certain entrenched urges. One might retort that the alcoholic's urge to drink is a case of pathological desire and that FP only works in cases of typically functioning cognitive apparatus. So let us take a more mundane case. Suppose the sun is shining outside, my colleagues are all drinking in the pub around the corner and I would really appreciate a cold beer and a good chat right now. However, I am scheduled to give a lecture on folk psychology during the next hour. I do not relish the prospect of giving the lecture and the beer is much more appealing. But I give the lecture anyway, the reason being that a commitment integral to my professional life over-rides an episodic inclination towards conversation and beer. Calling both states 'desires' obfuscates the difference between them, whereas just about any everyday description would serve to convey the nature of the conflict; 'I'd love a beer right now but I've got to give that darned lecture'. As Sen (1977, p. 327) argues, there is a difference between desires, construed as episodic or dispositional preferences, and commitments; the latter may involve 'counterpreferential choice'. There are different kinds of preference and a linear ranking of preference strength fails to capture the different kinds of motivation that everyday discourse is sensitive to.

Of course, Stich and Ravenscroft only say that a beer will typically be ordered. But who is to say what is typical? There are many varieties of motivation, which frequently conflict in all sorts of ways. FP examples tend to pass over such differences and replace them with the empty assumption that the strongest desire will be the one that wins out. If 'desire' is understood in a restrictive sense, this is untrue, as commitments and so forth can defeat desires. And, if a more encompassing sense is employed, it will trivially true, as the 'strongest desire' will be defined as whatever psychological state leads one to act as one does. The latter being the case, appeals to desire will be vacuous when it comes to explaining why one acted as one did.

The kinds of attitude that we sometimes refer to as 'commitments' and 'convictions' not only pose problems for the assumption that 'desire' picks out a distinctive psychological category. They also draw attention to the limits of propositional attitude descriptions of people's psychology and cast doubt on the view that there is a clear-cut distinction between informational and motivational states.

It is frequently assumed that belief, construed as a propositional attitude with an informational role, is central to intersubjective ability. Unless one is able to distinguish seeming from being, one will not be able to distinguish one's own perspective from that of someone else. Hence sophisticated psychological interpretation requires an appreciation of belief. This is why so much attention has been directed at the false belief task and why the ability to assign false beliefs is seen as such a developmental milestone. As I argued in Chapters 5 and 6, a sense of others as loci of agency and experience, rather than mere automata, can be grasped through perception. This involves a kind of bodily receptivity that is different from any practice of inferring psychological states on the basis of behaviour. Of course, we do make more complicated discriminations between how things might seem to someone and how they actually are, which will not be facilitated by a perceptual appreciation of people and their activities. However, this is not to suggest that a single, additional cognitive achievement underlies the ability to make such discriminations. As I have already suggested, in our everyday lives we distinguish various different psychological predicaments that get lumped together as 'belief' by FP. Studies such as false belief tasks generally presuppose a unitary conception of 'belief'. Hence it is not wholly clear what it is that they are supposed to be detecting. Even if the relevant achievement can be distinguished from other kinds of belief, the fact that the term 'belief' encompasses various different psychological predicaments still serves to downplay the developmental 'milestone' that false belief tasks are claimed to detect. Coming to understand one of the many predicaments that can be referred to as 'belief' is not quite as impressive as coming to understand *the* concept of belief.

However, a further concern with regard to such studies is that the information-motivation distinction, which they and FP more generally take to be central to psychological understanding from a very early age, is not respected by many of the attitudes that adults assign to each other. I have already indicated that this is so with certain emotional experiences.[11] However, the kinds of attitude that we refer to as 'convictions' or 'commitments' further compromise the distinction. Such attitudes have been largely neglected by FP, even though they are frequently talked about in everyday life.

An appreciation of commitments and convictions is apparent in, for example, various expressions and discussions of religious belief. Consider a belief in God. This might be claimed to take the form 'B believes that p', where p is the proposition 'God exists'. However, autobiographical and biographical narratives relating the nature of religious conviction often suggest otherwise. On 2nd January 2005, a week after the 26th December 2004 tsunami left hundreds of thousands of people dead, an article was published in the UK newspaper *The Sunday Telegraph*, written by the Archbishop of Canterbury, Rowan Williams. Williams addressed the age-old question of whether such events pose a challenge for religious belief and his answer was 'yes'. However, the challenge and, for him, its resolution do not involve musing over seemingly incompatible propositions. It is, he says, not a case of reconciling the proposition that there exists an omnipotent, omnibenevolent God with the proposition that much suffering exists, by cooking up a theodicy to explain why a being of this nature would initiate such terrible events or allow them to happen. Indeed, he remarks that he would feel 'something of a chill' at the prospect of such a being. Instead, he describes the religious predicament as follows:

> The extraordinary fact is that belief has survived such tests again and again – not because it comforts or explains but because believers cannot deny what has been shown or given to them. They have learned to see the world and life in the world as a freely given gift; they have learned to be open to a calling or invitation from outside their own resources, a calling to accept God's mercy for themselves and make it real for others; they have learned that there is some reality to which they can only relate in amazement and silence.

The 'belief' described here is not just a propositional attitude or a set of inter-related propositional attitudes, and this applies even if we accept that propositional attitudes are abstract placeholders for a wide range of states. It is not an attitude towards some object or set of objects but a general attitude towards life, an orientation or way of responding to things that shapes experience and thought regarding all manner of topics. And a belief in God is not something additional to this general attitude but constituted by it. As James argues in *The Varieties of Religious Experience*, the core conviction that underlies many instances of religious belief is not a propositional attitude but a deep-seated, inarticulate feeling of how things are with the world, around which articulate narratives are assembled.[12]

Commitments or convictions of this nature are certainly not exclusive to religion. Many uses of the term 'belief' do not convey an attitude towards a particular object but a guiding conviction that underlies a person's various 'desires' and more specific 'beliefs'. Here is how the British Prime Minister, Tony Blair (speaking at the Labour Party Annual Conference on 29th September 2004) expressed his view that the second Iraq war was just, even though no weapons of mass destruction had been found:

> Do I know I'm right? Judgements aren't the same as facts. Instinct is not science. I'm like any other human being, as fallible and as capable of being wrong. I only know what I believe.

He went on to outline two contrasting views about the current global situation. According to one, things are the same as ever, with isolated terrorists and small groups causing occasional death and destruction. According to the other, a new phenomenon of global terror has emerged. His use of 'believe' in this context suggests a general stance or way of interpreting the world, rather than a specific informational state that can be true or false. From Blair's words, it is also clear that he regards his belief as inextricable from his sense of moral conviction.[13]

Such beliefs are not wholly articulate in form; they are felt convictions that shape experience, thought and activity, which are not understood as a matter of assenting to a series of propositions. Indeed, belief as 'felt conviction' and belief as 'taking the state of affairs expressed by some proposition to be the case' can come apart. There is a sense in which people sometimes believe what they know to be false (Needham, 1972, p. 65). For example, a person might be informed that his spouse has died, recognise that it is true but still not quite believe it. People sometimes remark 'I know it's happened but I can't believe it', 'I still can't believe it' or 'I just can't believe it yet'. Closely associated is the expression 'it hasn't sunk in yet'. Such examples suggest that believing sometimes often involves not only recognising that something is the case but of also 'feeling' and accepting that it is (Ratcliffe, 2004b).

It is arguable that such 'beliefs' also play a role in structuring philosophical thought. For example, Van Fraassen (2002) argues that believing in a broad doctrine such as empiricism is not a matter of accepting certain propositions and patterns of reasoning. It is a matter of adopting a particular stance, a set of mostly inarticulate convictions concerning how the world is and how we relate to it. Rea (2002) advocates a similar position regarding a doctrine that often goes by the name 'naturalism'.

Naturalism, he suggests, consists of a largely implicit set of methodological dispositions that together comprise a general receptivity to certain kinds of argument and evidence. Hence not all 'beliefs' can be adequately described as attitudes towards specific propositional contents.

Talk of commitments and convictions is closely associated with talk of character and personality traits, general dispositions and temperaments. A conviction can be described as a 'belief' or as a 'temperament' and certain core commitments could be taken to partly constitute a person's 'character'. Thus there is a fine line between everyday talk about the specific beliefs and more general dispositions of a person.

Commitments and convictions do not respect the FP distinction between informational and motivational states. A commitment is both a way that one takes the world to be and a guide for action. Thus it is not just the situations that we take for granted which both inform and motivate. Various psychological predicaments that we attribute to people are understood to do so too. Of course, the line between informational and motivational factors can be more clearly drawn in many other cases. For example, if someone is asked why she did not attend Tim's party, a range of explanations might be offered, along the lines of:

I couldn't find the house.
I forgot about it.
I thought it was yesterday.
Nobody gave me the address.
I didn't feel like it.
I was just feeling a bit miserable that night and didn't want to meet people.
I don't like crowds.
I've never liked parties.[14]

The first four could all be categorised as informational and the rest as motivational. Even so, they do not fit neatly into homogeneous categories of 'belief' and 'desire'. Motivational states are very diverse in nature and also include a range of factors that are not captured by everyday or philosophical use of the term 'desire'. For example, someone might not attend because she was feeling tired, had a headache, had other commitments or because of a fear of crowds. Of course, we could say that such factors led to the formation of desires but it is arguable that they already incorporate motivations. It is not a case of having a headache plus a motive but of having a headache, which itself motivates in certain ways.

Interestingly, the assertion 'I didn't want to go' would not itself be acceptable as a reason but would instead serve as the beginning of a more specific explanation, with reasons ranging from a blend of situational and psychological factors, such as 'I can't cope with the way people are expected to behave at such events', to psychological/physiological factors, such as 'I was too tired'. Desires do not explain. Explanations instead involve identifying more specific motivating factors, personal dispositions, commitments and, quite often, lengthy narratives about a person's historical relations with others.

Potentially relevant informational considerations are perhaps not quite so varied. Nevertheless, 'I couldn't find the house' could involve a range of factors, including a lack of the practical ability to follow directions or an absence of clear signposting. Certain explanations, such as 'I thought it was on another street, with a similar-sounding name' and 'I thought it was yesterday', accord better with FP 'belief'. But there are others that do not distinguish so cleanly between informational and motivational factors. For example, 'it's against my religious beliefs/ moral principles to attend events that involve alcohol' involves offering, as a reason, both informational and motivational factors intertwined. That we distinguish the two in some cases does not imply that the distinction rests at the heart of everyday interpersonal understanding. And, even when explanations do conform to an informational/ motivational distinction, we discriminate between all manner of subtly different states and scenarios, which are not picked out by abstract talk of beliefs and desires. We also appeal to situational considerations ('it would have been inappropriate of me to attend, given the circumstances'), character traits ('I'm just not the kind of person who appreciates parties') and a range of other factors.

Beliefs as indeterminate dispositions

Davidson and Dennett, among others, have argued that 'belief' and other psychological terms do not refer to mental *entities* and also that attributions of belief involve indeterminacy. Davidson draws an analogy between assigning beliefs to people and assigning weights to objects:

> In thinking and talking of the weights of physical objects we do not need to suppose there are such things as weights for objects to have. Similarly, in thinking and talking about the beliefs of people we needn't suppose there are such entities as beliefs.
>
> (2001, p. 60)

He pursues this analogy further, by suggesting that there will be various equally legitimate ways of describing the contents of a person's beliefs. One can measure weight in kilograms, pounds or some other measure but entities have determinate weights, regardless of which measuring system is employed. Likewise, belief contents are determinate, despite the different ways in which they might be characterised.

Dennett (1987) makes a stronger claim on behalf of indeterminacy. According to his account of the 'intentional stance', we adopt a certain standpoint towards people and certain other complex objects, which resolves their behaviour into coarse-grained patterns. This simplifies the task of interpretation, relieving us of the considerable labour involved in attending to more fine-grained and detailed 'physical stance' interpretations of the same system. However, Dennett acknowledges that the patterns we discern in behaviour and characterise as the belief that p or the desire that q have 'imperfections', which are particularly salient when we interpret people with certain cognitive pathologies. In such cases and more generally, there may be genuine ambiguity in the pattern and 'no fact of the matter of exactly which beliefs and desires a person has' (p. 28). This is not to say that one can assign any belief one chooses but, rather, that there may be no way of arbitrating between two or more rival candidates for belief content.

Dennett (1991b, p. 143) also makes an interesting distinction between 'beliefs' and 'opinions'. The latter, he says, are not just beliefs but 'linguistically infected states' that feature in everyday conversational narratives. To assign a belief is not to assign an opinion; beliefs are more general patterns that we pick out in behaviour. Dennett's 'opinions' are what many proponents of FP call 'beliefs'. Thus, if we accept that referents of the term 'belief' are heterogeneous, his belief/opinion distinction is better construed as a distinction between different kinds of belief.

On the issue of indeterminacy, I side with Dennett over Davidson. 'Belief', in one sense of the term at least, picks out a very general disposition and there may be no fact of the matter to arbitrate between competing interpretations. I argued in Chapter 6 that some mental states and thought processes are not simply expressed in a person's behaviours and interactions with others but partly constituted by them. It is arguable that this applies to certain cases of believing and being disposed to believe. Perhaps holding a belief or no longer holding a belief are not fully realised prior to expression. Certain 'beliefs' may be partly constituted by changing bodily dispositions and by unfolding interactions with other people. They are not discrete entities or fully determinate states but multi-faceted dispositions, which are variably hazy.[15]

The view that belief, in one of its senses, refers to a general set of dispositions without rigid boundaries is, I think, most convincing when we consider the attribution of beliefs to collectives. Beliefs are not only assigned to people but also to companies, nations, cultures, peoples living in certain historical periods, religions and so forth. Collective beliefs often feature in historical explanations. It has been argued that the platitudes of FP are indispensable to such explanations, which are usually a matter of picking out the relevant propositional attitudes. For example, Stich and Ravenscroft offer the following example:

> Did Lincoln sign the Emancipation Proclamation because he wanted to abolish slavery? Or was it because he thought it would be a strategically useful move, helping to weaken the Confederacy?
>
> (1996, p. 115)

The same criticisms that apply to non-historical cases also apply here. The 'beliefs' and 'desires' of historical figures are as heterogeneous as those of anyone else. In addition, much of the interpretive work is directed at the tasks of describing interpersonal interactions and identifying relevant situational factors. A broader situational understanding is surely required in order to appreciate Lincoln's various motives and strategies. His personal 'wants' may also have parted company from what he 'wanted' in the context of his role as a politician. An account of individuals' personal preferences does not amount to a description of a historical situation and neither does it serve to make clear their various motivations. The history of humanity is not just a history of individuals and their psychological characteristics. Attitudes are embedded in situations and often formed or sustained by interactions between people. Did B manage to convince Lincoln of p or did interaction between Lincoln and B lead to formation of the shared conviction that p?

When historical explanations appeal to the beliefs of a collective, such as a government, culture, religious sect or nation, rather than an individual, the beliefs in question do not seem to be clearly bounded, fully determinate episodes or dispositions. For example, if one asserts 'The French believed that the Germans would come through the Maginot line', this is neither a matter of every French person possessing the belief that p nor of the French as a whole possessing between them one instance of the belief that p. Instead, it draws attention to the fact that the French (or, if we want to be more specific, the French government) failed to consider alternative possibilities, such as the Germans coming through Belgium. The 'belief' is an entrenched pattern of thinking and practice, manifested in different ways by different people at different times.

Appeals to collective beliefs are more widespread. As Needham (1972) points out, references to the beliefs of a culture are commonplace in anthropology. Saying that 'the Azande believe that p' surely does not amount to the claim that every member of that group possesses a specific propositional attitude or to the claim that the Azande amount to a group mind that possesses the belief that p. It may refer to the shared narratives of a culture, through which people regulate their activities, or perhaps to forms of largely inarticulate situational understanding. However, we do not need to tread on the treacherous territory of cultural anthropology to find further examples of collective beliefs. For instance, while writing a first draft of this chapter, I listened to a radio broadcast in which it was stated that 'British Airways believes it has been dragged into a dispute that is not of its own making'. Although this position may well have been explicitly formulated by an individual or small group of individuals working for British Airways and then conveyed by a spokesperson for British Airways, it would be wrong to assign the belief to these people alone. The belief is ascribable to British Airways. This need not entail that British Airways and the like be treated as individuals. Rather, as Meijers (2001, p. 167) suggests, certain beliefs are ascribed to 'collective agents'.

It might be argued that references to group 'beliefs' involve a metaphorical or at least different use of the term, suggesting that FP is not obliged to accommodate them. However, it is difficult to distinguish metaphorical from non-metaphorical uses of a term when that term is employed to refer to a variety of predicaments and has no core use. As 'belief' is frequently used to refer to rather hazy dispositions of collective entities (and, if Dennett is right, of individuals), without any explicit indication that such uses are metaphorical, I suggest that we take this use to be as literal as any of the others I have discussed. This entails that at least some kinds of 'belief' are not specific to people. Of course, belief, even in this sense, may be more typically applied to people. Nevertheless, there is the implication that any account focusing solely on this kind of belief will amount to an impersonal account of how we understand people. And this, I think, is one of the problems with Dennett's view. He understands all belief (and various other mental state terms) in this way and thus, as I will further discuss in Chapter 8, proposes an account of interpersonal understanding that is bereft of everything personal. Dennett admits that there will sometimes be no fact of the matter when it comes to arbitrating between different belief contents. However, what he does not acknowledge is that quite different kinds of 'believing' feature in everyday interpretations and explanations. The term 'belief' does not pick up on a single kind of pattern.

In contrast, Stich (1983), during his anti-folk psychology phase, does claim that 'belief' refers to different kinds of psychological state. He discusses cases where our 'verbal subsystem' says one thing while our 'non-verbal subsystem' contradicts it and does something compatible with a quite different assertion. Stich asks which of these response kinds we should call the 'belief' and suggests that there is no right answer. Thus there are *'no such things as beliefs'* (p. 231). However, he blames the poor 'folk' for the view that belief is a unified category, claiming that a pattern 'which looms large in our commonsense scheme of things is the one linking beliefs to their normal, sincere linguistic expression' (p. 231). But everyday discourse is quite compatible with the kinds of dissociation he discusses. Remarks such as 'she'll say one thing but do another', 'he doesn't think he's in love with her but he is', 'I don't think she really believes what she's saying' and so forth indicate that conflict between different kinds of response is not in tension with what the 'folk' think and say about each other.

What I suggest Dennett and Davidson are both quite right to stress is that 'I believe that p' is not a matter of possessing a discrete kind of mental state or entity. By analogy, 'I enjoy cycling' does not indicate that there is a mental state in my head called an enjoyment. This analogy highlights a further problem though. The term 'enjoy' does not identify a homogeneous category of mental state. Enjoyment might take the form of a buzz of adrenalin associated with exercise, a feeling of peace and tranquillity or a host of other experiential states. People enjoy sex, reading, life, roller-coasters, films, competition and a variety of other things in quite different ways. The same applies to belief and desire. We no more posit belief states than we do enjoyment states. As Needham (1972, p. 125) puts it, 'belief' is a 'peg word' that can refer to all manner of states, dispositions and circumstances in different contexts. Most if not all of these could be re-described using other terms that would make the differences between them explicit:

> . . . the phenomenon of belief consists in no more than the custom of making statements about belief. [. . .] The odd-job uses of 'belief' can be separately rendered by other words or by the substitution of other forms of expression, and the word can be so far translated away that the concept must disintegrate in correlation with the dispersal of its connotations.
>
> (1972, p. 131)

The use of abstract and artificial terms in philosophy is not in itself problematic. The problem arises because such terms are claimed to track distinctions that are central to everyday discourse and thought, when they do not. Furthermore, proponents of FP do not generally rest content with the claim that a distinction between informational and motivational propositional attitudes lie at the heart of our commonsense psychology. They frequently go further than this to suggest that such distinctions are even hardwired into the architecture of the brain. Nichols and Stich (2003) are among many who argue that behaviour and its interpretation are enabled by internal cognitive mechanisms that clearly distinguish beliefs from desires. In several diagrams, they represent components of these mechanisms as 'belief boxes' and 'desire boxes'. Heal (2005, p. 183) is critical of such practices:

> What we seem to need is the idea that concepts may be possessed, and beliefs may be formed, at lesser or greater levels of explicitness. And what that suggests is that the idea of there being only one sort of belief, one Belief box with a uniform sort of thing in it, is considerably too simple.
>
> (2005, p. 183)

We can add to her concerns that instances of belief not only vary along a continuum of explicitness but are also quite different in character. To offer a diagnosis of the problem, FP conflates general and specific senses of 'belief'. If one defines it as a propositional attitude, emphasising an essentially linguistic aspect, one gets a conception of belief that looks tidy enough. However, no such notion will be able to accommodate the many kinds of discrimination that we make in our day-to-day lives. Thus, when it comes to offering concrete examples, a much more general, heterogeneous notion of belief is slipped in.

A possible response to such criticisms would be to propose that FP be elaborated, to take account of more subtle distinctions made by the 'folk'. After all, a 'peg word' is only a peg on which to hang a limited range of concepts, rather than everything in our conceptual repertoire. FP belief could be broken down into various subcategories. Rather than simply attributing 'beliefs', it could be maintained that the 'folk' attribute p-type-beliefs, q-type-beliefs, r-type-beliefs and so forth. However, this response is unsatisfactory for a variety of reasons. First of all, proponents of FP do tend to operate with a unitary conception of belief, as exemplified by those who talk of 'belief boxes' and the like. So such a move would require revision of FP, rather than just elaboration.

Furthermore, it would not just be a matter of abandoning one FP assumption: that the 'folk' have a unitary conception of 'belief'. Accommodating the various different kinds of 'belief' would involve rejecting several other assumptions that are central to FP. For example, some beliefs will turn out to be habitual responses solicited by situations and FP has no account of situations. Others will be partly constituted by behaviour and so pose a problem for the commonplace assumption that beliefs and the like are internal states. Others will be formed through interactions between people and will therefore rest uneasily with the view that beliefs are 'attributed' by one person to another. And various beliefs will not respect the distinction between informational and motivational elements, thus requiring the rejection of another assumption that is central to FP. Hence little, if anything would remain of the orthodox account of FP.

Furthermore, it may well turn out that numerous other psychological predicaments are grouped together under the term 'belief' and that everyday distinctions are vague, variable or ambiguous in all sorts of ways. This being the case, describing 'folk' categories will turn out to be an extremely difficult philosophical and scientific project, a far cry from just stating what the 'folk' think. And the outcome of this work will be a debatable account of everyday thought, rather than an uncontentious description of everyday psychological concepts.

Narratives

I have suggested that, when we refer to people's psychological states in our everyday discourse, what we are referring to is singled out not just by the term that is used, such as 'belief' or 'want', but by the linguistic and non-linguistic context in which the term is employed. This and some of the other points I have made complement Bruner's (1990) account of the narrative structure of FP. According to Bruner, attribution of psychological states plays a distinctive role in our everyday discourse and interaction with each other, which can only be appreciated if we recognise the extent to which social life is regulated by culture. People behave and interpret behaviour in the context of a shared background of normative, symbolic systems. When everyone behaves in accordance with this established framework, activities do not require explanation. However, when an observed behaviour fails to cohere with it, we construct explicit narratives, which refer to beliefs and desires. As Bruner puts it:

. . . it is only when constituent beliefs in a folk psychology are violated that narratives are constructed. (1990, p. 39) When things 'are as they should be', the narratives of folk psychology are unnecessary. (p. 40) Thus, while a culture must contain a set of norms, it must also contain a set of interpretive procedures for rendering departures from those norms meaningful in terms of established patterns of belief.

(p. 47)

The aim of such narratives is to show how the behaviour is, after all, intelligible in terms of the shared framework ('the constituent beliefs in a folk psychology') that gives behaviour its meaning. For example, someone wearing a silly costume and singing loudly on a shopping street might seem incongruous, given the patterns of activity that we associate with such contexts. However, the explanation 'he believes that it is carnival day' reintegrates, to some extent, the behaviour into a shared framework of meaning by making it intelligible in terms of norms concerning carnivals. As Bruner puts it, the function of such stories is *'to find an intentional state that mitigates or at least makes comprehensible a deviation from a canonical cultural pattern'* (1990, p. 50). Explanation, in the form of a narrative, is not always a matter of showing how seemingly incongruous activities *conform* to pre-established norms. There is also the possibility of 'negotiating communal meanings' (p. 47). Hence, according to Bruner, the assignment of mental states is not something that we need do all the time in order to explain or predict the internal workings and behaviour of others. It is an occasional activity, the purpose of which is to reunite seemingly anomalous activities with a normative cultural context.

I am sympathetic to Bruner's suggestions that (a) understanding psychological states and actions involves situating them in contexts of shared norms and (b) most of the time, explicit narratives along FP lines are just not needed. As I argued in Chapter 4, social interpretation and interaction are regulated by shared, normatively structured situations. Bruner too takes the constituent 'beliefs' of a culture to be a matrix of norms that regulate behaviour and render it meaningful. His own use of the term 'folk psychology' does not conform to FP. Instead, he uses it to refer to this matrix of norms. However, he does accept that our folk psychology includes concepts of 'belief' and 'want', which operate in the context of a particular kind of narrative. What I want to show is that Bruner's account of narrative understanding, though plausible in various respects, does not give us any grounds for accepting that 'belief' and the like are unitary concepts or that they have distinctive roles to play in certain kinds of narrative. Hence his view does not preserve FP, even in a limited role.

In order to assess Bruner's claim that belief-desire psychology plays the occasional but distinctive role of uniting incongruous behaviour with established cultural norms, we need to establish what is meant by 'narrative'. A narrative presumably takes a linguistic form or has a structure that is in some respects isomorphic with certain linguistic forms. This alone is not very restrictive. Also associated with the term 'narrative' are more specific linguistic constructions that take the form of stories. Given the criteria that Bruner (1990, Chapter 2) offers for something's having a narrative structure, it would seem that he adopts this more specific sense. Here are some features of narratives that he outlines:

a. Sequentiality: A narrative is composed of a sequence of events.
b. Plot: The sequence of events has an organised structure.
c. Indifference to reality: The influence that narratives can have on us need not depend on whether we take them to involve a real or fictitious chain of events.
d. Accommodation of shared norms: Convention and tradition have an important influence on predominant narrative forms.
e. Linking of the ordinary and the extraordinary: A narrative can make the extraordinary intelligible by relating it to the ordinary.
f. Dramatic quality: Deviations from the ordinary have significant repercussions, often moral ones.

First of all, it is worth noting that various narratives account for seemingly strange behaviours without referring to any psychological states. As I argued in Chapter 4, pointing out a relevant feature of the situation is often enough. In other cases, we might appeal to habitual tendencies, character traits, commitments and so forth, rather than to beliefs or desires. Furthermore, many of the 'narratives' we construct to make sense of a behaviour in terms of a shared context are fairly brief and fail to meet most of Bruner's criteria. Of course, it could be argued that responding to the question 'why's she running towards the fire with a hose pipe?' with 'she's a fire fighter; it's her job' serves to draw attention to a more elaborate narrative about fire fighters which, although not explicitly mentioned, plays a role in interpreting the fire fighter's behaviour by supplying the relevant norms. However, this kind of background situational understanding does not conform to Bruner's criteria for narrative form, at least not in most cases. It seldom involves or originates in intricate tales with plots, dramatic events and so forth. For example, people might come to accept norms like 'drive on the left', having been briefly informed of simple prescriptions, rather than as a result of being told dramatic stories about people who drive on the right and meet with moral disapproval or come to a sticky end. In addition, as suggested in Chapter 4, many norms are partly embedded in the shared world, in the form of artefact configurations. These configurations are not themselves narratives, even though narratives contribute to our understanding of how artefacts are to be used in certain contexts. Hence situational understanding is more encompassing than narrative understanding.

But let us consider those cases where we do offer narrative accounts of behaviour. First of all, it is clear that the narratives we construct in such cases do not always re-unite an activity with shared norms. Consider a dramatic and distressing behaviour, such as a person hitting her head against a wall repeatedly, until it bleeds profusely and she loses consciousness. One could relate such events in the form of a detailed, evocative and tragic narrative without showing how the behaviour in question cohered with established norms of behaviour. The narrative might contextualise the behaviour by construing it as the result of a psychotic episode, extreme drunkenness or a consequence of that person having endured terrible emotional suffering. So certain narrative explanations of unusual behaviour do not involve the pattern indicated by Bruner. Indeed, the more anomalous the behaviour, the less likely it is that it will be rendered intelligible in terms of shared norms.

Thus various narratives concerning behaviour do fit the criteria listed by Bruner but do not refer to beliefs or involve rationalisation through an appreciation of relevant shared norms. Not all narratives concerning anomalous behaviour attempt to rationalise it and, what is more, many of those that do take the form of situational rather than psychological narratives. To add to this, talk of beliefs and desires is not restricted to cases of deviation from the norm. People gossip about all sorts of activities, not all of which are unusual. Hence Bruner's account does not secure a specific role for 'belief' and the like or show that use of such terms is associated with a particular kind of narrative. And Bruner does not offer anything to challenge the view that, when the terms 'belief' and 'desire' are employed as part of a rationalising narrative, they refer to a range of predicaments, including engrained habits, commitments, various experiences and sentential attitudes.

Another claim made by Bruner (1990, Chapter 3) is that growing narrative competence plays a central role in children's social development. I do not want to dispute this. As discussed in Chapter 6, at least some norms of activity are created or acquired through dialogical interactions between parents and children, which often have a narrative form along the lines indicated by Bruner. However, this is not to suggest that the relevant narratives embody the key concepts or generalisations of FP. Adult discourse involves neither unified concepts of belief and desire nor an appreciation of systematic relations between them. Hence, given that FP is never acquired, there are no good grounds for imposing it upon the narratives that children construct and are exposed to.

There is a further problem with the view that an appreciation of the core concepts of FP resides in the narratives we construct around behaviour. Many great works of literature display a depth and breadth of psychological insight that would be extremely difficult, to say the least, to exhaustively summarise in the form of a long list of interrelated assumptions about human psychology and social situations. The question arises as to whether great works, such as *Wuthering Heights, War and Peace* and *King Lear*, should be regarded as conveying a folk psychology or an appreciation of psychology that reaches beyond folk understanding. If it is claimed that they embody an unusually clear articulation of what the 'folk' think, FP is, by implication, a terribly unsophisticated caricature of 'folk' thinking. Try translating *Othello* into FP terms and then ask anyone familiar with the text whether the translation contains anything like the same level of psychological insight as the play. I think it is safe to say that the predominant answer will be an emphatic no. The problem is nicely expressed by Strawson, who remarks that the term 'folk psychology' is employed, 'with apparently pejorative intent', to refer to:

> the ordinary explanatory terms employed by diarists, novelists, biographers, historians, journalists, and gossips, when they deliver their accounts of human behavior and human experience – the terms employed by such simple folk as Shakespeare, Tolstoy, Proust and Henry James.
>
> (1985, p. 56)

A sophisticated personal story related by a great novelist is arguably no more of a 'folk' view than an impersonal story formulated by the best scientists in a given field. But, if works by Shakespeare and the like are claimed to fall outside the scope of FP, there is the question of which narratives do exemplify it and where to draw the line. There is surely a continuum of psychological sophistication in literature and a variety of different, often incompatible insights, rather than a neat division between folk and expert psychological narratives. Furthermore, if we want to chart the full richness of a 'folk' understanding, we should surely attend to the most sophisticated examples of it. Analogously, if we want the best account of the structure of the universe, we would be advised to scrutinise the work of leading cosmologists, rather than interviewing somebody who has been taught elementary physics at school. Hence it is arguable that great novelists and the like are the best people to turn to. However, an account of 'folk psychology' that adequately accommodates all of the many subtle distinctions found in great psychological novels has not been formulated. If it had, the study of literature would be a very unrewarding pursuit. Translating these narratives into belief-desire psychology is trivially easy to do but loses most of what is conveyed by them in the process. Such artificial impositions are not always strictly speaking false. For example, if it is asserted that 'Othello believed that Desdemona had been unfaithful and desired to kill her', the right response is not to counter by saying that Othello did not have such beliefs and desires. Indeed, it is the implausibility of such responses that proponents of FP take to vindicate their case for the intuitive and inevitable role of belief and desire in everyday interpretation. A better response might be to point out that an essay written along such lines would receive a very low mark, due to its crudeness, lack of insight and utter insensitivity to the various meanings that may or may not be embodied in the text. When we survey everyday life and literature, we ought to do so with a philosophical eye, rather than assuming that simple psychological patterns can be lifted from it without effort.[16]

Understanding reasoning

That an action has a reason does not imply that it is the outcome of reasoning. An action performed in response to a situation, without any reasoning, can still be understood and explained in terms of reasons. However it is important to consider whether FP at least applies to those actions that are preceded by chains of reasoning.[17] After all, when someone acts in a particular way, we do sometimes wonder what she might have been thinking. Could FP, with its emphasis on systematic relations between kinds of mental states, underlie our ability to interpret people's reasoning? Consider this example from Stich and Ravenscroft (1996, p. 126):

> If a person believes that all scorpions are poisonous, and if she comes to believe that Henry's pet is a scorpion, then she will typically come to believe that Henry's pet is poisonous.

This could be taken to indicate that an appreciation of how people are likely to reason is grounded in an understanding of structured connections between states such as beliefs. However, understanding reasoning is not a matter of understanding how *belief* operates. The person in the above case is following a simple pattern of deductive reasoning:

All p's are q
x is a p
Therefore x is q

When we attribute this pattern of reasoning to, say, Henrietta, we are not just speculating as to what she will think but also what she should think. And why should she? The answer is because *one* ought to reason in such a way. The norms of good reasoning are there for all to follow, just like situational norms. Furthermore, such norms are not just used to anticipate people's behaviour but also to criticise and correct their reasoning or to teach them how to reason in a particular way. The standards in question are shared standards, rather than being psychological processes that are assigned to individuals. The judgement that x is a good piece of reasoning can be made without attributing x to anyone in particular. You can look at an argument on a page and appraise it without inferring anything about the psychology of its originator. Norms of reasoning take the form 'what one should do', rather than 'what I would do' and then 'what Henrietta would do'. It is not a matter of understanding relationships between beliefs but of assuming, teaching, learning or debating a competence.

Understanding why Henrietta would reason in a particular way often involves no more work than understanding why one would reason in such a way oneself. In both cases, it is just a matter of appreciating what one ought to think or do when presented with a given situation. The norms of good reasoning are a subset of the more general norms that we take for granted in the form of a situation. And, when one sets out to explain why a person did something that people would not generally do, in the context of a given situation, the factors cited are often idiosyncratic dispositions and characteristics, which one gets to know about through familiarity with that person, rather than radical differences in styles of reasoning. In cases where people's actions fail to accord with any shared standards of reasoning, despite consideration of such additional factors, the tendency is to attribute them to a lack of reasoning or even a pathological state, rather than to an idiosyncratic reasoning process that is interpreted by deploying FP.

An appreciation of standards of good reasoning need not amount to an explicit or implicit theory of what it is to reason well. We can take certain patterns of reasoning to be good or bad on a case-by-case basis. To do so, we do not need a general account of what it is to reason well; we can rely instead on what Heal calls co-cognition. People appreciate 'what one should do' or 'how one should think' in various situations and presuppose, for the most part, that others participate in the same norms. This can proceed without any need to model, simulate or imagine the mental lives of people, at least when they are sufficiently similar to each other in the relevant respects. Thus an appreciation of good reasoning has the same structure as situational understanding. As noted in Chapter 4, patterns of social explanation and interpretation do not make a clear distinction between norms of good reasoning and situational norms. Both serve as reasons for action and take the form 'one ought to say or do y' or, sometimes, 'where x applies, one ought to say or do y'.

It is questionable whether a competence with the norms of deductive logic is actually assumed by most people in most situations, as Stich himself has noted elsewhere (Stich, 1990). In any case, it is not actually clear what inference ought to be made in the scorpion case. Perhaps Henrietta will revise her initial belief in all scorpions being poisonous, given her knowledge that Henry is very safety-conscious and has a phobia of poisonous organisms. Or perhaps, having seen Henry take his scorpion to the vet shortly after purchase, she will assume that he has had its sting removed or modified. Maybe she will conclude that Henry has failed to accord with shared standards and explain his behaviour in terms of eccentricity or psychopathology. The explanation that is offered will be determined not just by a generic appreciation of how people ought to reason but also by broader situational factors and what Henrietta knows about Henry.

In addition to appreciating how one *ought to* reason in a given situation, we also sometimes consider how specific people *will* reason. I certainly do not wish to deny that psychological understanding has a role to play here; there are many cases where we attempt to understand a person's psychology, what she is actually thinking or feeling. However, I have argued that psychological understanding is quite unlike FP. We interpret people in the context of situations and often through our interactions with them. Many mental states are perceivable, as opposed to being internal causes of behaviour. And, as argued in this chapter, 'belief' and 'desire' as conceived of by FP, are not unitary concepts residing at the heart of some 'folk' view.

When it comes to interpreting what people are thinking and feeling, I suggest that there is no place for anything like a 'theory of mind'. This is partly because theory of mind is offered as an explanation of how we apply FP and it turns out that we do not apply FP at all. In addition to this, a theory of mind is surplus to requirements. Most of the systematic structure we need to interpret people comes from an appreciation of interrelated situational norms. Thus the job that theory of mind is alleged to perform has already been done by the world. I do, however, acknowledge a role for simulation. Although simulation, like theory, is offered as an account of how we accomplish FP, some of the imaginative practices that have been referred to as 'simulations' can be extricated from the FP framework and recontextualised. Even so, the role of 'simulation' turns out to be very limited. We perceive others as loci of experience and agency. We also perceive the structure of specific actions and the meanings of various expressions and gestures. Hence, as with theory, the task that implicit simulation is alleged to perform has already been done by something else. I also argued, in Chapter 6, that certain examples of simulation misconstrue imagined interaction between A and B as a modelling or imagining of B by A. That said, when thinking about people, we do perform various other imaginative exercises on occasion. For example:

a. One sees or hears about someone in a certain situation, imagines how one would feel and assumes that they feel something similar. This might involve brief reflection or, alternatively, it could take the form of a lengthy imaginative exercise. It might also involve adjustments that take account of differences between one's own priorities, commitments, character traits and so forth, and theirs.
b. One embarks upon the same exercise as in (a) but actually feels the relevant feeling. One might also have further feelings *towards* the other person.
c. One tries to understand someone's actions by literally putting oneself in a similar situation or imaginatively doing so and letting events unfold.
d. One perceives or hears about another person in a situation, imagines what one would do in that situation and attributes the same activity to him.
e. One performs the same exercise as in (d) but also takes the other person's idiosyncratic traits into account and then contemplates what she will do.
f. One reflects upon a person's situation and decides what ought to be done in that situation.

g. One starts with (f) and then considers whether the other person will
   do what ought to be done.

Admitting all of the above might seem like a big concession to simulation theory. But it really is not. It is worth reiterating that such imaginative activities need not be interpreted through the framework of FP.
In addition, they are not just *accompanied* by the kinds of abilities I have
claimed to be central to interpersonal understanding but partly or wholly
constituted by them. Indeed, cases (d) to (g) do not involve anything
more than a combination of situational understanding, perception of
activity and knowledge of person-specific traits. Cases (a) to (c) do seem
to involve an additional imaginative exercise. However, they will also
incorporate situational understanding, a characteristic kind of bodily
responsiveness to people and person-specific knowledge. And many
such cases will involve simulated interaction, rather than simply modelling. When all this is taken into account, it appears that 'simulation'
does not refer to a single, distinctive kind of cognitive ability but,
rather, a disparate range of achievements that draw, in different ways,
on the kinds of abilities I have already outlined in earlier chapters.
There is no such thing as 'simulation'.

It might be argued that what is distinctive about at least some of the
exercises listed above is the use of imagination. However, there are
insufficient grounds for insisting that the imaginative abilities
employed to understand people are any different in character from
imaginative abilities that are employed more generally. It could well be
that such practices only have a distinctively personal or social character
in so far as they involve the kinds of bodily responses discussed in
Chapters 5 and 6, in addition to situational understanding. It is also
worth noting that an ability to deploy the imagination in these various
ways is not a universal 'folk' competence, demonstrated by all people to
a similar degree. Tolstoy, Dostoyevsky and Jane Austin are a far cry from
certain other 'folk'. And some people's imaginative skills will be particularly well refined with respect to only some kinds of interpersonal and
social imagination. The same point applies when it comes to imagining
various impersonal scenarios. There is no unitary, distinctive kind of
folk psychological imaginative sensitivity to others; people can be sensitive, insensitive, socially inept, considerate, inconsiderate, perceptive,
egocentric, open to others or distant from them in all sorts of ways.

So, in summary, I have not been able to find any evidence for the
claim that the 'folk', whoever they are, take there to be entities in people's heads that fall into two general categories and play distinct roles in

the generation of behaviour, let alone for the view that belief-desire psychology, construed in this way, is the basis of all social life. The problems with FP remind me of Austin's well-known concerns about sense data theories of perception which, he warned, both caricature and distort the view of the 'plain man':

> . . . it is quite plain that the philosophers' use of 'directly perceive', whatever it may be, is not the ordinary, or any familiar use; for in *that* use it is not only false but simply absurd to say that such objects as pens or cigarettes are never perceived directly. But we are given no explanation or definition of this new use – on the contrary, it is glibly trotted out as if we were all quite familiar with it already.
>
> (1962, p. 19)

The same, I suggest, applies to 'belief' and 'desire', and to other FP terms, such as 'internal' for example. Is it really part of a 'folk' view that mental states are 'internal' in the same way that a liver is 'internal'? It would seem not. Indeed, when explanations of behaviour do appeal to episodes and dispositions that are not *of a person* but *internal to a person*, they are usually not personal explanations at all. For example, internal mental states are frequently postulated in contexts such as psychiatry, in such a way as to indicate that the relevant patterns of behaviour warrant medical or biological, rather than personal, explanations.[18]

8
The Personal Stance

What is left of FP? Stich and Ravenscroft (1996) distinguish three different senses of the term 'folk psychology'. It can be employed to refer to the various platitudes about beliefs and desires. It can also be used in a more specific sense, to refer to the view that our familiarity with these platitudes is symptomatic of a systematically organised 'theory of mind', embedded in the architecture of the human brain. The third option is that 'folk psychology' refers neither to the platitudes nor to an internalised theory that facilitates our appreciation of them. Rather, it is an externally imposed systematisation of the platitudes that is not part of everyday social life but a framework through which certain people think about social life. In this sense, folk psychology is still a 'theory'. But it is not a theory that the 'folk' implicitly or explicitly depend upon when interpreting each other. If 'folk psychology' is understood in this way alone, there are no issues as to which processes facilitate it, how they develop or how they evolved, given that it is not something people actually do but a way of thinking about what people do. As Stich and Ravenscroft recognise, everyday practices could be systematised in a variety of different ways. Some systematisations will be more or less useful than others and the utility of any one systematisation may be restricted to only certain contexts of enquiry.

My use of the term FP is closest to Stich and Ravenscroft's first sense. An ability to attribute propositional attitudes in order to predict and explain behaviour is something that is said to be exemplified by the various platitudes. It is presupposed by internal theory theories, which are offered as accounts of *how* we do it, and it is taken to be something we actually do, rather than an externally imposed systematisation of what we do. I have argued that FP, so construed, is not an adequate description of something central to everyday interpersonal understanding and that the 'platitudes' offered on its behalf are often quite misleading. So my position can be summed up in terms of the distinctions offered by Stich and Ravenscroft: 'folk psychology', construed in terms of the platitudes, is actually 'folk psychology' in the third sense of the term. It is a structure imposed on everyday practice by philosophers of mind, cognitive scientists and others. Imposing order on phenomena is by no means a bad thing; it serves an important pragmatic role in numerous theoretical and practical contexts. But the problem with FP is that it is not acknowledged as an external imposition and is instead taken to be something that people actually do, by deploying internal cognitive abilities to theorise and/or simulate. Furthermore, in abstracting from the complexities of social life, FP omits much that is central to it, principally:

a. The role of situational understanding, which is often sufficient for the facilitation of social interpretation, interaction and coordination.
b. The manner in which we perceive the goal structures of actions, the meanings of expressions and gestures, and even something of people's thought processes.
c. The extent to which interpersonal understanding relies upon relatedness between people and mutual facilitation through interaction, rather than detached observation.
d. The sense of the personal, which is constituted by a distinctive kind of bodily responsiveness to people.
e. The diversity of ways in which terms like 'belief' and 'desire' are employed.

So FP is a misleading simplification of things that passes over much that is characteristic of any distinctively *personal* or *social* understanding. It is conceivable that FP descriptions will be useful in some areas of enquiry and practice. For example, perhaps they could serve as a kind of shorthand in certain philosophical contexts. However, the question of whether and where 'folk psychology', conceived of as an artificial abstraction, might be a convenient way of talking needs to be disentangled from the assumption that it is something that people actually do when they understand each other. Construed in the latter way, it serves not to facilitate but to obfuscate the attempt to characterise interpersonal understanding, interaction and coordination.

The problem with FP stems in part from the projection of philosophical presuppositions, associated with functionalism and closely related doctrines, onto social life. In conjunction with this, the FP literature has not given due attention to what we actually do and say or to the broader contexts that we take for granted when interpreting each other.[1] FP imposes a theoretically motivated abstraction upon social life and then takes it to be the central ability upon which social life depends. It is not plain *false*; 'A believes that p and desires that q' is not to be met with the retort 'it is not the case that A believes that p and desires that q'. However, it accommodates neither the personal nor the social, as it fails to distinguish the personal from the impersonal and does not recognise the role of situational understanding. Furthermore, it groups together a range of different psychological predicaments, distinguished by everyday discourse, under the labels 'belief' and 'desire'. Thus it is an impoverished abstraction and, even if it turns out to be of use in some context, it will be of no use when it comes to the task of studying how people understand each other. The labels 'folk' and 'commonsense' are thus quite misleading.

My conclusions amount to a form of eliminativism concerning FP. However, my version of eliminativism is very different from that of Churchland and others. Churchland assumes that FP is an adequate characterisation of folk practice and proceeds to address the questions of (a) whether we should be realists about what the 'folk' postulate and (b) whether FP is an effective way of predicting and explaining what people do. His answer to both questions is 'no'. With regard to the former, he remarks that 'perhaps the internal kinematics and dynamics of human and animal cognition is not at all like the sentential dance portrayed by FP' (1998a, p. 15). I wholly agree. However, the FP that portrays it as such is not our everyday discourse and interpretive practices but something cooked up by philosophy and cognitive science.[2] Churchland's eliminativism recommends the elimination of something that was not part of social life to begin with. It is the elimination of what certain philosophers and cognitive scientists think that the 'folk' think, rather than what the 'folk' actually think.

In the remainder of this final chapter, I will tie up two loose ends. The FP literature includes much discussion of the evolution of human social cognition and I want to briefly indicate how my alternative account of interpersonal understanding fits in with some recent thinking about human evolution. Then, to conclude my discussion, I will address the question of how the relationship between personal and impersonal stances should be construed.

Evolution and development

The positive account I have offered emphasises the extent to which interpersonal interpretation, interaction and coordination depend upon the relatedness between people. This relatedness involves various abilities, including emotional resources, perceptual abilities, learning processes that contribute to a competence with norms, bodily sensitivities to the actions, gestures and expressions of others and so forth. I have also argued that interpersonal understanding will not be wholly explicable in terms of internal mechanisms possessed by individuals, given that it is partly constituted by relations and interactions between people in shared situations. Given the range of abilities implicated in interpersonal understanding, an evolutionary account of intersubjectivity will not take the form of a story about a single, underlying 'core' ability. It will need to refer to a variety of evolved characteristics, historical periods and selection pressures. And it will need to emphasise the roles of interaction and the shared social environment.

Much of what I have said in earlier chapters is complemented by the speculative account of human cognitive evolution that Donald (1991) proposes. Donald suggests that recent human evolution involved three key stages, which together endowed us with the cognitive characteristics that distinguish us from our closest primate relatives. These stages were the development of:

1. Mimesis (an ability to re-enact events).
2. Speech (with an emphasis on the ability to construct narratives).
3. The ability to use the environment as an external storage system for symbolic representations.

Although Donald's aim is to offer a general account of human cognitive evolution, rather than a more specific account of the evolution of intersubjectivity, all three of his proposed stages centrally involve changes in how our ancestors interacted with each other. The first two shifts, Donald claims, occurred at a biological level and involved genetic changes, whereas the third involved a restructuring of the cultural environment, with consequent changes in brain development. His account of mimesis implicates the kinds of ability that I discussed in Chapters 5 and 6. According to Donald, mimesis is an ability to re-enact events and actions. A range of bodily capabilities together serve to facilitate it:

> Tones of voice, facial expressions, eye movements, manual signs and gestures, postural attitudes, patterned whole-body movements of various sorts, and long sequences of these elements can express many aspects of the perceived world.
>
> (p. 169)

He also emphasises the expressiveness of the face and the subtle ways in which feelings are communicated through expressive interaction (pp. 190–181).

Donald suggests that a great deal can be accomplished through mimetic abilities, even in the absence of language. Indeed, mimesis was not just an evolutionary precursor to modern human social abilities but remains central to social life:

> No matter how evolved our oral-linguistic culture, and no matter how sophisticated the rich varieties of symbolic material surrounding us, mimetic scenarios still form the expressive heart of human social interchange.
>
> (p. 189)

Certain complicated mimetic acts, which people understand easily, are much harder to communicate in words and a reliance on bodily, expressive communication is prevalent even in modern societies. For example, much of what we take from watching a good film is very difficult to convey in words (p. 170). Donald also suggests that many linguistic performances, in church services, crowds, demonstrations and various other contexts, are not primarily about conveying linguistic meaning. They involve shared enactment and a synchrony of feeling that depend on mimetic, rather than linguistic, ability. In many cases, participants' understanding of word meanings does not in any way supplement their sense of the 'meaningfulness' of the practice they are engaged in. Donald also suggests that mimesis can facilitate the establishment of shared norms, in the form of 'customs, games, skills and representations' (p. 173). This has much in common with Hobson's suggestion that gestural and expressive exchanges between parent and child involve the construction of shared norms that regulate further exchanges between them. If Donald is right, bodily, affective interaction between our ancestors, involving re-enactment of gesture and action, facilitated at least some degree of what I have called situational understanding, in the absence of spoken language.

Donald's second stage of human cognitive evolution is the arrival of spoken language. This, he suggests, not only developed after mimesis but also *within* a mimetic framework or scaffolding. Mimesis incorporates much of the structure that is central to spoken language, such as 'intentionality, generativity, communicativity, reference, autocueing, and the ability to model an unlimited number of objects' (p. 171). So the evolution of language, Donald claims, was facilitated by earlier mimetic ability. Furthermore, the linguistic abilities of modern humans remain embedded in a framework of bodily, affective communicative abilities. He argues that spoken language is not primarily an adaptation for the communication of information between individuals. Rather, it has a regulative social function. Invoking Bruner's distinction between paradigmatic and narrative modes of thought, Donald suggests that the primary role of language was (and perhaps still is) the construction of mythological narratives, which prescribe shared patterns of conduct and give an overall narrative coherence to otherwise disparate contexts of social activity (pp. 214–217). The mythology of a culture takes the form of a presupposed reality, which operates as a framework for the interpretation and mutual regulation of behaviour. Donald does not try to account for what I have called situational understanding solely in terms of these narratives. His first stage allows for an inarticulate situational appreciation, acquired through mimesis. And his third stage acknowledges the regulative role of the shared social environment. This stage, Donald claims, took the form of a radical reshaping of the external environment, with consequent changes in patterns of human cognitive development. The reshaping involved using the environment as an 'external symbolic storage system' (ESS) (p. 306). In other words, it was a matter of moving towards what others have called 'embodied, embedded' cognition. Information is encoded in the abiotic, biotic and cultural environment, thus changing and often simplifying the demands made on internal cognitive processes:

> The skilled user of ESS does not try to carry around too much fine detail in biological memory but has learned to be very adept in accessing and utilizing the relevant parts of the external symbolic storage system.
>
> (p. 321)

His account thus accommodates situational understanding, which is construed as something that was originally embedded in mimetic exchange but grew in sophistication with the arrival of mythological narratives and then the ESS. Donald also acknowledges the bodily, felt, expressive aspects of interpersonal relations. Hence there is no tension between what I have said in earlier chapters and an evolutionary approach to human social ability. Something along the lines of Donald's account is just what is needed.

But what is the prognosis for Machiavellian intelligence, of the kind often associated with orthodox conceptions of FP? Throughout my discussion, I have emphasised the role of shared situations in regulating behaviour. An implication of this is that social interaction and coordination will not be comprehensively explained by any account that focuses solely on the cognitive abilities of individuals and how they are brought to bear on the activities of other individuals. Given the pervasive role of shared regulative structures, it would seem that many failures of interpretation and interaction do not stem from the shortcomings of Machiavellian efforts at mind-reading. Confusion instead arises from a failure to appreciate some of the norms that regulate a person's activity. Indeed, it may well be that unsuccessful communication often arises from an *excessive* emphasis on what others might be thinking, which obfuscates a participant situational understanding (Schmitt and Grammer, 1997). Another limitation of Machiavellian intelligence is the emphasis that many theories, which go by that name, place on deception and strategic cunning. As Schmitt and Grammer observe, although there is considerable emphasis on tactical deception in the literature, there is insufficient evidence to discern whether deception is the norm or whether it is even commonplace. Several studies indicate that superficially friendly behaviour is much more prevalent and that, despite difficulties in reading people's underlying motives, there is every reason to suspect that this kind of behaviour is just what it seems to be. Many behaviours, they suggest, are just 'aimed at socialising' (1997, p. 93). I suspect that this view will be corroborated by most responses to the question 'what are you up to over the weekend?'

Another problem for Machiavellian intelligence is that, as discussed, human social interaction involves a wide range of abilities. Machiavellian intelligence will only involve some of them. In addition, it is unclear that Machiavellian intelligence involves a deception-specific skill or set of skills. Deceiving people and detecting deception will both draw upon a wide range of information sources and abilities, suggesting that they do not comprise a distinctive kind of social achievement. Cosmides and Tooby (1992) hypothesise that we have an adaptation for 'cheater detection', a modular social contract logic embedded in our brains. However, a social contract logic, operating in isolation from a broader situational and personal understanding, would be ineffective when it comes to dealing with deceit. In face to face encounters, it could well be that subtle anomalies in the reciprocity of expression, gesture and gaze add up to the *feeling* that another person is not to be trusted. An appreciation of when deception is likely will also involve an understanding of those situations in which deceit is frequent and of how certain deceitful tactics are associated with certain social roles, such as 'politician' and 'estate agent'. To add to this, we can obtain information about the past behaviour of a person, regulate exchanges in various ways so as to make deceit unlikely and so forth. Hence, even if the kinds of cognition often referred to as Machiavellian intelligence did have some role to play in human social evolution, they will only be a small part of the story and will most likely draw on a mixed bag of abilities, most or all of which are also integral to non-Machiavellian social relations.

A question closely associated with discussion of human social evolution is that of how much commonality there is between us and other species. Throughout this book, I have restricted my discussion of FP to the social abilities of humans and have not considered other species. My reason for this is that we need some account of what humans actually do before we can enquire as to whether certain other species do it too. However, my account does have some repercussions for the study of non-human social cognition. First of all, it implies that the question of whether other species have FP or some part of it is misplaced. Given that we do not employ FP ourselves, a comparison between human and non-human FP abilities will be uninformative. What I have said also has implications for the question of whether other species have 'beliefs'. I have argued that the term 'belief' is a placeholder for a range of different states. Thus the appropriate question is not whether members of a given species do or do not have beliefs but which, if any, kinds of belief they have. People do talk about what animals 'think' and, sometimes, 'believe' and I am reluctant to regard such talk as merely metaphorical. As noted in Chapter 7, it is difficult to distinguish literal from metaphorical uses of the term 'belief' when we do not have a clear account of the various ways in which the term is employed. And, if it has many different literal uses, the warrant for labelling certain other uses metaphorical is unclear. I thoroughly doubt that cats and dogs have felt convictions or stances that permeate their lives in the way that a person's belief in God might and they almost certainly do not have beliefs in a more specifically linguistic sense of the term. However, if we accept that a complex, multi-faceted, indeterminate, bodily disposition is a 'belief', then many species of organisms may have beliefs, in this sense.[3]

It is clear that nothing approximating the complex, systematic, normative structure of human situational understanding exists in any other species on this planet. And the intricacy of expressive and gestural reciprocity that characterises human relations is not observed elsewhere. Nevertheless, I tentatively suggest that acknowledgement of the multi-faceted nature of interpersonal understanding, and of the extent to which it is bodily, perceptual and affective, may well serve to lessen perceived differences between ourselves and other species. Once it is acknowledged that human social abilities are multi-faceted, there can be no single, simple yes/no answer to the question of whether certain other species of organism do or do not possess human-like social abilities. In addition, given that understanding people is not generally a matter of understanding internal mental states but of perceiving experiences *in* situated behaviours, the contrast between mind readers and behaviour-readers is thrown into question. FP suggests that the differences between our social abilities and those of our closest primate relatives are largely a matter of our ability to attribute complex internal mental states on the basis of behavioural observations. But, as interpersonal understanding is mostly practical, affective and perceptual, we should perhaps attend to various other individually unremarkable differences, such as humans' more diverse range of facial expressions and more refined affective receptivity to action, gesture, expression and tone.[4]

The impersonal personal stance

More pressing than the task of wedding my account to a particular evolutionary narrative is that of clarifying the relationship between personal and impersonal stances. I have argued that a serious problem with FP is its tendency to misconstrue personal understanding as a variant of mechanistic understanding. My complaint is not that proponents of FP make use of mechanistic thinking but that many of them, especially theory theorists, mistakenly construe our everyday social achievements in such terms. There is a difference between offering a mechanistic account of certain processes involved in interpersonal understanding and construing interpersonal understanding itself as a species of mechanistic understanding. The former involves *first* formulating an adequate description of the phenomenon to be explained and *then* supplying a mechanistic explanation of what that ability consists of. The latter, however, involves failing to acknowledge the relevant phenomenon to begin with, offering an account of complicated mechanistic thinking in its place. In this section, I will further emphasise the way in which the personal is frequently misconstrued in terms of the impersonal. Then, in the final section of the chapter, I will consider whether, having distinguished the personal stance and what it discloses from the mechanistic stance and its deliverances, we should strive to assimilate the former into the worldview that has been constructed through the latter.

A failure to acknowledge the personal is evident in various discussions of FP. For example, it is conspicuous in some of Dennett's writings. As quoted in Chapter 1, Dennett describes the intentional stance as follows:

> . . . first you decide to treat the object whose behaviour is to be predicted as a rational agent; then you figure out what beliefs that agent ought to have, given its place in the world and its purpose. Then you figure out what desires it ought to have, on the same considerations, and finally you predict that this rational agent will act to further its goals in the light of its beliefs. A little practical reasoning from the chosen set of beliefs and desires will in many – but not all – instances yield a decision about what the agent ought to do; that is what you predict the agent will do.

He refers to the entity that is interpreted as an 'object' and his description of the stance suggests detached scrutiny of a thing, rather than bodily relatedness between people. I suspect that this emphasis on the detached contemplation of complicated objects stems from Dennett's more general commitment to 'mechanistic naturalism' (2005, p. 5). According to Dennett, the intentional stance and closely associated design stance are devices that we adopt to interpret the behaviour of certain complicated, systematically organised mechanisms, which could also be interpreted in a more detailed but less convenient way through a physical stance.

Dennett does briefly consider the possibility that there might be something distinctive about second-person interpretation:

> What about the second-person point of view? What people seem to have in mind by this suggestion is either some sort of *empathy*, or a sort of *trust* that is distinct from the admittedly weird, unnaturally noncommittal attitude adopted by heterophenomenology.
>
> (2005, p. 50)

He goes on to ask, 'is there more to empathy than just good, knowledgeable interpretation from the intentional stance? If so, what is it?' (2005, p. 55). I have argued here that there is a great deal more to interpersonal experience and interpretation than what Dennett allows for in 'the intentional stance' and the practice of 'heterophenomenology' (by which he means interpretation of third-person experience through the intentional stance). His failure to recognise such possibilities stems from his imposing the stance of detached, mechanistic theorising upon interpersonal understanding from the outset. I am sympathetic to his claim that there are different stances involved in personal and impersonal understanding. But the problem is that the intentional stance conflates them, the result being an 'impersonal personal stance'. I have argued that what is central to a *personal* understanding is best exemplified by certain second-person interactions, which involve the greatest degree of bodily responsiveness and reciprocity. However, even experiencing someone in the third-person involves a kind of bodily relatedness to them, which constitutes the sense that one is experiencing something quite different from an inanimate object and from most kinds of non-human organisms.

This kind of stance has been recognised by others and referred to in various ways. For example, Thompson (2001, p. 12) describes it as an 'openness of the self to the other' and Hobson (2002, p. 59) suggests that 'experience of affectively patterned personal relatedness is *constitutive* of the concept of persons' (1993b, pp. 211–212). The key point is that revelation of someone as a person requires the adoption of a kind of embodied attitude; without this attitude one would not be open to the possibility of people. Thus, any account that starts by assuming the ubiquity of a rather distant understanding of objects will end up neglecting the personal altogether. Heider, back in 1958, acknowledged that the personal has pride of place in any commonsense psychology and also that the ability to perceive others as people depends upon having a certain kind of receptivity to them:

> Phenomenologically orientated psychologists have stressed that for one person to be in contact with another and to perceive and react to the other's sentiments and wishes, it is not enough that he is exposed to certain stimulus configurations. A general readiness to perceive psychologically is necessary; this receptivity makes possible the arousal of such percepts as 'he is angry', or 'he wants to tell me something'. As we know, people vary widely in such social-psychological receptivity.
>
> (p. 57)

However, the point seems to have been lost somewhere along the way since then. It is worth considering what it would actually be like to take a detached, objective stance towards somebody and understand her in terms of connections between internal mental episodes and behaviours. Perhaps some autistic people experience others like this. However, the difference between a personal understanding and an appreciation of complex mechanisms is perhaps better exemplified by the autobiographical reports offered by certain schizophrenic patients, given that these people are able to emphasise the contrast between their impersonal experiences of others and what their healthy social experiences used to be like. Stanghellini (2004, p. 103) suggests that a conspicuous symptom of schizophrenia is anomalous social experience, structured in terms of objective 'it-it' relations, rather than the 'I-you' relations that more usually characterise social life. He remarks of the contrast between typical interpersonal experience and the social experiences of schizophrenic people:

> What do I share with someone who says that she can perceive her thoughts as quasi-material objects in her head? Or that she experiences the body or some part of it not as her own, but as a mechanism capable of feeling, perceiving and acting? Or that she feels so disconnected from all the others that she is trying to find out an algorithm suitable for interacting with other people?
>
> (2004, p. 111)

If FP, especially in the guise of theory theory, is anything to go by, then the answer would seem to be that we share an awful lot. Stanghellini goes on to say:

> It is not uncommon that schizophrenics become naïve ethologists or naïve psychologists to overcome their separateness from the human world and establish a quasi-mathematical system of key-rules to appropriately interact with the others.
>
> (2004, p. 115)

Again, this sounds remarkably like theory theories of FP.

Here is how 'Renee', in *Autobiography of a Schizophrenic Girl* (Sechehaye, 1970), describes how, during the early stages of schizophrenia, she experienced other people:

> I look at her, study her, praying to feel the life in her through the enveloping unreality. But she seems more a statue than ever, a manikin moved by mechanism, talking like an automaton. It is horrible, inhuman, grotesque.
>
> (p. 38)

Later on in the book, Renee describes her partial recovery as follows:

> The people whom we encountered were no longer automatons, phantoms, revolving around, gesticulating without meaning; they

were men and women with their own individual characteristics, their own individuality.

(pp. 105–106)

Such descriptions complement Stanghellini's claims and, I think, serve to further illustrate the poverty of FP's emphasis on detached observation of complicated objects.[5] The estranged predicament that Renee goes on to describe, in which both the personal and situational have drained away from experience, is not easily distinguishable from the predicament that the theory theorist assumes to be characteristic of typical social relations.[6] If one starts by tacitly assuming the ubiquity of an impersonal, detached, theoretical stance and then attempts to accommodate interpersonal understanding within such a framework, the result is an account that better describes some of the most severe pathologies of intersubjectivity.

Any enquiry into the nature of interpersonal understanding ought to begin with an adequate explanandum, an account of what is distinctive and central to a typical understanding of *people*. The incautious imposition of implicit theoretical assumptions upon the object of one's enquiry leads only to confusion, amounting to the surreptitious denial of a stance that is constitutive of our sense of the personal.[7] But why has this denial become so commonplace? I think it owes much to a general outlook on the world, entrenched in certain philosophical and scientific circles, of which an over-emphasis on mechanistic thinking is symptomatic.

Phenomenology, science and naturalism

The detached, theoretical stance characteristic of FP and the associated tendency to interpret people as complicated objects are both incorporated into a more general standpoint that is frequently adopted as a starting point for philosophical enquiry and often goes by the name 'naturalism'. The term 'naturalism' is used to refer to several different doctrines.[8] In its broadest sense, it amounts to no more than the premise that philosophical theories should not appeal to anything irrevocably mysterious. However, it has also acquired a more specific meaning, involving epistemological and metaphysical theses along the following lines:

i. Epistemological: The standpoint and method/s of empirical science are the best way to acquire knowledge of every aspect of the world, including ourselves.

ii. Metaphysical: The world is comprised solely of the kinds of objects, properties and causal relations posited by scientific theories.

Acceptance of such theses fuels the project of exhaustive 'naturalisation', whereby understanding something is identified with integrating it into the scientifically described world. Anything that exists but does not seem to fit requires reinterpretation in objective, physical, scientific terms or, alternatively, elimination from our ontology. I suspect that the tendency to misinterpret interpersonal understanding is, in part, a symptom of this kind of naturalism. Regardless of whether or not such assumptions are more generally defensible, they have been misapplied in the case of FP. An acceptable naturalisation of a phenomenon at least requires that one start off with an adequate characterisation of it, before going on to address whether and how it can be integrated into a naturalistic account of the world. The problem with FP is that it characterises interpersonal understanding from the outset in terms of a detached standpoint towards an impersonal object, much like the standpoint that naturalism itself places on a pedestal. So the relevant phenomenon is not confronted at all.

Naturalism cannot legitimately claim credibility by ignoring or misinterpreting anything that does not accord with its own presuppositions. The issue is whether, once the personal has been properly acknowledged, the project of further understanding it should involve the goal of naturalisation. Once the structure of interpersonal understanding has been described, can it or should it then be naturalised, through a mechanistic account encompassing both the processes that enable an appreciation of people and the entities that those processes reveal?

The question of how impersonal and personal stances might be reconciled is closely related to that of how we should think about the interaction between phenomenology and empirical science. In this book, I have drawn both on phenomenological descriptions and empirical scientific claims. It is not simply the case that phenomenology acknowledges the personal while science does not. The empirical claims of Hobson, Trevarthan and others are made in the context of a more general recognition of the personal. So the question of how we relate the personal and the impersonal does not map neatly onto that of how we relate the phenomenological and the scientific. The impersonal view is not characteristic of all scientific thought. Rather, it is symptomatic of a particular conception of what science should aspire to, according to which its goal (or one of them, at least) is to construct a comprehensive, mechanistic, impersonal picture of the world, by employing epistemic practices that presumably exclude emotional connectedness, gestural responsiveness and having a nice conversation with the phenomenon in question. So the question to address is whether we should seek to further understand the personal, as described by phenomenologists and others, by integrating it into a wholly impersonal, scientific picture of the world. I will address this question by considering the more general relationship between phenomenology and naturalism.

My view is that the interaction between phenomenology and science need not and should not be construed exclusively in terms of the integration of phenomenological accounts into an increasingly encompassing naturalistic world-view, the reason being that an acknowledgement of the distinctive nature of personal understanding serves to erode epistemological and ontological assumptions that are constitutive of naturalism. In short, not everything is best revealed through a detached, objective standpoint. However, the naturalisation of phenomenology is an option that many take seriously. For example, Roy, Petitot, Pachoud and Varela (1999) focus on Husserlian phenomenology and suggest that:

> . . . when provided with adequate characterizations such as those conducted along the lines of Husserlian phenomenology, phenomenological data can be adequately reconstructed on the basis of the main tenets of Cognitive Science, and then integrated into the natural sciences.[9]
>
> (p. 48)

Hence phenomenology is to be 'integrated into an explanatory framework where every acceptable property is made continuous with the properties admitted by the natural sciences' (1999, pp. 1–2). In so far as there are 'phenomenological data', they need to be re-interpreted so as to cohere with an objective, scientific view of the world that makes no ultimate appeal to the character of experience (1999, p. 48). This presumably also applies to more specifically *interpersonal* experiences, regardless of whether or not the relevant descriptions are acquired by means of explicit phenomenological methods.[10]

In order to insist on the requirement of 'naturalisation', naturalism must involve some quite rigid metaphysical and epistemological assumptions. It is not just that the world consists of *whatever science ultimately reveals*. The demand for reinterpretation and integration into a scientific view is only compelling if the *current scientific worldview* is taken to be metaphysically authoritative. And this can only be accepted on the grounds that (a) current science *does* reveal the world to be that way and (b) certain kinds of epistemic access, characteristic of the relevant areas of scientific enquiry, are privileged over all others. Hence, when I refer to naturalism here, I have in mind a doctrine incorporating contestable assumptions about the nature of science and the way the world is, which legitimate the goal of naturalisation. This can be distinguished from the more accommodating view that philosophy should be in some sense continuous with science, a version of which I will support.

Phenomenology, broadly construed, includes many different approaches, all of which seek to describe the structure of experience. Phenomenologists offer very different methods for charting this structure. For example, as discussed in Chapter 2, Husserl's central methodological innovation is the 'epoché'. Despite there being different phenomenological methods and many conflicting phenomenological claims, there is general consensus among phenomenologists that, in studying the structure of experience, we at least find that objective scientific knowledge does not comprise our most fundamental understanding of the world. Phenomenology is thus opposed to naturalism.

As mentioned in Chapter 2, Husserl (1970) claims that science draws its meaning from a presupposed 'life world' [*Lebenswelt*]. The empirical sciences, according to Husserl, are to be understood instrumentally, as sets of concepts and methods that organise the life-world so as to enhance our practical negotiation of it in various contexts. For example, geometry, he claims, has its source in the 'practical art of surveying' (p. 49), from which it continues to draw its meaning. Geometry is analogous to a map; its role is to abstract from and simplify the life-world in such a way as to facilitate certain kinds of activity. However, it remains a tool and cannot take the place of the life-world within which it operates.

Husserl claims that various methods and concepts have historically come to rest upon others, resulting in a 'sedimented' history of forgotten achievements. As science builds on top of what came before, there is a tendency to lose sight of the fact that these accomplishments only make sense in so far as they are anchored in an underlying world of everyday experience. Naturalism, he claims, mistakes contingent conceptual innovations for the taken-for-granted world upon which they rest. Scientific practices do not provide us with all-encompassing epistemic access to the way things are, enabling us to transcend the everyday world and replace it with the product of scientific enquiry. So naturalism, for Husserl, is not an inevitable complement to scientific theorising. It is a misinterpretation of science that involves an unwarranted over-reliance on certain historically contingent forms of understanding that are actually quite limited in scope. Scientific activities draw their meanings and goals from a pre-understood world; they are necessarily embedded in this world and cannot coherently aspire to assimilate it in its entirety. Such assimilation would be analogous to a road map of the British Isles, which is useful only in relation to certain means of transport, assimilating or replacing the British Isles.

A similar view is voiced by Merleau-Ponty. Like Husserl, he regards naturalistic interpretations of science and the world as confused, in failing to acknowledge that objective scientific descriptions are not all-embracing or fundamental. According to Merleau-Ponty, restricting one's enquiry to the methods and discoveries of empirical science involves a failure to recognise their grounding in a more fundamental experiential disclosure of the world. He construes the structure of perceptual experience as a context of intelligibility for all thought, scientific or otherwise; it is the source of 'all rationality, all value and all existence' (1964a, p. 13). Perception constitutes a foundational 'openness to *something*', within which scientific thought is nested.

Heidegger too emphasises the manner in which scientific practices and theories presuppose a pre-scientific, practical familiarity with the world:

> The basic structures of any such area [a science] have already been worked out after a fashion in our pre-scientific ways of experiencing and interpreting that domain of Being in which the area of subject-matter is itself confined.
>
> (1962, p. 29)

Hence, according to these phenomenologists, and others that I have referred to in earlier chapters, an objective, mechanistic picture of the world, extracted from certain areas of scientific enquiry that are held in high esteem, is contingent on a standpoint that inevitably remains founded on a more basic mode of access to things.

Such themes do not entail that phenomenology is anti-*scientific*. For example, Merleau-Ponty, in *Phenomenology of Perception*, makes extensive use of neuropsychological case studies. And Husserl (1970) takes one of his central tasks to be the *clarification* of natural science. Science still has a place in phenomenology, despite the rejection of naturalism. Science does not contain its own interpretation and naturalism is not sewn into its structure. However, despite the claim that phenomenology clarifies, rather than criticises, changes or repudiates science, a rejection of naturalism would surely have some influence on the practicalities of science. Much of scientific practice does not hinge upon a naturalistic interpretation. Nevertheless, naturalism does structure at least some scientific projects. For example, the pursuit of a comprehensive biological account of human mental life draws its rationale from the assumption that objective science can, in principle, provide exhaustive descriptions of mental phenomena.

Whether phenomenological claims can be developed into a legitimate case against naturalism is another matter. The question therefore arises as to how the interaction between phenomenology and science should be conceived, the tension being between two contrasting viewpoints; naturalism and anti-naturalism. Which one of these, if either, is adopted will significantly influence the course of further enquiry concerning the structures of interpersonal and social understanding that I have sketched in earlier chapters.

Should phenomenology surrender to naturalism or can it go some way towards repudiating naturalism? Roy, Petitot, Pachoud and Varela lean towards the former view. They suggest that, although Husserl's overall phenomenology is resolutely anti-naturalistic, it is possible to extract some of his numerous phenomenological insights from their philosophical context and put them to good use in a naturalistic cognitive science. Phenomenology supplies us with a rich archive of intricate, accurate and insightful descriptions of various aspects of experience. And there is considerable common ground between some of Husserl's phenomenological descriptions and recent findings in neurobiology. Thus Husserlian phenomenology can supply explananda for cognitive science. The job of the science is then to provide objective, naturalistic models of cognitive processes in order to explain the phenomenology. Petitot, Varela, Pachoud and Roy construe their project as a 'reciprocal movement' between Husserlian phenomenology and cognitive science (xiii). Phenomenological descriptions are fed into cognitive science and re-interpreted in the process, so as to accord with naturalism. This conception does not allow for the possibility of the naturalist's ontology or epistemology undergoing significant reappraisal and reinterpretation through the interaction between phenomenology and science. Instead, a fairly orthodox conception of naturalisation is assumed, according to which phenomenological properties are to be rendered non-mysterious through their 'reconstruction' and integration into an objective, scientific description (pp. 48–49).

I agree with the view that phenomenology is a rich resource that we can borrow from to describe structures of experience, including interpersonal experience, which have been neglected or caricatured by mainstream Anglophone philosophy of mind. And, in earlier chapters,

I indicated a number of ways in which phenomenological descriptions and neurobiological findings can complement each other. Phenomenology provides descriptions of intersubjective experience, which indicate just what it is that scientific accounts are required to explain. These descriptions can serve as a directive and interpretative framework for scientific enquiry, as in the case of mirror neurons for example. Conversely, neurobiological findings can provide support for phenomenological descriptions. For example, the discovery of an intermodal link between perception and action illustrates how the kind of non-inferential bond between self and other, characterised by Husserl and others, might be possible. Furthermore, in emphasising perception of *action*, neuroscience can aid phenomenological interpretation, by clarifying the *nature* of the achievements that certain phenomenological descriptions allude to. So mutually enlightening interaction between phenomenological description and scientific investigation is certainly possible.

When discussing the relationship between phenomenology and neuroscience in Chapter 5, I assumed that neuroscience need accept neither phenomenological methods nor phenomenological accounts of science. For example, it can draw insights from Husserl's account of intersubjectivity, without insisting on adoption of the epoché or on an instrumentalist interpretation of scientific concepts and methods. Does this then entail the kind of view sketched by Petitot, Varela, Pachoud and Roy (1999), according to which specific phenomenological insights are pillaged in the service of naturalism? I suggest not.

The interaction between phenomenology and neuroscience can lead to significant revision of the way in which we think about certain cognitive processes. And science is not a mysterious, non-worldly, transcendent activity; it is something that we do *in the world*, which relies upon some of the same cognitive processes that comprise the subject matter of cognitive science. So, in rethinking the nature of processes that we employ in our interactions with the world, by drawing on both phenomenology and science, we should also be open to the possibility of rethinking the kinds of cognition involved in science, the very nature of science, and how the world is most fundamentally revealed to us. The relationship between phenomenology and science is not simply a matter of one being put to work to serve the other. It can also be construed as an ongoing process of mutual re-interpretation, which is not legitimately constrained by inflexible metaphysical and epistemological assumptions about the nature of science that are imposed in advance of empirical enquiry. If one rejects the imposition of phenomenology as an inflexible *a priori* framework for the interpretation of science, it does not follow that naturalism, as outlined above, is the only viable alternative.

Naturalism itself rests upon specific assumptions concerning the nature of our cognitive processes. The world, as disclosed through a particular epistemic standpoint, is taken to be ontologically privileged or indeed exhaustive. Hence naturalism is committed to the assumption that processes exist which *do* disclose the world in such a way, and which also constitute *the best way* of disclosing it. If naturalism is to be coherent, our understanding of cognition will be vulnerable to revision, as cognitive processes are not just a means whereby science is accomplished but also an object of scientific enquiry. Scientific findings could well prompt us to revise our conception of what various cognitive achievements consist of and of which processes enable us to understand various aspects of the world, like people. A potential outcome of this is that the kind of epistemic standpoint taken as basic by naturalism will turn out not to be characteristic of the ability to encounter many or even most phenomena. This being the case, the following argument against naturalism would apply:

1. Naturalism takes processes of type A to be universally epistemically privileged.
2. A-type processes disclose the world as fundamentally x.
3. But empirical research suggests that B-type processes carry the primary burden of disclosing some aspect of the world. A-type processes impede this disclosure.
4. B-type processes reveal that aspect of the world to be y and not x.

The question then arises as to why that aspect of the world should be reinterpreted, so as to be accommodated by the limitations of a naturalistic standpoint. Unless a compelling case can be formulated, we have:

5. There is no good argument for the universal primacy of A.
6. Reinterpretation of y as x is therefore not warranted.
7. That A and x are all-encompassing is a premise of naturalism.
8. Therefore naturalism should be rejected.

If naturalism is not fallible in the above sense, then it is a transcendent doctrine, which imposes metaphysical and epistemological assumptions upon science that are not drawn from science, revisable in the light of science or necessarily compatible with what science reveals about the world. Such a position would explicitly contradict the aim of naturalism, which is to integrate everything into the scientifically described world. If science *can* tell us about epistemic processes, it must surely allow for the possibility of significant metaphysical revision, given that claims about how the world most fundamentally is are mortgaged on claims about the structure of our epistemic abilities. We thus have an ongoing hermeneutic between the discoveries and metaphysical presuppositions of science.

Now it might be argued that, even if the epistemological and metaphysical assumptions of naturalism are revisable, the result is still the world-view adopted by most naturalists, according to which a world of physical objects, best surveyed from a theoretical standpoint, is metaphysically complete. Naturalism is not a rigid epistemological and metaphysical doctrine; it only puts forward its current claims about the world and how it is known as contingent *results* of scientific enquiry.

However, I suggest that a specific version of the general argument against naturalism outlined above can be formulated regarding our understanding of people, given the picture of our intersubjective accomplishments proposed in earlier chapters. In our everyday interactions with the world, we experience things through all sorts of standpoints. Naturalism involves an epistemological assumption to the effect that the world is best disclosed from a standpoint of theoretical detachment (through which it is resolved as a collection of objective entities, processes, properties and relations, extricated from one's own concerns and practical engagements). But other people are disclosed as people through a very different stance. People can only be appreciated as what they are through a bodily, affective receptivity that is constitutive of our sense of the personal. Hence, in the case of people, at least, the naturalistic standpoint is not the way in which we access the way things are.

Despite this, the assumption that people are understood through a detached, objective stance is commonplace in the literature on intersubjectivity. Theory and simulation theories both implicitly presuppose that a certain kind of standpoint towards things, including people, is most conducive to the acquisition of knowledge. As Thompson (2001, p. 12) puts it, 'the presupposition both theories share is that mind-reading is primarily a "spectatorial" process of explanation and prediction'. The epistemic standpoint allegedly characteristic of our best science is taken as primary. However, assuming the universal applicability of a detached, spectatorial standpoint is precisely what eclipses that fact that people are not ordinarily experienced and understood as complex objects.

Hence I suggest that phenomenological descriptions, in conjunction with neuroscientific findings, call into question the epistemic practices and objective ontology presupposed by the project of naturalisation. Naturalism makes assumptions about the way in which we understand the world. However, we do not understand other people like that. Hence the stance presupposed by naturalism is not all-embracing.

Now, one might argue that a theoretical stance and the world of inanimate objects it discloses have a more general or ultimate priority. So our appreciation of people will eventually be accommodated into such a picture and what I have described is just a hurdle en route. However, there is a troubling circularity here:

Why should certain cognitive processes have authority?
Because the world is such and such a way.
Why do you think the world is like that?
Because those processes reveal it to be.

We ought to allow for the possibility of breaking out of this loop. Why assume that what a personal stance reveals is ultimately better understood in a very different way through a detached, impersonal, objective stance? Perhaps, as Buber suggests, an I-Thou relation is a more fundamental way of accessing the way things are than an I-it relation. In any case, there are, I suggest, no good grounds for assuming that the impersonal, objective stance is the only one through which things are adequately revealed. Much of what a personal stance discloses may not be accessible from an objectivist standpoint. Characteristically 'naturalistic' thinking, incorporating an emphasis on mechanism, is partly responsible for a misleading denial of the personal. And, once we have recovered the personal from its grasp, there are insufficient grounds for maintaining that further study must involve the pursuit of naturalisation.

What I do not want to deny is that mechanistic understanding of certain processes may well turn out to be illuminating. But what I do deny is that we should dismiss from the outset the possibility of a personal stance being our best way of accessing how certain things are, on the basis that naturalism, of some description, will ultimately triumph.[11] So my modest conclusion is that, given our current state of knowledge, there are insufficient grounds for adopting, as a premise, the view that the pursuit of understanding the personal should involve attempting to comprehensively integrate it into the realm of the impersonal. We can allow for interaction between various areas of enquiry, such as phenomenology and neuroscience, involving mutual illumination and revision, without adopting from the outset the assumption that some contingent set of ontological and epistemological presuppositions will prevail. Philosophical and scientific enquiry can quite happily accommodate interaction between impersonal and personal standpoints, without adopting the inflexible assumption that one will ultimately swallow up the other. Whatever the outcome of this interaction, I suggest that we should at least start by acknowledging the personal. And ditching FP will be a significant move in the right direction.

Notes

1 Commonsense Psychology, Theory of Mind and Simulation

1. I will briefly return to the question of how we interpret non-human animals in Chapter 8.
2. I employ the term 'person' in a noncommittal sense here, as I do not wish to begin this discussion by adopting a host of metaphysical assumptions about personhood that might presuppose answers to the questions I address. Indeed, it would be premature at this stage to suppose that there is a unitary conception of personhood or that we understand others primarily as 'persons'. I will use the plural 'people', rather than 'persons', so as to emphasise an everyday rather than specialist use of the term.
3. For example, Botterill and Carruthers (1999, Chapters 1 and 2) claim that the 'folk' take beliefs and desires to be internal states of agents, with distinct causal roles, and that they adopt a realist view of these states.
4. What I have offered here is only a brief overview of the debate concerning realism and eliminativism. For detailed discussions of the nature of eliminativism and a range of arguments for and against it, see the essays in Greenwood ed. (1991).
5. Dennett is a holist concerning intentional states and thinks that any attribution of belief entails attribution of a host of other beliefs. However, not all proponents of belief-desire psychology are holists. For example, Fodor argues that propositional attitudes are discrete entities. For a discussion of holism and individualism with regard to propositional attitudes, see the essays in Greenwood ed. (1991), especially the contributions by Dennett and Fodor. In Chapters 4 and 7, I will suggest that the role allegedly performed by a presumption of rationality and an associated holistic network of intentional states is actually played by an understanding of shared social situations.
6. For various reasons, Davidson (for example, 2001) also rejects the assumption that propositional attitudes are internal mental entities. I will not be addressing Davidson's position in detail here. He does emphasise the centrality of propositional attitudes to interpersonal interpretation, in conjunction with an assumption of rationality, and I will offer a more general critique of both these assumptions. However, other aspects of Davidson's work distinguish his view from the claim that we employ a discrete 'folk psychology'. For example, in articles such as 'Three Varieties of Knowledge' (2001, pp. 205–220), he argues that objectivity, knowledge of one's own mental states and knowledge of others' mental states are mutually constitutive. Thus propositional attitude psychology is not a stance that we adopt, an ability that we employ or a theory that we apply *within* a pre-established world. Rather, it is presupposed by the possibility of having any knowledge about anything. Although I will challenge the centrality of propositional attitudes in what follows, I will be agreeing with Davidson at least in so far

as our understanding of self, other and world are more intimately connected than most formulations of belief-desire psychology acknowledge them to be.

7. For a similar account of what it is for something to be a theory, see Wellman (1990, pp. 6–7).

8. The debate between 'theory theory' and 'simulation theory' commenced in 1986, when accounts of simulation by Heal and Gordon appeared in the journal *Mind & Language* 1/2. These articles are referred to here as Gordon (1995a) and Heal (1995a).

9. Heal also indicates that the role of simulation may be more encompassing than this (for example, 1995b, p. 44).

10. Heal expresses reservations about the term 'off-line' (1995b, p. 34), as she takes simulation to be an activity that people engage in and are aware of, rather than something that is achieved by a sub-personal mechanism.

11. Heal relates this problem to the Frame Problem in artificial intelligence. There are many different statements of the problem but it is essentially that of how our considerable knowledge of the world is organised in such a way that only certain factors, usually the relevant ones, come into play when we think about and respond to situations. For a clear discussion of the Frame Problem, see Dennett (1998, Chapter 11).

12. In a response to Heal (1998), Nichols and Stich at least agree that the term 'simulation' 'needs to be retired' (1998, p. 500).

13. See Nichols and Stich (2003, Chapter 4) for a detailed discussion of differences between first- and third-person uses of FP.

14. Another term often used in place of FP is 'mind-reading', which Nichols and Stich (2003, p. 2) take to be less committal than FP, given that the latter is suggestive of the theory theory. I will take the term 'mind-reading' to be synonymous with (b), given that mature mind-reading is assumed to centrally involve the attribution of propositional attitudes.

15. I will discuss the false belief task in more detail in Chapters 2 and 4.

16. There is considerable debate over the relationship between autism and folk psychological ability, which is further complicated by the question of whether the symptoms specific to autism cohere better with theory or simulation theory. See the essays in Carruthers and Smith eds (1996, Part III) and Baron-Cohen, Tager-Flusberg and Cohen eds (1993) for several different views.

17. For discussions of modularity in evolutionary psychology, see Segal (1996), Samuels (2000) and Ratcliffe (2005b).

18. It is arguable that the role of simulation is not limited to propositional attitude attribution or even to interpersonal understanding more generally (Nichols, Stich, Leslie and Klein, 1996). Nevertheless, it could still be maintained that the ability to simulate involves a dedicated functional architecture, even though that architecture is put to a variety of uses. Simulation could be a modular *process*, despite the inputs to that process being quite wide-ranging.

19. See Baron-Cohen and Swettenham (1996) for a discussion of how the shared attention mechanism is related to the later theory of mind mechanism.

20. See Ratcliffe (2006b) for a survey of different accounts of biological function, including variants of the evolutionary account assumed by Cosmides and Tooby.

21. See Leslie and German (1995) for one such account.
22. The term 'deceit' as I am using it here, refers to 'intentional deceit', rather than 'functional deceit' (see Hauser, 1997, for this distinction). The former involves deliberately concealing one's beliefs whereas the latter includes cases like camouflage in butterflies, which do not involve cognitive ability.

2   Where is the Commonsense in Commonsense Psychology?

1. After I presented an earlier version of this section at a conference in January 2005, Beata Stawarska gave these and additional questions to a group of students in the form of a questionnaire. Like me, she found no consistent pattern of response, with a similar number of 'yes' and 'no' answers to most questions and slightly more 'don't know' answers.
2. Strawson also argues that the ability to conceive of one's own mental states is inextricable from the ability to conceive of the mental states of others: 'it is a necessary condition of one's ascribing states of consciousness, experiences, to oneself, in the way one does, that one should also ascribe them, or be prepared to ascribe them, to others who are not oneself' (p. 99). In what follows, my own methods will differ from the kind of conceptual analysis offered by Strawson. However, my conclusions will have much in common with his. For example, I will argue that, in everyday life, we take mental states to be states of *persons*, rather than of minds or brains. I will suggest that an understanding of one's own mental states is bound up with an understanding of others' mental states, but in ways that are not mentioned or implied by Strawson. And I will argue that psychological states are not all 'internal'. See Sacks (2005) for a detailed discussion of Strawson's views on these matters.
3. For a more detailed discussion of Husserl's method in *Cartesian Meditations*, see Ratcliffe (2002a).
4. As Merleau-Ponty (1962, xiv) famously remarks, 'the most important lesson which the reduction teaches us is the impossibility of a complete reduction'.
5. Schutz (1967) and Gurwitsch (1974) build on Husserl's account. Both stress the social, public nature of the life world. I will return to these authors in Chapter 3.
6. Stanghellini (2004) adopts a phenomenological conception of commonsense to explore the nature of psychopathology. He remarks that commonsense is not 'readily definable' (p. 79) and discusses various different conceptions of it (Chapter 4). For his own purposes, he takes it to be a framework of interpretive procedures that comprise the taken-for-granted reality or life world that we ordinarily inhabit. Pathologies such as schizophrenia, he argues, erode this background of commonsense.
7. In fact, Sellars was not only the first to propose that mental state terms are unobservables postulated by a theory. In the same article, he also notes approvingly that this view accommodates the possibility of scientifically driven eliminativism, encompassing not just folk psychology but our everyday ontology more generally (pp. 172–173).
8. Lewis approvingly cites Sellars' story as a 'good myth' (1980, p. 213). Sellars concludes his essay by indicating that it is not, after all, a myth and asking

whether the reader recognises Jones 'as Man himself in the middle of his journey from the grunts and groans of the cave' (1963, p. 196).

9. All comments are quoted verbatim. The students participating in these exercises were informed that what they wrote might be published and that their names would be withheld.

10. The term 'understanding' might have been employed as a synonym for 'explanation' but this is not something that we take for granted. After all, an explicit contrast is often drawn between a hermeneutic social science, which seeks understanding, and a naturalistic social science, whose task is to explain.

11. In Chapter 4, I will argue that a lot of work is done by the kind of understanding described under 2. However, as I will not be suggesting that this is 'obvious to the folk', the fact that nobody selected this option is not an objection to my argument.

12. Wellman, Cross and Watson (2001, p. 665) claim that whether one uses a person, a puppet or a doll has no effect on the result. Even if this is so, it is arguable that person-specific characteristics contribute to other aspects of our intersubjective ability and that excessive focus upon an ability to detect 'beliefs', in abstraction from the complexities of interpersonal interaction, leads to an impoverished picture of intersubjectivity.

3 The World We Live in

1. The people to whom Baker refers as 'us' are presumably philosophers and scientists, rather than the 'folk' more generally.

2. I will refer throughout to Macquarrie and Robinson's 1962 translation of *Being and Time*, and to Hofstadter's 1982 translation of *Basic Problems of Phenomenology*.

3. See Cooper (2005) for a discussion of this passage and of the shift in Heidegger's later work towards the idea that an aesthetic disclosure of things is more fundamental than his earlier categories of presence-at-hand and readiness-to-hand.

4. See Glazebrook (2001) for a detailed discussion of Heidegger on science, phenomenology and everyday life.

5. Although Heidegger regards both 'Das Man' and 'Leaping in' as inauthentic modes of being with others, his conception of the relationship between them is unclear. Leaping in retains the 'solicitude' that is distinctive of understanding others as people. However, it is not clear that Das Man involves even this much. Losing oneself in a situation, failing to differentiate oneself from others and doing 'what one does' is perhaps a predicament that does not require any distinctively *personal* understanding.

6. I am grateful to Shaun Gallagher for pointing out to me the relevance of Gurwitsch's work to both FP and the question of how others are ordinarily encountered.

4 Letting the World Do the Work

1. Botterill and Carruthers (1999, p. 45) make some similar points about the same passage by Fodor.

2. I do not want to claim that all norms are embodied in artefact configurations. Many are but some are not. For example, 'one does not sing loudly late at night in residential neighbourhoods' is a norm that is often not supported by means of signs or other equipment.

3. Bermúdez distinguishes between broad and narrow accounts of the role of FP. He challenges the broad conception, according to which FP underlies all social understanding, but concedes that FP does have a more limited role to play.

4. See also Dennett (1987, p. 21).

5. McGeer (2001, p. 111) suggests that 'psycho-practical know-how' might be a better term for commonsense social understanding than 'folk psychology' (2001, p. 111). As she puts it, it is something we 'feel in our bones', rather than something that we first conceptualise and then use to navigate the world (p. 121).

6. Although my discussion of situations takes its lead from Heidegger and Gurwitsch, similar lessons can be drawn from the work of Wittgenstein (1953) and many others. See Rouse (2002) for a discussion of different accounts of shared normative practice. See McDonough (1991) for an approach that takes its lead from Wittgenstein.

7. The point is also noted by Heal (1996), who argues that any such account would encounter a version of the Frame Problem. A conceptual knowledge base able to accommodate all the constraints of relevance involved in inter-personal interpretation would be so vast and complex as to be cognitively impossible.

8. See Ratcliffe (2004a) for a discussion of Searle, intentionality and the Background. Searle accounts for the Background in terms of the biological capacities of individuals. As the remainder of this chapter will make clear, I do not think that such an interpretation is plausible. What Searle calls the Background is partly out there in the world.

9. Coltheart and Langdon (1998, p. 138) suggest that autism is a heterogeneous condition with many possible causes, as does Gerrans (2002). Boucher (1996, p. 228) argues that increasing emphasis on the precursors to FP leads to a convergence between FP theories and 'socio-affective' theories of autism of the kind proposed by Hobson (1993a,b, 2002) among others. If autism is caused by abnormalities in early abilities that are required for emotional interaction in social contexts *and* for the attribution of mental states, both theories end up appealing to the same underlying causes.

10. See also Astington (1996) for a Vygotskian approach.

11. In support of the claim that the social environment contributes to FP development, Garfield, Peterson and Perry cite a range of evidence, including data showing that the extent of family conversation affects the rate of FP development in typical children (2001, p. 513).

12. Strum, Forster and Hutchins did not coin the term 'situated cognition' but they do offer a history of it, tracing it back to Vygotsky.

13. Wheeler (2005) offers an extensive discussion of the parallels between Heideggerian phenomenology and embodied, embedded cognitive science. He offers a naturalistic account of how the two are to be united.

14. See Rowlands (1999, Chapter 5) for a discussion of Gibson's work in the context of a more general study of embodied cognition. See Noë (2004) for a discussion of how skilful bodily activity might participate in perception.

15. Hutchins and Hazelhurst (1995) also emphasise the role of artefacts in social cognition and argue for a situated approach to cognition.

5 Perceiving Actions

1. See Noë (2004, Chapter 2) for an account of object perception that complements Husserl's discussion.
2. See Steinbock (2001) for a survey and discussion of Scheler's *The Nature of Sympathy*.
3. Zahavi (2001, p. 164) discusses neonate studies and suggests that they offer empirical confirmation of some of Merleau-Ponty's claims.
4. See Gallagher (2005a, Chapters 3 and 7) for a discussion of Meltzoff's findings.
5. See Rizzolatti, Craighero and Fadiga (2002, pp. 40–42) for a discussion of the evidence for mirror neurons in humans.
6. See also Zahavi (2007) for the view that neither simulation nor theory provides our most primary access to others.
7. Petit (1999) and Thompson (2001) also discuss Husserl's unpublished later work on intersubjectivity and movement.
8. Happé and Loth (2000) similarly claim that an understanding of communicative gesture is psychologically distinct from an understanding of intentional action. However, they focus on ostensive gestures, rather than the kinds of gestures that accompany most conversation.
9. In cases of congenital blindness, it seems that there are delays in the development of certain intersubjective competences. However, the developmental outcome is unaffected (Garfield, Peterson and Perry, 2001, p. 512).
10. See Ratcliffe (2005c, forthcoming) for a discussion of our tactile phenomenology.
11. See Ratcliffe (2005c, forthcoming) for a discussion of such feelings.
12. See also Gallagher (2005a, pp. 121–122) for a discussion of the inter- and intra-personal roles of gesturing.
13. A largely complementary view is offered by Melser (2004). Melser adopts a very broad conception of 'thinking' and argues that it is a mistake to construe thinking as a wholly internal process that occurs inside brains or minds. Various activities, such as 'muttering words, adopting facial expressions, making eye movements as if inspecting things, tensing specific muscles, feinting gestures (e.g. drawing in the air)' (p. 8) are not symptoms of thinking but constituents of thinking. His positive account construes thinking as a kind of action, which is acquired as a 'learned skill' (p. 12).

6 The Second Person

1. The claim that second-person interaction involves different cognitive achievements to third-person observation is complemented by studies of how autistic children use pronouns. Loveland (1993, pp. 244–245) observes that autistic children have problems using first- and second-person pronouns but not third-person pronouns or proper names. She relates this to the movement of 'I' and 'you' in interpersonal exchanges. See also Hobson (2002, p. 224).

2. See also Jopling (1993) for a critique of the tendency in philosophy of mind to emphasise the internal constituents of individuals, rather than the relations between people.
3. See also Gallagher (2005a, Chapter 9) for an account of intersubjectivity as interaction. Bermúdez (2003) similarly suggests that regulating behaviour in response to the affective states of others plays an important role in enabling social relations. Like Gallagher, he claims that FP is a 'last resort' that we turn to only once all our more commonplace interpretive strategies have failed (p. 47). See also Stanghellini (2004) for the view that intersubjectivity is essentially intercorporeality and Thompson (2001, p. 4) for the complementary thesis of 'self-other co-determination'.
4. I should stress that I certainly do not want to claim that a typically functioning human body is a necessary condition for a fully rich interpersonal life. Many impairments can be compensated for in social contexts by substituting or modifying other bodily responses. Indeed, there is considerable variety in the means by which people express themselves. So it need not be the case that a substantial proportion of those people labelled 'disabled' have less developed social lives. Indeed, what my argument suggests is that interpersonal relations require work on the part of both parties. Thus many of the social problems that people with certain impairments face may be just as much, if not more so, due to the activities of others.
5. See Ratcliffe (forthcoming) for a detailed discussion of such feelings.
6. The view that an understanding of mental states is acquired through development of a competence with shared narratives is elaborated and defended by Hutto (2004, 2007, forthcoming).
7. Hutto (2007) makes the similar point that reasons for action are embedded in first- to second-person dialogue, which has an in-built sensitivity to each participant's explanatory requirements.
8. See Langdon, Davies and Coltheart (2002) for a discussion of Grice's principle and some of the alternatives that have been proposed in response to Grice's work.
9. One question that I have left unanswered here is that of what norms actually are. I have avoided this question, as my aim is to characterise the structure of everyday interpersonal understanding, rather than to offer a comprehensive metaphysical analysis of the various ingredients of social life, such as norms. However, I cannot resist tentatively suggesting that an appreciation of the normative, of the 'ought', originates in patterns of felt, bodily responsiveness between people, in bodily dispositions that constitute a sense of how to respond to the gestures and expressions of others. Given the permeability between people, it is possible to have a shared, bodily appreciation of appropriateness, of 'what is to be done by someone' in a given context of interaction. Once this bodily sense of appropriateness is acquired, it becomes possible to acquire specific norms through explicit prescription and instruction, as well as by participating in contexts of interaction.
10. Kusch regards folk psychology not as an interpretive framework possessed by discrete individuals but as a shared social institution to which they belong. Indeed, he argues that it is our most fundamental social institution. In so doing, he is not committed to a narrow conception of 'folk psychology' as propositional attitude attribution but uses the term to mean whatever the

most fundamental psychological concepts that we employ to interpret and regulate behaviour turn out to be.

11. A complementary argument is proposed by Wheeler (2005), who distinguishes between on-line and off-line intelligence, the former being intelligence that is embodied in a context of activity and the latter being a more detached, theoretical affair. Wheeler, like Vygotsky, argues that on-line intelligence is primary. Cognitive abilities are first embedded in contexts of activity. More detached forms of intelligence are derived from these.

7 Beliefs and Desires

1. As J. L. Austin (1962, p. 3) remarks, 'our ordinary words are much subtler in their uses, and mark many more distinctions, than philosophers have realized'.
2. But see Lewis (1979) for the claim that belief and desire are unified psychological categories that have properties, rather than propositions, as objects. Lewis conceives of propositions as sets of possible worlds. He does not challenge the view that beliefs and desires have sentence-like objects but suggests that, if they do, these objects will not be limited to those that express propositions. Although my argument that 'belief' and 'desire' are heterogeneous categories will be directed primarily at propositional attitude views, many of my criticisms will also apply to the view that they have properties as their objects.
3. I use the term 'state' in a metaphysically noncommittal way. I do not want to imply that mental states are 'states' in a sense to be contrasted with episodes, properties, entities, processes, dispositions, experiences or anything else.
4. For an overview of debates concerning the nature of mental representation, see, for example, Stich and Warfield eds (1994).
5. Thanks to Suilin Lavelle for drawing my attention to the relevance of this joke.
6. Goldie (2007) distinguishes between 'thin' and 'thick' reason explanations. The former restrict themselves to psychological states but are, Goldie suggests, too skeletal to constitute satisfactory reason explanations in most cases. 'Thicker' explanations refer to factors such as motives, character and personality traits, emotions and emotional dispositions, and narrative-historical context. Such factors are often more pragmatically salient than propositional attitudes and, where this is the case, explanations need not make any explicit references to propositional attitudes.
7. See also Dancy (2000) for the view that reasons are features of a situation, rather than beliefs or desires.
8. See, for example, most of the essays collected in Solomon ed. (2004) for the view that emotions are neither propositional attitudes nor combinations of propositional attitudes and feelings but, rather, ways in which things are experienced. Even if it is claimed that emotions are not 'cognitive' states but feelings, it can still be maintained that they are ways in which the world or parts of it are experienced. See Ratcliffe (2005c,d, forthcoming) for further discussion of both points.
9. See, for example, Solomon (2003, Chapters 4 and 5) for a critique of the view that emotions can be adequately described in terms of propositional attitudes.

10. Morton argues that flexibility over what is meant by terms such as 'belief' itself plays a role in facilitating interpersonal coordination. Context and other factors, he argues, help us to determine or perhaps negotiate what is meant by such terms on a given occasion (2003, Chapter 4).

11. Heal (2005, p. 183) also questions the assumption that there is 'a clear-cut distinction between beliefs and desires', pointing out that cases such as x being frightening are informational under one description and motivational under another.

12. See Ratcliffe (2005d) for a discussion of James on religion and feeling.

13. Despite the frequency with which people express and act upon moral beliefs, work on FP is curiously isolated from ethics. For two approaches that criticise this neglect and offer correctives, see Morton (2003) and Knobe (2007).

14. Thanks to Tim Lewens for this example.

15. Gallagher (2001a, p. 96) similarly suggests that 'beliefs' are general dispositions, which are often ambiguous, even from the first-person perspective. Likewise, Baker (2001, p. 34) claims that 'to have a belief that p is to be ready to do, say or think various things in various circumstances'.

16. For a defence of the view that propositional attitude psychology is acquired through exposure to narratives, see Hutto (2007, forthcoming). Hutto's 'narrative practice hypothesis' appeals to a more encompassing conception of 'narrative' than that of Bruner. Although Hutto and I disagree with regard to the importance of narratives, we share many other concerns about the shortcomings of FP. See Hutto and Ratcliffe eds (2007, forthcoming).

17. Thanks to Daniel Hutto for drawing my attention to this possibility.

18. As McGeer (2001, p. 119) observes, we do not ordinarily understand people by adopting an impersonal stance towards them and positing internal states; we do so only when we suppose a person to be 'mad' or at least 'eccentric'.

8 The Personal Stance

1. Jopling (1993, p. 298) offers a succinct summary of the problem: 'Before engaging in theory construction and model building, it is essential to attend to the phenomena in question and to describe them as accurately as possible. Without this preliminary empirical work, and the ecological and phenomenological validity it assures, the questions with which we begin our investigations will be theory-driven and our solutions will be implausible abstractions with little bearing on reality. It is from such skewed starting points that pseudoproblems arise'.

2. McDonough (1991, p. 263) makes the complementary point that eliminativists 'mischaracterise FP by reading into it the internalist metaphysics of their own mechanistic worldview'. He goes on to emphasise the extent to which interpersonal understanding is embedded in culture.

3. My position has changed since Ratcliffe (2002b), where I assumed 'belief' to be a unitary concept.

4. See Andrews (2007) for a discussion of how a broader conception of FP, as a mixed bag of social abilities, might impact upon the comparative study of human and non-human social cognition.

5. See Ratcliffe (2005c, forthcoming) for further discussion of the phenomenology of schizophrenia.

6. Schizophrenic subjects do often have problems with so-called 'theory of mind' tests (Langdon, Davies and Coltheart [2002]). But, as suggested in earlier chapters, the social achievements required to pass these tests need not and should not be characterised in FP terms.

7. Others have suggested a diagnosis along similar lines. See, for example, Trevarthan (1993, p. 161) and McGeer (2001, p. 118).

8. See Rouse (2002) for a discussion of different kinds of naturalism and for a conception of naturalism very different from the doctrine discussed here.

9. Roy, Petitot, Pachoud and Varela understand the term 'cognitive science' in a general sense, to include various projects in neuroscience, rather than just the attempt to explain the psychological in information-processing terms.

10. Although Roy, Petitot, Pachoud and Varela advocate this view in their introduction, it is not shared by all other contributors to *Naturalizing Phenomenology*, a book that recognises a range of different views concerning the nature of phenomenology-science interaction.

11. There are other problems with naturalism. For example, although I have provided an account of some broad metaphysical and epistemological leanings that characterise it, the specific commitments of naturalism and the rationale for adopting them are not entirely clear. Indeed, Rea (2002) argues that naturalism is largely a matter of adopting an implicit, inarticulate set of assumptions, which he claims amount to a sort of pre-reflective 'research programme' that is insulated from rational critique. Others do claim to identify clear methodological, epistemological and ontological elements, along the lines I have sketched above. For example, Moser and Yandell (2000, p. 10) list the core commitments of what they call 'Core Scientism', 'scientism' being an alternative term for 'naturalism' adopted by some of its various detractors. For several different critiques of naturalism, offered from various standpoints, including theism, see the essays collected in Craig and Moreland eds (2000). See Olafson (2001, Chapter 4) for a phenomenological critique of naturalism, based around the argument that our experiential openness to things is un-thing-like and evades naturalistic characterisation.

References

Andrews, K. 2007. 'Critter Psychology: On the Possibility of Nonhuman Animal Folk Psychology'. In Hutto, D. and Ratcliffe, M. eds (forthcoming).

Astington, J. 1996. 'What is Theoretical about the Child's Theory of Mind?: A Vygotskian View of its Development'. In Carruthers, P. and Smith, P. K. eds: 184–199.

Austin, J. L. 1962. *Sense and Sensibilia*. Oxford: Clarendon Press.

Ayer, A. J. 1940. *Foundations of Empirical Knowledge*. London: Macmillan.

Baker, L. R. 1999. 'What is this Thing called "Commonsense Psychology"?' *Philosophical Explorations* 2: 3–19.

Baker, L. R. 2001. 'Are Beliefs Brain States?' In Meijers, A. ed.: 17–38.

Barkow, J., Cosmides, L. and Tooby, J. eds. 1992. *The Adapted Mind: Evolutionary Psychology and the Generation of Culture*. Oxford: Oxford University Press.

Baron-Cohen, S. 1995. *Mindblindness: An Essay on Autism and Theory of Mind*. Cambridge, Mass.: MIT Press.

Baron-Cohen, S., Leslie, A. and Frith, U. 1985. 'Does the Autistic Child have a "Theory of Mind"?' *Cognition* 21: 37–46.

Baron-Cohen, S. and Swettenham, J. 1996. 'The Relationship between SAM and ToMM: Two Hypotheses'. In Carruthers, P. and Smith. P. K. eds: 158–168.

Baron-Cohen, S., Tager-Flusberg, H. and Cohen, D. 1993. *Understanding Other Minds: Perspectives from Autism*. Oxford: Oxford University Press.

Bartsch, K. and Wellman, H. 1995. *Children talk about the Mind*. Oxford: Oxford University Press.

Bateson, P. and Hinde, R. eds. 1976. *Growing Points in Ethology*. Cambridge: Cambridge University Press.

Bermúdez, J. 2003. 'The Domain of Folk Psychology'. In O'Hear, A. ed.: 25–48.

Blackburn, S. 1995. 'Theory, Observation and Drama'. In Davies, M. and Stone, T. eds (a): 274–290.

Block, N. ed. 1980. *Readings in Philosophy of Psychology: Volume I*. London: Methuen.

Bloom, P. 2002. 'Mindreading, Communication and the Learning of Names for Things'. *Mind and Language* 17: 37–54.

Bloom, P. 2004. *Descartes' Baby: How the Science of Child Development explains what makes us Human*. London: William Heinemann.

Bloom, P. and German, T. 2000. 'Two Reasons to abandon the False Belief Task'. *Cognition* 77: 25–31.

Boker, S. and Rotondo, J. 2002. 'Symmetry Building and Symmetry Breaking in Synchronized Movement'. In Stamenov, M. and Gallese, V. eds: 163–171.

Botterill, G. 1996. 'Folk Psychology and Theoretical Status'. In Carruthers, P. and Smith, P. K. eds: 105–118.

Botterill, G. and Carruthers, P. 1999. *The Philosophy of Psychology*. Cambridge: Cambridge University Press.

Boucher, J. 1996. 'What could possibly explain Autism?' In Carruthers, P. and Smith, P. K. eds: 223–241.

Bruner, J. 1990. *Acts of Meaning*. Cambridge, Mass.: Harvard University Press.

Bruner, J. and Feldman, C. 1993. 'Theories of Mind and the Problem of Autism'. In Baron-Cohen, S., Tager-Flusberg, H. and Cohen, D. eds: 267–291.

Buber, M. 1958. *I and Thou* (Trans. Smith, R. G.). Edinburgh: T & T. Clark.

Buck, R. 1993. 'Spontaneous Communication and the Foundation of the Interpersonal Self'. In Neisser, U. ed.: 216–236.

Byrne, R. 1997. 'The Technical Intelligence Hypothesis: An Additional Evolutionary Stimulus to Intelligence?' In Whiten, A. and Byrne, R. eds: 289–311.

Byrne, R. and Whiten, A. eds. 1988. *Machiavellian Intelligence: Social Expertise and the Evolution of Intellect in Monkeys, Apes and Humans*. Oxford: Oxford University Press.

Byrne, R. and Whiten, A. 1997. 'Machiavellian Intelligence'. In Whiten, A. and Byrne, R. eds: 1–23.

Campbell, S. 1997. *Interpreting the Personal: Expression and Formation of Feelings*. Ithaca: Cornell University Press.

Carruthers, P. 1996. 'Simulation and Self-Knowledge: A Defence of the Theory-Theory'. In Carruthers, P. and Smith, P. K. eds: 22–38.

Carruthers, P. and Chamberlain, A. eds. 2000. *Evolution and the Human Mind: Modularity, Language and Meta-Cognition*. Cambridge: Cambridge University Press.

Carruthers, P. and Smith, P. K. 1996. 'Introduction'. In Carruthers, P. and Smith P. K. eds: 1–8.

Carruthers, P. and Smith, P. K. eds. 1996. *Theories of Theories of Mind*. Cambridge: Cambridge University Press.

Churchland, P. M. 1981. 'Eliminative Materialism and the Propositional Attitudes'. *Journal of Philosophy* 78: 67–90.

Churchland, P. M. 1991. 'Folk Psychology and the Explanation of Human Behaviour'. In Greenwood, J. ed.: 51–69.

Churchland, P. M. 1998a. 'Folk Psychology'. In Churchland, P.M. and Churchland, P.S.: 3–16.

Churchland, P. M. 1998b. 'Evaluating our Self Conception'. In Churchland, P.M. and Churchland, P.S.: 25–38.

Churchland, P. M. and Churchland, P. S. 1998. *On the Contrary: Critical Essays 1987–1997*. Cambridge, Mass.: MIT Press.

Clark, A. 1997. *Being There: Putting Brain, Body and World Together Again*. Cambridge, Mass.: MIT Press.

Clark, A. 2001. 'Reasons, Robots and the Extended Mind'. *Mind and Language* 16: 121–145.

Clark, A. 2003. *Natural-Born Cyborgs: Minds, Technologies and the Future of Human Intelligence*. Oxford: Oxford University Press.

Clark, A. and Chalmers, D. 1998. 'The Extended Mind'. *Analysis* 58: 7–19.

Cole, J. 1998. *About Face*. Cambridge, Mass.: MIT Press.

Cole, J. 2001a. 'Empathy needs a Face'. *Journal of Consciousness Studies* 8 (5–7): 51–68.

Cole, J. 2001b. 'The Contribution of the Face in the Development of Emotion and Self'. In Kaszniak, A. ed.: 478–482.

Coltheart, M. and Langdon, R. 1998. 'Autism, Modularity and Levels of Explanation in Cognitive Science'. *Mind & Language* 13: 138–152.

Cooper, D. E. 2005. 'Heidegger on Nature'. *Environmental Values* 14: 339–351.

Cosmides, L. and Tooby, J. 1992. 'Cognitive Adaptations for Social Exchange'. In Barkow, J., Cosmides, L. and Tooby, J. eds: 163–228.

Craig, W. L. and Moreland, J. P. 2000. *Naturalism: A Critical Analysis*. London: Routledge.

Cummins, D. 2001. 'The Impact of the Social Environment on the Evolution of the Mind'. In Holcomb III, H. R. ed.: 85–118.

Currie, G. and Sterelny, K. 2000. 'How to Think about the Modularity of Mind-Reading'. *Philosophical Quarterly* 50: 145–160.

Dancy, J. 2000. *Practical Reality*. Oxford: Oxford University Press.

Davidson, D. 1980. *Essays on Actions and Events*. Oxford: Clarendon Press.

Davidson, D. 2001. *Subjective, Intersubjective, Objective*. Oxford: Oxford University Press.

Davies, M. and Stone, T. 1995a. 'Introduction'. In Davies, M. and Stone, T. eds (a): 1–18.

Davies, M. and Stone, T. 1995b. 'Introduction'. In Davies, M. and Stone, T. eds (b): 1–44.

Davies, M. and Stone, T. eds. 1995a. *Mental Simulation: Evaluations and Applications*. Oxford: Blackwell.

Davies, M. and Stone, T. eds. 1995b. *Folk Psychology: The Theory of Mind Debate*. Oxford: Blackwell.

Dennett, D.C. 1987. *The Intentional Stance*. Cambridge, Mass.: MIT Press.

Dennett, D.C. 1991a. 'Real Patterns'. *Journal of Philosophy* LXXXVIII: 27–51.

Dennett, D.C. 1991b. 'Two Contrasts: Folk Craft versus Folk Science, and Belief versus Opinion'. In Greenwood, J. ed.: 135–148.

Dennett, D.C. 1998. *Brainchildren*. London: Penguin.

Dennett, D.C. 2005. *Sweet Dreams: Philosophical Obstacles to a Science of Consciousness*. Cambridge, Mass.: MIT Press.

Donald, M. 1991. *Origins of the Modern Mind: Three Stages in the Evolution of Culture and Cognition*. Cambridge, Mass.: Harvard University Press.

Dreyfus, H. and Dreyfus, S. 1999. 'The Challenge of Merleau-Ponty's Phenomenology of Embodiment for Cognitive Science'. In Weiss, G. and Haber, H. eds: 103–120.

Dreyfus, H. and Wrathall, M. eds. 2006. *A Companion to Phenomenology and Existentialism*. Oxford: Blackwell.

Ekman, P. 2003. *Emotions Revealed: Understanding Faces and Feelings*. London: Weidenfeld and Nicholson.

Embree, L. ed. 2005. *Gurwitsch's Relevancy for Cognitive Science*. Dordrecht: Kluwer.

Fodor, J. 1968/1980. 'The Appeal to Tacit Knowledge in Psychological Explanation'. In Block, N. ed.: 627–640.

Fodor, J. A. 1983. *The Modularity of Mind*. Cambridge, Mass.: MIT Press.

Fodor, J. A. 1987. *Psychosemantics*. Cambridge, Mass.: MIT Press.

Fodor, J. A. 1991. 'Fodor's Guide to Mental Representation: The Intelligent Auntie's Vade-mecum'. In Greenwood, J. ed.: 22–50.

Fodor, J. A. 1995. 'A Theory of the Child's Theory of Mind'. In Davies, M. and Stone, T. eds (a): 109–122.

Fogassi, L. and Gallese, V. 2002. 'The Neural Correlates of Action Understanding in Non-Human Primates'. In Stamenov, M. and Gallese, V. eds: 13–35.

Frith, U. and Happé, F. 1999. 'Theory of Mind and Self-Consciousness: What is it like to be Autistic?' *Mind and Language* 14: 1–22.

Gallagher, S. 2001a. 'The Practice of Mind: Theory, Simulation, or Interaction?' *Journal of Consciousness Studies* 8 (5–7): 83–107.

Gallagher, S. 2001b. 'Emotion and Intersubjective Perception: A Speculative Account'. In Kaszniak, A. ed.: 95–100.

Gallagher, S. 2005a. *How the Body Shapes the Mind*. Oxford: Clarendon Press.

Gallagher, S. 2005b. 'Situational Understanding: A Gurwitschian Critique of Theory of Mind'. In Embree, L. ed.: 25–44.

Gallagher, S. 2007. 'Logical and Phenomenological Arguments against Simulation Theory'. In Hutto, D. and Ratcliffe, M. (forthcoming).

Gallagher, S. and Meltzoff, A. 1996. 'The Earliest Sense of Self and Others: Merleau-Ponty and Recent Developmental Studies'. *Philosophical Psychology* 9: 213–236.

Gallese, V., Fadiga, L., Fogassi, L. and Rizzolatti, G. 1996. 'Action Recognition in the Premotor Cortex'. *Brain* 119: 593–609.

Gallese, V. and Goldman, A. 1998. 'Mirror Neurons and the Simulation Theory of Mind-Reading'. *Trends in Cognitive Sciences* 2: 493–501.

Garfield, J. L., Peterson, C. C. and Perry, T. 2001. 'Social Cognition, Language Acquisition and the Development of the Theory of Mind'. *Mind and Language* 16: 494–541.

Gascoigne, P. (with Davies, H.) 2004. *Gazza: My Story*. London: Headline.

Gerrans, P. 2002. 'The Theory of Mind Module in Evolutionary Psychology'. *Biology and Philosophy* 17: 305–321.

Gibson, J. J. 1979. *The Ecological Approach to Visual Perception*. Boston: Houghton Mifflin.

Glazebrook, P. 2001. 'Heidegger and Scientific Realism'. *Continental Philosophy Review* 34: 361–401.

Goffman, E. 1982. *Interaction Ritual: Essays on Face-to-Face Behaviour*. New York: Pantheon Books.

Goldie, P. 1999. 'How We think of Others' Emotions'. *Mind & Language* 14: 394–423.

Goldie, P. 2000. *The Emotions: A Philosophical Exploration*. Oxford: Clarendon Press.

Goldie, P. 2007. 'There are Reasons and Reasons'. In Hutto, D. and Ratcliffe, M. eds (forthcoming).

Goldman, A. 1995. 'Interpretation Psychologized'. In Davies, M. and Stone, T. eds (b): 74–99.

Goldwin-Meadow, S. 1999. 'The Role of Gesture in Communication and Thinking'. *Trends in Cognitive Sciences* 3: 419–429.

Goody, E. 1995. *Social Intelligence and Interaction: Expressions and Implications of the Social Bias in Human Intelligence*. Cambridge: Cambridge University Press.

Gopnik, A. 1996a. 'Theories and Modules: Creation Myths, Developmental Realities and Neurath's Boat'. In Carruthers, P. and Smith, P. K. eds: 169–183.

Gopnik, A. 1996b. 'The Scientist as Child'. *Philosophy of Science* 63: 485–514.

Gordon, R. 1995a. 'Folk Psychology as Simulation'. In Davies, M. and Stone, T. eds (b): 60–73.

Gordon, R. 1995b. 'Simulation without Interpretation or Inference from Me to You'. In Davies, M. and Stone, T. eds (a): 53–67.

Gordon, R. 1995c. 'The Simulation Theory: Objections and Misconceptions'. In Davies, M. and Stone, T. eds (b): 100–122.

Gordon, R. 1996. '"Radical" Simulation'. In Carruthers, P. and Smith, P.K. eds: 11–21.

Greenwood, J. ed. 1991. *The Future of Folk Psychology: Intentionality and Cognitive Science*. Cambridge: Cambridge University Press.

Greenwood, J. 1991. 'Reasons to Believe'. In Greenwood, J. ed.: 70–92.

Greenwood, J. 1999. 'Simulation, Theory-Theory and Cognitive Penetration: No Instance of the Fingerpost'. *Mind and Language* 14: 32–56.

Grice, P. 1989. *Studies in the Way of Words*. Cambridge, Mass.: Harvard University Press.

Griffiths, P. and Stotz, K. 2000. 'How the Mind Grows: A Developmental Systems Perspective on the Biology of Cognition'. *Synthese* 122: 29–51.

Gurwitsch, A. 1974. *Phenomenology and the Theory of Science*. (Embree, L. ed.). Evanston: Northwestern University Press.

Gurwitsch, A. 1979. *Human Encounters in the Social World*. Pittsburgh: Duquesne University Press.

Happé, F. and Loth, E. 2002. '"Theory of Mind" and Tracking Speakers' Intentions'. *Mind & Language* 17: 24–36.

Haugeland, J. 1998. *Having Thought*. Cambridge, Mass.: MIT Press.

Hauser, M. 1997. 'Minding the Behaviour of Deception'. In Whiten, A and Byrne, R. eds: 112–143.

Heal, J. 1995a. 'Replication and Functionalism'. In Davies, M. and Stone T. eds (b): 45–59.

Heal, J. 1995b. 'How to Think about Thinking'. In Davies, M. and Stone, T. eds (a): 33–52.

Heal, J. 1996. 'Simulation, Theory and Content'. In Carruthers, P. and Smith, P.K. eds: 75–89.

Heal, J. 1998. 'Co-Cognition and Off-line Simulation: Two Ways of Understanding the Simulation Approach'. *Mind & Language* 13: 477–498.

Heal, J. 2005. 'Review of Nichols and Stich (2003). *Mindreading: An Integrated Account of Pretence, Self-Awareness and Understanding Other Minds*'. *Mind* 114: 181–184.

Heidegger, M. 1962. *Being and Time* (Trans. Macquarrie, J. and Robinson, E.). Oxford: Blackwell.

Heidegger, M. 1982. *The Basic Problems of Phenomenology*. (Trans. Hofstadter, A.) Bloomington: Indiana University Press.

Heider, F. 1958. *The Psychology of Interpersonal Relations*. London: John Wiley & Sons.

Hobson, P. 1993a. *Autism and the Development of Mind*. Hove: Erlbaum.

Hobson, P. 1993b. 'Understanding Persons: The Role of Affect'. In Baron-Cohen, S., Tager-Flusberg, H. and Cohen, D. eds: 204–227.

Hobson, P. 2002. *The Cradle of Thought*. London: Macmillan.

Holcomb III, H. R. ed. 2001. *Conceptual Challenges in Evolutionary Psychology: Innovative Research Strategies*. Dordrecht: Kluwer.

Hull, J. 1990. *Touching the Rock: An Experience of Blindness*. New York: Pantheon Books.

Humphrey, N. 1976. 'The Social Function of the Intellect'. In Bateson, P. and Hinde, R. eds: 303–317.

Husserl, E. 1960. *Cartesian Meditations: An Introduction To Phenomenology* (Trans. Cairns, D.). The Hague: Martinus Nijhoff.

Husserl, E. 1970. *The Crisis of European Sciences and Transcendental Phenomenology* (Trans. Carr, D.). Evanston: Northwestern University Press.

Hutchins, E. and Hazelhurst, B. 1995. 'How to invent a Shared Lexicon: The Emergence of Shared Form-Meaning Mappings in Interaction'. In Goody, E. ed.: 53–67.

Hutto, D. 2004. 'The Limits of Spectatorial Folk Psychology'. *Mind and Language* 19: 548–573.

Hutto, D. 2007. 'Folk Psychology without Theory or Simulation'. In Hutto, D. and Ratcliffe, M. eds (forthcoming).

Hutto, D. forthcoming. *Folk Psychological Narratives*. Cambridge, Mass.: MIT Press.

Hutto, D. and Ratcliffe, M. eds. 2007, forthcoming. *Folk Psychology Reassessed*. Springer.

James, W. 1902. *The Varieties of Religious Experience*. New York: Longmans, Green and Co.

Jopling, D. 1993. 'Cognitive Science, Other Minds, and the Philosophy of Dialogue'. In Neisser, U. ed.: 290–309.

Kaszniak, A. ed. 2001. *Emotion, Qualia and Consciousness*. London: World Scientific.

Knobe, J. 2007. 'Folk Psychology: Science and Morals'. In Hutto, D. and Ratcliffe, M. eds (forthcoming).

Knoblich, G. and Jordan, J. 2002. 'The Mirror System and Joint Action'. In Stamenov, M. and Gallese, V. eds.: 115–124.

Kusch, M. 1999. *Psychological Knowledge: A Social History and Philosophy*. London: Routledge.

Kusch, M. 2007. 'Folk Psychology and Freedom of the Will'. In Hutto, D. and Ratcliffe, M. eds (forthcoming).

Langdon. R., Davies, M. and Coltheart, M. 2002. 'Understanding Mind and Understanding Communicated Meanings in Schizophrenia'. *Mind and Language* 17: 68–104.

Leslie, A. and German, T. 1995. 'Knowledge and Ability in "Theory of Mind": A One-Eyed Overview of the Debate'. In Davies, M. and Stone, T. eds (a): 123–150.

Lewis, D. 1972/1980. 'Psychophysical and Theoretical Identifications'. In Block, N. ed.: 207–215.

Lewis, D. 1979. 'Attitudes De Dicto and De Se'. *Philosophical Review* 88: 513–543.

Libet, B. 2004. *Mind Time: The Temporal Factor in Consciousness*. Cambridge, Mass.: Harvard University Press.

Lord, C. 1993. 'The Complexity of Social Behaviour in Autism'. In Baron-Cohen, S., Tager-Flusberg, H. and Cohen, D. eds.: 292–316.

Loveland, K. 1993. 'Autism, Affordances, and the Self'. In Neisser, U. ed.: 237–253.

McDonough, R. 1991. 'A Culturalist Account of Folk Psychology'. In Greenwood, J. ed.: 263–288.

McGeer, V. 2001. 'Psycho-practice, Psycho-theory and the Contrastive Case of Autism: How Practices of Mind become Second-nature'. *Journal of Consciousness Studies* 8 (5–7): 109–132.

Meijers, A. 2001. 'Collective Beliefs and Practical Realism: Giving Relations their Proper Metaphysical Due'. In Miejers, A. ed.: 163–182.

Meijers, A. ed. 2001. *Explaining Belief: Lynne Rudder Baker and her Critics*. Stanford: CSLI Publications.

Melser, D. 2004. *The Act of Thinking*. Cambridge, Mass.: MIT Press.

Meltzoff, A. 1995. 'Understanding the Intentions of Others: Re-Enactment of Intended Acts by 18-Month-Old Children'. *Developmental Psychology* 31: 838–850.

Meltzoff, A and Moore, M. 1977. 'Imitation of Facial and Manual Gestures by Human Neonates'. *Science* 198: 75–78.

Merleau-Ponty, M. 1962. *Phenomenology of Perception* (Trans. Smith, C.). London: Routledge.

Merleau-Ponty, M. 1964a. *The Primacy of Perception. And Other Essays on Phenomenological Psychology, and Philosophy of Art, History and Politics*. (Edited with Introduction by Edie, J. M.). Evanston: Northwestern University Press.

Merleau-Ponty, M. 1964b. *Sense and Non-Sense*. (Trans. Dreyfus, H. and Dreyfus, P.). Evanston: Northwestern University Press.

Moore, G. E. 1959. 'A Defence of Commonsense'. In his *Philosophical Papers*. London: George Allen and Unwin Ltd: 32–59.

Morton, A. 1980. *Frames of Mind: Constraints on the Common-Sense Conception of the Mental*. Oxford: Clarendon Press.

Morton, A. 1995. 'Game Theory and Knowledge by Simulation'. In Davies, M. and Stone, T. eds(a): 235–246.

Morton, A. 1996. 'Folk Psychology is not a Predictive Device'. *Mind* 105: 119–137.

Morton, A. 2003. *The Importance of being Understood: Folk Psychology as Ethics*. London: Routledge.

Moser, P. and Yandell, D. 2000. 'Farewell to Philosophical Naturalism'. In Craig, W. L. and Moreland, J. P. eds: 3–23.

Needham, R. 1972. *Belief, Language, and Experience*. Oxford: Blackwell.

Neisser, U. 1993. 'The Self Perceived'. In Neisser, U. ed.: 3–21.

Neisser, U. ed. 1993. *The Perceived Self: Ecological and Interpersonal Sources of Self-Knowledge*. Cambridge: Cambridge University Press.

Nichols, S. and Stich, S. 2003. *Mindreading*. Oxford: Clarendon Press.

Nichols, S and Stich, S. 1998. 'Rethinking Cognition: A Reply to Heal'. *Mind & Language* 13: 499–512.

Nichols, S., Stich, S., Leslie, A. and Klein, D. 1996. 'Varieties of Off-Line Simulation'. In Carruthers, P. and Smith, P. K. eds: 39–74.

Noë, A. 2004. *Action in Perception*. Cambridge, Mass.: MIT Press.

O'Hear, A. ed. 2003. *Minds and Persons* (Royal Institute of Philosophy Supplement 53). Cambridge: Cambridge University Press.

O'Hear, A. ed. 2005. *Philosophy, Biology and Life* (Royal Institute of Philosophy Supplement 56). Cambridge: Cambridge University Press.

Olafson, F. 2001. *Naturalism and the Human Condition: Against Scientism*. London: Routledge.

Papafragou, A. 2002. 'Mindreading and Verbal Communication'. *Mind & Language* 17: 55–67.

Petit, P. 1999. 'Constitution by Movement: Husserl in Light of Recent Neurobiological Findings'. In Petitot, J., Varela, F. J., Pachoud, B. and Roy, J. M. eds: 220–224.

Petitot, J., Varela, F. J., Pachoud, B. and Roy, J. M. eds. 1999. *Naturalizing Phenomenology: Issues in Contemporary Phenomenology and Cognitive Science*. Stanford: Stanford University Press.

Premack, D. and Woodruff, G. 1978. 'Does the Chimpanzee have a Theory of Mind?' *Behavioral and Brain Sciences* 1: 515–526.

Ramachandran, V. S. 2000. 'Mirror Neurons and Imitation Learning as the Driving Force behind 'the great leap forward' in Human Evolution'. *Edge*. (www.Edge.org/documents/archive/edge69.html)

Ratcliffe, M. 2002a. 'Husserl and Nagel on Subjectivity and the Limits of Physical Objectivity'. *Continental Philosophy Review* 35: 353–377.

Ratcliffe, M. 2002b. 'Evolution and Belief: The Missing Question'. *Studies in History and Philosophy of Biological and Biomedical Sciences* 33: 133–150.

Ratcliffe, M. 2004a. 'Realism, Biologism and "the Background"'. *Philosophical Explorations* 7: 149–166.

Ratcliffe, M. 2004b. 'Interpreting Delusions'. *Phenomenology and the Cognitive Sciences* 3: 25–48.

Ratcliffe, M. 2005a. 'Folk Psychology and the Biological Basis of Intersubjectivity'. In O'Hear, A. ed.: 211–233.

Ratcliffe, M. 2005b. 'An Epistemological Problem for Evolutionary Psychology'. *International Studies in the Philosophy of Science* 19: 47–63.

Ratcliffe, M. 2005c. 'The Feeling of Being'. *Journal of Consciousness Studies* 12 (8–10): 43–60.

Ratcliffe, M. 2005d. 'William James on Emotion and Intentionality'. *International Journal of Philosophical Studies* 13: 179–202.

Ratcliffe, M. 2006a. 'Phenomenology, Neuroscience and Intersubjectivity'. In Dreyfus, H. and Wrathall, M. eds: 327–343.

Ratcliffe, M. 2006b. 'Function'. In Sarkar, S. and Pfeifer, J. eds: 315–322.

Ratcliffe, M. 2006c. 'Folk Psychology is not Folk Psychology'. *Phenomenology and the Cognitive Sciences* 5: 31–52.

Ratcliffe, M. 2007. 'From Folk Psychology to Commonsense'. In Hutto, D. and Ratcliffe, M. eds (forthcoming).

Ratcliffe, M. forthcoming. *Feelings of Being: Phenomenology, Psychopathology and Taken-for-Granted Reality*. Oxford: Oxford University Press.

Ravenscroft, I. 1998. 'What is it like to be Someone Else? Simulation and Empathy'. *Ratio* XI: 170–185.

Rea, M. 2002. *World without Design: The Ontological Consequences of Naturalism*. Oxford: Clarendon Press.

Rizzolatti, G. and Arbib, M. A. 1998. 'Language within our Grasp'. *Trends in Neuroscience* 21/5: 188–194.

Rizzolatti, G. and Craighero, L. 2004. 'The Mirror-Neuron System'. *Annual Review of Neuroscience* 27: 169–192.

Rizzolatti, G., Craighero, L. and Fadiga, L. 2002. 'The Mirror System in Humans'. In Stamenov, M. and Gallese, V. eds: 37–59.

Rizzolatti, G., Fadiga, L., Fogassi, L. and Gallese, V. 1996. 'Premotor Cortex and the Recognition of Motor Actions'. *Cognitive Brain Research* 3: 131–141.

Rotondo, J. L. and Boker, S. M. 2002. 'Behavioral Synchronization in Human Conversational Interaction'. In Stamenov, M. and Gallese, V. eds: 151–162.

Rouse, J. 2002. *How Scientific Practices Matter: Reclaiming Philosophical Naturalism*. Chicago: University of Chicago Press.

Rowlands, M. 1999. *The Body in Mind: Understanding Cognitive Processes*. Cambridge: Cambridge University Press.

Roy, J. M., Petitot, J., Pachoud, B. and Varela, F. J. 1999. 'Beyond the Gap: An Introduction to Naturalizing Phenomenology'. In Petitot, J., Varela, F.J., Pachoud, B. and Roy, J.M. eds: 1–80.

Sacks, M. 2005. 'Sartre, Strawson and Others'. *Inquiry* 48: 275–299.

Samuels, R. 2000. 'Massively Modular Minds: Evolutionary Psychology and Cognitive Architecture'. In Carruthers, P. and Chamberlain, A. eds: 13–46.

Sarkar, S. and Pfeifer, J. eds. 2006. The *Philosophy of Science: An Encyclopedia, Volume I*. London: Routledge.

Sartre, J. P. 1989. *Being and Nothingness*. (Trans. Barnes, H. E.). London: Routledge.

Scheler, M. 1954. *The Nature of Sympathy* (Trans. Heath, P.). London: Routledge.

Schmitt, A. and Grammer, K. 1997. 'Social Intelligence and Success: Don't be Clever in order to be Smart'. In Whiten, A. and Byrne, R. eds: 86–111.

Scholl, B. J. and Leslie, A. M. 1999. 'Modularity, Development and 'Theory of Mind''. *Mind and Language* 14: 131–153.

Schutz, A. 1967. *The Phenomenology of the Social World* (Trans. Walsh, G. and Lehnert, F.). Evanston: Northwestern University Press.

Searle, J.R. 1992. *The Rediscovery of the Mind*. Cambridge, Mass.: MIT Press.

Sechehaye, M. ed. 1970. *Autobiography of a Schizophrenic Girl*. New York: Signet.

Segal, G. 1996. 'The Modularity of Theory of Mind'. In Carruthers, P. and Smith, P. K. eds: 141–157.

Sellars, W. 1963. 'Empiricism and the Philosophy of Mind'. In his *Science, Perception and Reality*. London: Routledge: 127–196.

Sen, A.K. 1977. 'Rational Fools: A Critique of the Behavioral Foundations of Economic Theory'. *Philosophy & Public Affairs* 6: 317–344.

Smith, A. D. 2003. *Routledge Philosophy Guidebook to Husserl and the* Cartesian Meditations. London: Routledge.

Solomon, R. C. 2003. *Not Passion's Slave: Emotions and Choice*. Oxford: Oxford University Press.

Solomon, R. C. ed. 2004. *Thinking about Feeling: Contemporary Philosophers on Emotions*. Oxford: Oxford University Press.

Sperber, D. and Wilson, D. 2002. 'Pragmatics, Modularity and Mind-reading'. *Mind and Language* 17: 3–23.

Stamenov, M. 2002. 'Some Features that make Mirror Neurons and Human Language Faculty Unique'. In Stamenov, M. and Gallese, V. eds: 249–271.

Stamenov, M. and Gallese, V. eds. 2002. *Mirror Neurons and the Evolution of Brain and Language*. Amsterdam: John Benjamins.

Stanghellini, G. 2004. *Disembodied Spirits and Deanimated Bodies: The Psychopathology of Common Sense*. Oxford: Oxford University Press.

Stawarska, B. 2007. 'Persons, Pronouns and Perspectives'. In Hutto, D. and Ratcliffe, M. eds (forthcoming).

Steinbock, A. J. 2001. 'Interpersonal Attention through Exemplarity'. *Journal of Consciousness Studies* 8 (5–7): 179–196.

Stern, D. 1993. 'The Role of Feeling for an Interpersonal Self'. In Neisser, U. ed.: 205–215.

Stich, S. 1983. *From Folk Psychology to Cognitive Science: The Case Against Belief*. Cambridge, Mass.: MIT Press.

Stich, S. 1990. *The Fragmentation of Reason*. Cambridge, Mass.: MIT Press.

Stich, S. P. and Ravenscroft, I. 1996. 'What *is* Folk Psychology?' In Stich's *Deconstructing the Mind*. Oxford: Oxford University Press: 115–135.

Stich, S. and Warfield, T. eds. 1994. *Mental Representation: A Reader*. Oxford: Blackwell.

Stone, T. and Davies, M. 1996. 'The Mental Simulation Debate: A Progress Report'. In Carruthers, P. and Smith, P. K. eds: 119–137.

Strawson, P. F. 1959/1990. *Individuals*. London: Routledge.

Strawson, P. F. 1985. *Skepticism and Naturalism*. London: Methuen.

Stone, T. and Davies, M. 1996. 'The Mental Simulation Debate: A Progress Report'. In Carruthers, P. and Smith, P. K. eds: 119–137.

Strum, S., Forster, D. and Hutchins, E. 1997. 'Why Machiavellian Intelligence may not be Machiavellian'. In Whiten, A. and Byrne, R. eds: 50–85.

Studdert-Kennedy, M. 2002. 'Mirror Neurons, Vocal Imitation, and the Evolution of Particulate Speech'. In Stamenov, M. and Gallese, V. eds: 207–227.

Thompson, E. 2001. 'Empathy and Consciousness'. *Journal of Consciousness Studies* 8 (5–7): 1–32.

Tooby, J. and Cosmides, L. 1995. 'Foreword'. In Baron-Cohen, S.: xi–xviii.

Trevarthan, C. 1993. 'The Self Born in Intersubjectivity: The Psychology of an Infant Communicating'. In Neisser, U. ed.: 121–173.

Van Fraassen, B. 2002. *The Empirical Stance*. New Haven: Yale University Press.

Varela, F. J., Thompson, E. and Rosch, E. 1991. *The Embodied Mind: Cognitive Science and Human Experience*. Cambridge, Mass.: MIT Press.

Vygotsky, L. 1978. *Mind in Society: The Development of Higher Psychological Processes*. Cambridge, Mass.: MIT Press.

Warren, D. 1999. 'Externalism and Causality: Simulation and the Prospects for a Reconciliation'. *Mind and Language* 14: 154–176.

Weiss, G. and Haber, H. eds. 1999. *Perspectives on Embodiment: The Intersections of Nature and Culture*. London: Routledge.

Wellman, H. M. 1990. *The Child's Theory of Mind*. Cambridge, Mass.: MIT Press.

Wellman, H., Cross, D., and Watson, J. 2001. 'Meta-analysis of Theory-of-Mind Development: The Truth about False Belief'. *Child Development* 72: 655–684.

Wheeler, M. 2005. *Reconstructing the Cognitive World: The Next Step*. Cambridge, Mass.: MIT Press.

Whiten, A. 1997. 'The Machiavellian Mindreader'. In Whiten, A. and Byrne, R. W. eds: 144–173.

Whiten, A. and Byrne, R. W. eds. 1997. *Machiavellian Intelligence II: Extensions and Evaluations*. Cambridge: Cambridge University Press.

Wimmer, H. and Perner, J. 1983. 'Beliefs about Beliefs: Representation and Constraining Function of Wrong Beliefs in Young Children's Understanding of Deception'. *Cognition* 13: 103–128.

Wittgenstein, L. 1953. *Philosophical Investigations* (Trans. Anscombe, G.E.M.). New York: Macmillan.

Wohlschläger, A. and Bekkering, H. 2002. 'The Role of Objects in Imitation'. In Stamenov, M. and Gallese, V. eds: 101–113.

Zahavi, D. 2001. 'Beyond Empathy: Phenomenological Approaches to Intersubjectivity'. *Journal of Consciousness Studies* 8 (5–7): 151–167.

Zahavi, D. 2007. 'Expression and Empathy'. In Hutto, D. and Ratcliffe, M. (forthcoming).

Index

action
  explanation of, 95, 97, 121, 149–51,
    191, 193–7, 205, 207, 211–18
  interpretation of, 85–98, 147,
    149–51, 157, 165, 170, 175–7,
    191, 193–4, 206–7, 212–14,
    218–19, 227–8, 231
  perception of, 121–4, 129–49, 171
  varieties of, 138–9
affect, 77–8, 124, 144, 153, 155,
  159–74, 183, 226
  see also emotion; feeling
Andrews, K., 253
animals, nonhuman, 104, 229–30
Arbib, M.A., 140
artefacts,
  see functions, of artefacts
Astington, J., 249
Austin, J. L., 43, 221, 252
autism, 17, 44, 101–3, 165, 173, 232
Ayer, A. J., 43

Baker, L. R., 59–61, 119, 248, 253
Baron-Cohen, S., 17–18, 44, 102, 167,
  246
Bartsch, K., 52
Bekkering, H., 132
belief
  collective beliefs, 207–8
  and commitment, 199–205
  everyday uses of the term, 23,
    187–9, 193, 198–201, 203–5,
    208–10
  and experience, 197–9
  as an indeterminate disposition,
    205–11
  literal and metaphorical uses of the
    term 'belief', 208, 229
  as a propositional attitude, 3, 23,
    187–92, 197–204, 208, 210
  relationship to desire, 199–205, 210
belief-desire psychology,
  see folk psychology

Bermúdez, J., 94, 101, 114, 117, 249,
  251
Blackburn, S., 99
Blair, T., 203
Bloom, P., 29–35, 101–2, 104
Boker, S., 140
Botterill, G., 9, 14, 18, 28, 44, 85, 245,
  248
Boucher, J., 249
Bruner, J., 103, 173–4, 211–14, 227, 253
Buber, M., 154–6, 161, 243
Buck, R., 170
Byrne, R., 20

Campbell, S., 146–7
Carruthers, P., 14, 16–18, 28, 44, 85,
  245–6, 248
Cartesian dualism
  see dualism as commonsense
Chalmers, D., 107, 111–12
character, 96, 149, 183, 189, 204–5
Churchland, P.M., 2, 6–8, 43, 51, 123,
  153, 224
Clark, A., 107, 109, 111–12, 116, 180,
  183
co-cognition, 14, 134, 218
Cole, J., 168–9
Coltheart, M., 249, 251, 254
commitments, 189–90, 199–205
commonsense
  the commonsense world, 59–61, 67,
    70
  different conceptions of, 21, 27–45,
    55–7, 60
  and everyday intuitions about men-
    tal states, 21, 46–52, 211
  and folk psychology, 27–57
  and philosophical enquiry, 31–46,
    51–2, 55, 72, 74, 79, 82, 211,
    215–16, 221
  relationship between commonsense
    psychology and commonsense
    more generally, 59–61, 98

commonsense – *continued*
  and scientific views, 27, 52–7, 60, 98
commonsense psychology,
  see folk psychology
concepts, nature of, 171–3
constraints on interpretation
  cooperative creation of constraints
    through interaction, 166–7,
    173–80
  the shared social world, 58, 73,
    85–98, 116–20, 177–80
conversation, 157, 164–5, 173–80
convictions,
  see commitments
Cooper, D.E., 248
Cosmides, L., 18–19, 228, 246
craft, versus ideology, 55–6
Craig, W. L., 254
Craighero, L., 130–2, 142, 250
Cross, D., 17, 55, 100, 248
Cummins, D., 119
Currie, G., 19, 85, 100–1

Dancy, J., 190, 252
Davidson, D., 96, 138, 205–6, 209,
  245
Davies, M., 3, 13, 19, 132, 251, 254
Dennett, D.C., 7–8, 33, 55–7, 82, 86–7,
  96, 205–9, 231, 245–6, 249
Descartes, R., 37, 67
descriptive metaphysics, 33, 36
desire
  and commitment, 199–205
  everyday uses of the term, 23,
    189–90, 198–200, 204–5
  as a propositional attitude, 3, 23,
    187, 190–1, 197–9
  relationship to belief, 199–205, 210
development, of social ability, 16–19,
  52–5, 98–107, 128–9, 153,
  173–4, 214
Donald, M., 175, 224–9
Dreyfus, H., 115
Dreyfus, S., 115
dualism, as commonsense, 29–35

Ekman, P., 146
eliminativism, concerning folk psychology, 6–7, 15, 209, 224

embodied, embedded cognition,
  107–18, 164–5, 227
emotion, 77, 127, 143–6, 181, 198
empathy, 125, 127, 160, 181, 231
enactive cognition, 107, 133–4
  see also embodied, embedded cogni-
    tion
epoché, phenomenological, 37–41,
  237, 240
evolution, of social ability, 16–20,
  224–9
experience, its relationship to understanding, 25
explanation, of behaviour, 4, 25, 95,
  97, 149–51, 191, 193–7, 205,
  207, 211–14, 216–18, 221
expression, 121–32, 137–48, 165–6,
  168–71, 175–6, 206, 226
extended cognition, 107
  see also embodied, embedded cogni-
    tion

Fadiga, L., 130–2, 250
false belief task, 16–17, 52–6, 100–6,
  174, 201
feeling, 77, 127, 144–7, 159–61, 163,
  167, 169–71, 198, 202–3, 226,
  228
Feldman, C., 103, 173–4
first-person access to mental states, in
  contrast to third-person, 15
Fodor, J. A., 3, 6–9, 17–18, 28, 44, 47,
  56, 85–7, 187, 245, 248
Fogassi, L., 130–1, 134, 136
folk psychology
  central concepts of, 3–5, 186–221
  and commonsense, 27–57, 59–61,
    79, 215–16
  definition adopted here, 16, 222–3
  and development, 16–19, 98–107,
    173
  different senses of the term, 16,
    222–3
  and evolution, 16–20
  and interaction between people,
    79–80, 105–18, 139–41, 152–4,
    160–85
  internal and external accounts of,
    222–3

and modularity, 18–19
orthodox account of, 2–7, 15–16,
    42–6
and perception of mental states,
    121–51
and the phenomenology of the
    social world, 62–84
philosophical origins of, 42–6
and scientific psychology, 27, 52–7
and understanding the social world,
    58–60, 89–99, 107–20, 149–51
as a theoretically motivated abstrac-
    tion from social life, 23, 199,
    216, 222–4, 230–4
in relation to theory and simulation
    theories, 6–15, 28, 44
Forster, D., 107, 249
FP, acronym for 'folk psychology', 16
Frith, U., 5, 44, 52, 55, 193
functionalism, and folk psychology,
    43–5
functions
    and modularity, 18–19
    of artefacts, 21–2, 61, 66–9, 71, 74,
        78, 84, 86–92, 96, 98, 108–19,
        165, 214

Gallagher, S., 53, 77–8, 101, 124,
    133–4, 136–7, 145, 149, 152–3,
    156–7, 167–8, 172, 248, 250–1,
    253
Gallese, V., 130–2, 134, 136
Garfield, J. L., 19, 101, 106, 249–50
Gascoigne, P., 115–16
German, T., 101, 104, 247
Gerrans, P., 102, 249
gesture, 121–4, 127–32, 137–48,
    165–6, 170–2, 175–6, 226
Gibson, J. J., 91, 110, 133–4, 249
Glazebrook, P., 248
Goffman, E., 177–8
Goldie, P., 96, 156, 181, 252
Goldman, A., 3, 10–14, 16, 28, 45,
    132
Goldwin-Meadow, S., 138, 147–8
Gopnik, A., 17, 19
Gordon, R., 11–12, 14–16, 18, 28, 44,
    89–94, 118, 181–2, 246
Grammer, K., 228

Greenwood, J., 33, 42, 105, 245
Grice, P., 178, 251
Griffiths, P., 112–3
Gurwitsch, A., 59, 74–8, 89–94, 179,
    247, 249

Happé, F., 5, 18, 52, 55, 193, 250
Haugeland, J., 107–8, 117
Hauser, M., 247
Hazelhurst, B., 250
Heal, J., 10–14, 44, 134, 210, 218,
    246, 249, 253
Heidegger, M.
    on authenticity and inauthenticity,
        72–4
    on Being, 62, 64
    on being-in-the-world, 59, 61–70,
        238, 248–9
    on being-with-others, 70–4
    on 'das Man', 73–4
    on equipment, 64–70, 89, 96
    on phenomenological method, 41–2
Heider, F., 42, 143, 232
Hobson, P., 33, 106, 137, 153–4, 157,
    165–6, 170, 173–4, 179, 226,
    232, 235, 249–50
horizons, in Husserlian phenomenol-
    ogy, 124–5, 144–5, 175
Hull, J., 169
Humphrey, N., 20
Husserl, E.
    on intersubjectivity, 124–6, 136–7,
        142, 144–5, 175, 240
    on phenomenological method,
        36–42, 237, 247
    on science and the life world,
        39–41, 61, 237–8, 240
Hutchins, E., 107, 249–50
Hutto, D., 251, 253
hybrid theories, 13–15

ideology, versus craft, 55–6
imagination, 11, 14, 219–20
informational states, as distinct from
    motivational states, 4, 45, 190,
    192, 198–205, 210
innateness, of social ability, 16–19
intentional stance, 7–8, 86, 206,
    231–2

interaction
  contrast with spectatorial folk psy-
    chology, 79–80, 105–6, 139–41,
    152–4, 160–85, 232
  conversational interaction, 157,
    164–5, 172–80
  and intersubjective development,
    101–7, 153, 173–4
  and simulated interaction, 153,
    180–4, 219–20
  and social understanding, 22–3, 86,
    105–18, 126, 139–41, 152–4,
    160–85
  see also Thou-orientation
internal, mental states as internal,
    4–8, 32, 34–5, 43, 45, 94,
    107–8, 122, 145–9, 163, 176,
    186, 195, 221, 230, 232
internalisation, of cognitive abilities,
    106–8, 111–15, 119, 164, 180–4

James, W., 202, 253
Jopling, D., 251, 253
Jordan, J., 141

Kant, I., 56
Klein, D., 246
Knobe, J., 253
Knoblich, G., 141
Kusch, M., 118, 180, 251

Langdon. R., 249, 251, 254
Lavelle, J. S., 252
Leslie, A. M., 44, 197, 246–7
Lewens, T., 253
Lewis, D., 43, 44, 247, 252
Libet, B., 115
life world, in phenomenology, 39–41,
    61, 237–8
Lord, C., 103
Loth, E., 18, 250
Loveland, K., 250

M-predicates, 34–5
Machiavellian intelligence, 20, 227–9
McDonough, R., 249, 253
McGeer, V., 97, 249, 253–4
mechanistic understanding, of peo-
    ple, 184

Meijers, A., 208
Melser, D., 250
Meltzoff, A., 100, 122, 130, 137, 250
Merleau-Ponty, M., 128–9, 133, 137,
    146–7, 162, 175, 238, 247, 250
mimesis, 225–6
mirror neurons, 130–43, 170, 240
Mobiüs syndrome, 168
modularity, 17–19
Moore, G. E., 56
Moore, M., 130
Moreland, J. P., 254
Morton, A., 44, 97, 116–18, 174, 177,
    253
Moser, P., 254
motivational states, as distinct from
    informational states, 4, 45, 190,
    192, 198–205, 210

narratives, 173–4, 176–9, 187, 193,
    202, 205, 208, 211–16, 227
natural attitude, in phenomenology,
    37–41, 79
naturalisation,
  see naturalism
naturalism, 23, 203–4, 231, 234–44
Needham, R., 23, 187–8, 203, 208–9
Neisser, U., 166
Nichols, S., 15, 210, 246
Noë, A., 134, 172, 249–50
norms, social, 21–2, 60–1, 73–4, 78,
    84, 87–98, 108–9, 114–17, 119,
    165, 177–80, 192, 194–5, 211,
    213–14, 217–18, 226, 228

Olafson, F., 254
opinions, in contrast to beliefs, 206

P-predicates, 34–5
Pachoud, B., 41, 236, 239–40, 254
Papafragou, A., 100
peg words, 23, 209–10
perception
  of action, 80, 121–4, 129–48, 171
  of experience, 80–81, 127–8, 138,
    143–6, 162
  of expression, 75, 80, 121–4,
    127–8, 130–2, 137–48, 165,
    168–9, 171

of gesture, 75, 80, 121–4, 127–32, 137–48, 165, 171
Perner, J., 16, 44, 52–4, 104
Perry, T., 19, 101, 106, 249–50
personal stance, 23, 82, 84, 139, 153–61, 166, 171, 176, 180, 184, 223–4, 230–6, 242–4
persons, 23–4, 33–5, 78–9, 82–3, 141, 153–61, 166, 171, 176, 180, 184, 231–2, 234, 242–4
see also personal stance
Peterson, C. C., 19, 101, 106, 249–50
Petit, P., 124, 250
Petitot, J., 41, 236, 239–40, 254
Phenomenology
  and commonsense, 36–42, 82
  and embodied, embedded cognition, 108–9
  and folk psychology, 26, 36, 82
  and intersubjectivity, 70–84, 123–9, 133, 136–8, 141–2, 144–6, 158–64
  and naturalism, 234–44
  and science, 39–41, 68, 109, 124, 136–8, 141, 234–44
  of the social world, 62–84
  see also Gurwitsch, Heidegger, Husserl, Merleau-Ponty, Sartre, Scheler, Schutz
physicalism, and the commonsense view, 60–1, 75
platitudes, of folk psychology, 13, 193, 222–3
prediction, of behaviour, 4, 7–8, 10, 12, 24–5, 85–7, 89, 96, 107, 114–18, 177, 212
Premack, D., 44
projection, in simulation, 92–4
propositional attitudes, nature of, 3–8, 187, 190–3, 197–9, 202–3, 208, 210
propositional attitude psychology, *see* folk psychology

Ramachandran, V. S., 141
Ratcliffe, M., 170, 203, 246–7, 249, 251–3
rational choice theory, 116
rationality, 7, 13, 96–8

Ravenscroft, I. , 28, 43, 44, 181, 191, 193, 199–200, 207, 216, 222–3
Rea, M., 203, 254
realism, concerning the posits of folk psychology, 6–8
reasoning, 13, 216–19
reasons
  kinds of reasons offered for actions, 95, 97, 139, 149–51, 195–7, 204–5, 216
  motivating and normative reasons, 197
  social situations as reasons, 96–8, 122, 149–51, 195–6, 216
reciprocity, between people, 158, 162–3, 166–70, 175, 228, 232
regulation, of behaviour, 107–8, 112–18, 166–70, 173, 175, 177, 180, 208, 211, 226–8
relations
  kinds of social relation, 79–84
  relatedness between people, 49, 79, 81–2, 141, 153–70, 184, 232
relevance, 12
revisionary metaphysics, 33
Rizzolatti, G., 130–2, 140, 142, 250
roles, social, 21–2, 61, 74–8, 83–90, 94–8, 108–9, 119, 165, 177
Rosch, E., 107
Rotondo, J. L., 140
Rouse, J., 98, 249, 254
Rowlands, M., 107–8, 249
Roy, J. M., 41, 236, 239–40, 254

Sacks, M., 247
Samuels, R., 246
Sartre, J. P., 129, 158–64, 174, 179
scaffolding, 106, 112, 226
Scheler, M., 127–8, 137, 250
schizophrenia, 232–3
Schmitt, A., 228
Scholl, B. J., 197
Schutz, A., 44, 59, 78–84, 149–51, 179, 247
Searle, J.R., 99, 249
Sechehaye, M., 233
second-person understanding, 22, 81–2, 152–85, 231–3
  see also third-person understanding

Segal, G., 246
Sellars, W., 43, 45, 247
Sen, A.K., 200
simulation theory
  and development, 16–19
  and interaction, 23, 153, 168,
      180–4, 219–20
  and modularity, 18–19
  and the shared social world, 92–4,
      219–20
  tacit simulation and perception,
      132–5
  and theory of mind, 10–15, 44–5
  varieties of, 9–15, 219–20
situated cognition, 107
  see also embodied, embedded cogni-
      tion
situational understanding
  development of, 98–107
  evolution of, 226–7
  and explanation, 95–7, 121,
      149–51, 191, 194–7, 205, 207,
      212–14, 216–18
  nature and scope of, 85–98, 107–20
  phenomenology of, 73–8
  in place of simulation, 92–4, 219
  in place of theory of mind, 96–8,
      219, 228
situations,
  as normative, shared contexts, 73,
      89–98, 107–18, 121, 149–51,
      191, 212–14
  as reasons, 96–8, 122, 149–51,
      195–7, 205, 216–18
Smith, A. D., 125, 136, 142
Smith, P. K., 16, 246
Solomon, R. C., 252
spectatorial stance, of folk psycholo-
      gy, 104–7, 118, 124, 126,
      139–41, 152–8, 161, 166,
      168–9, 173, 177, 184, 231–5,
      242
Sperber, D., 18
Stamenov, M., 141
Stanghellini, G., 233–4, 247, 251
Stawarska, B., 157–8, 247
Steinbock, A. J., 250
Sterelny, K., 19, 85, 100–1
Stern, D., 144, 167

Stich, S., 15, 28, 43–4, 191, 193,
      199–200, 207, 209–10, 216,
      218, 222–3, 246, 252
Stone, T., 3, 13, 19, 132
Stotz, K., 112–13
Strawson, P. F., 33–6, 215, 247
Strum, S., 107, 249
Studdert-Kennedy, M., 132
Swettenham, J., 102, 246
sympathy, 127, 160, 181

temperament, 96, 204
theory of mind
  and development, 16–19
  different senses of the term 'theory
      of mind', 16, 44
  folk psychology as a theory, 6, 8–9,
      43–4
  and interpersonal interaction,
      152–3, 156, 168, 178, 180, 233
  and modularity, 18–19
  and simulation theory, 10–15, 44–5
  and social norms, 96–8
theory theory,
  see theory of mind
third-person access to mental states,
      in contrast to first-person, 15
third-person understanding, 22, 81–2,
      152–85, 231–3
  see also second-person understand-
      ing
Thompson, E., 107, 124, 232, 242,
      250–1
Thou-orientation
  and dialogue, 157–8
  in Buber, 154–5
  in Schutz, 81–4, 155
Tooby, J., 18–19, 228, 246
Trevarthan, C., 144, 167, 174, 176,
      235, 254

understanding, nature of, 25–6

Van Fraassen, B., 203
Varela, F. J., 41, 107, 236, 239–40, 254
Vygotsky, L., 106, 112, 249, 252

Warfield, T., 252
Warren, D., 28

Watson, J., 17, 55, 100, 248
Weber, M., 79
Wellman, H. M., 5, 17, 31–2, 35, 52, 55, 100, 144, 150, 187, 246, 248
Wheeler, M., 66, 107, 115, 249, 252
Whiten, A., 20, 104
Williams, R., 202
Wilson, D., 18

Wimmer, H., 16, 44, 52–4, 104
Wittgenstein, L., 249
Wohlschläger, A., 132
Woodruff, G., 44
Wundt, W., 42

Yandell, D., 254

Zahavi, D., 136, 250

·

Breinigsville, PA USA
11 June 2010
239700BV00003B/9/P